Medieval History and Archaeology

General Editors

JOHN BLAIR   HELENA HAMEROW

Early Medieval Settlements

EARLY MEDIEVAL SETTLEMENTS

The Archaeology of
Rural Communities in
Northwest Europe
400–900

HELENA HAMEROW

OXFORD
UNIVERSITY PRESS

OXFORD
UNIVERSITY PRESS

Great Clarendon Street, Oxford OX2 6DP

Oxford University Press is a department of the University of Oxford.
It furthers the University's objective of excellence in research, scholarship,
and education by publishing worldwide in

Oxford New York

Auckland Bangkok Buenos Aires Cape Town Chennai
Dar es Salaam Delhi Hong Kong Istanbul Karachi Kolkata
Kuala Lumpur Madrid Melbourne Mexico City Mumbai Nairobi
São Paulo Shanghai Taipei Tokyo Toronto

Oxford is a registered trade mark of Oxford University Press
in the UK and in certain other countries

Published in the United States
by Oxford University Press Inc., New York

British Library Cataloguing in Publication Data
Data available

Library of Congress Cataloging in Publication Data
Hamerow, Helena.
Early medieval settlements: the archaeology of rural communities in Northwest
Europe, 400–900/Helena Hamerow.
p. cm.
Includes bibliographical references and index.
1. Europe, Western—Antiquities. 2. Land settlement—Europe, Western.
3. Agricultural geography—Europe, Western. 4. Agriculture—Europe,
Western—History. 5. Europe, Western—Rural conditions—History. I. Title.
D125 .H36 2002 940.1—dc21 2002067186
ISBN 0-19-924697-1

1 3 5 7 9 10 8 6 4 2

Typeset in Sabon
by SNP Best-set Typesetter Ltd., Hong Kong
Printed in Great Britain
on acid-free paper by
T.J. International Ltd,
Padstow, Cornwall

To Eric and Max

Preface and Acknowledgements

The idea for this book sprang from doctoral research undertaken in the 1980s into the development of the Anglo-Saxon settlement at Mucking, in Essex. At that time, no early medieval settlement had been excavated in Britain on a scale comparable to Mucking, where, in the 1960s and 1970s, some 18 hectares of a multi-period landscape had been investigated (Jones and Jones 1975; Hamerow 1993). Published reports of large-scale settlement excavations in northwest Europe—especially Germany, Denmark, and the Netherlands—and conversations with continental colleagues about their interpretations of these settlements provided the key to understanding Mucking's development. They also convinced me that a greater familiarity with the innovative research being undertaken on the other side of the North Sea would enrich our interpretations of early medieval settlements in England, despite certain differences in excavation methods and in the character of the settlements themselves.

It is difficult, however, to introduce Anglophone—and often monoglot—students (and colleagues, for that matter), with limited access to foreign publications, to these sites; this crucial body of evidence for how the peoples of early medieval northwest Europe lived has therefore been largely neglected by Anglo-Saxon archaeologists and historians. While countless pages have been devoted to early medieval burial rites and how social identity and social structure may (or may not) be reflected in cemeteries, there is little in the way of a general overview of the evidence for rural settlements between the collapse of the western Empire and the rise of the 'Successor States'.[1] Yet the history of this period is in fundamental ways the history of rural settlements. This book was written in the hope that such a survey will provide a way into the rich and rapidly increasing archaeological evidence for early medieval settlements, and will encourage us to examine Anglo-Saxon settlements within their wider European context.[2]

In seeking to provide a synthesis and overview of archaeological sites in several different countries, I have relied heavily upon colleagues who have shown unstinting generosity in providing access to unpublished material and information. This book is based to a very large extent on their work, both

---

[1] Chapelot and Fossier's *The Village and House in the Middle Ages* (first published in 1980 and translated into English in 1985) forms a notable exception, but it deals with the whole of the Middle Ages, draws heavily on later written sources and is now over twenty years out of date.

[2] It is in the nature of any book dealing primarily with archaeological evidence, that the rate of discovery of that evidence outstrips the author's ability to write about it. Indeed, some of the interpretations offered in the following pages may already have been superseded or overturned by new work. I have, regrettably, been unable in all but a few cases to take account of work published after 1999.

published and unpublished, and I have benefited greatly from their hospitality and readiness to respond to countless queries. I am particularly indebted to Danny Gerrets, Anthonie Heidinga, Hauke Jöns, Claude Lorren, Michael Müller-Wille, Palle Ø. Sørensen, Jan Lanting, Peter Vang Petersen, Arno Verhoeven, Uta von Freeden, H. T. Waterbolk, Rotraut Wolf, and Haio Zimmerman. I am also grateful to the Arbeitsgemeinschaft für Sachsenforschung, whose Sachsensymposia have been a vital source of stimulating ideas and whose members have provided both assistance and friendship. Those colleagues who kindly read parts or all of earlier drafts have, by their comments, improved my original text enormously and I am greatly indebted to Debbie Banham, John Blair, Tania Dickinson, Ros Faith, David Hinton, Catherine Mortimer, Marijke van der Veen, and Chris Wickham for their encouragement and insights. The following institutions generously made available their libraries and expertise: Niedersächsisches Institut für historische Küstenforschung, Wilhelmshaven; Römisch-Germanische Kommission, Frankfurt; the Groningen Institute of Archaeology; National Museet, Copenhagen; Centre de Recherches Archéologiques Médiévales, Université de Caen; Amsterdam Archaeological Centre; Württembergisches Landesmuseum, Stuttgart; Institut für Ur- und Frühgeschichte der Christian-Albrechts Universität, Kiel; Rijksdienst voor het Oudheidkundig Bodemonderzoek, Amersfoort. The following also generously provided unpublished information: Torben Egeberg Hansen, Gill Hey, Hauke Jöns, John Newman, Jörn Schuster, Ian Scott, Astrid Tummuscheit, and Hermann Witte.

The illustrations were drawn by Yvonne Beadnell and Alison Wilkins, to whom I am grateful not only for their skills as illustrators, but also for their patience when faced with pleas for 'just one more' alteration.

The research for this book was supported by a Special Research Award from the University of Durham and by the Institute of Archaeology, University of Oxford. I am grateful to colleagues in both institutions for providing the support, moral and practical, needed to see this project to completion.

Contents

List of Illustrations

Table

1

Rural Communities in Early Medieval Europe: Archaeological Approaches and Frameworks

INTRODUCTION

The primary aim of this book is to provide an overview of the evidence for the settlements and everyday life of rural communities in northwest Europe from *c.* AD 400 to 900, broadly the period from the collapse of the western Roman Empire to the rise of early states in its former provinces and Scandinavia. Its secondary purpose is to relate this evidence, which comes mainly from archaeological excavations, to Anglo-Saxon England and to consider its implications for our understanding of settlements here. Each chapter concludes, therefore, with a brief discussion of the comparable evidence from England, even though detailed comparisons cannot always be drawn due to differences in the quantity and nature of the data available. The evidence is examined under five broad topics: buildings and what the 'built environment' tells us about the household and its activities; the layout of farmsteads and settlements and how these may reflect the social structure of communities; the formation of territories and demographic developments; farming strategies; and, finally, the role of non-agrarian production and exchange in the economies of rural settlements.[1]

Working with evidence spanning such a broad chronological and geographical range is naturally beset with methodological difficulties. One obvious complication is introduced by the different traditions of periodization and terminology used by scholars working in different countries. Thus, a settlement dating to the sixth century might be described as 'Germanic Iron Age', 'Migration period', 'early Anglo-Saxon', or 'Merovingian', depending on its location. The chapters which follow draw primarily on evidence from a large

---

[1] The focus of this book is on settlements. Burial evidence (which continues to form the basis of most archaeologically derived models of society during the first few post-Roman centuries) is only drawn on in a limited way, usually where a settlement has been excavated together with associated burials. Integration of settlement and cemetery evidence for a particular community, while it remains the ideal, is rarely attainable due to the often serendipitous discovery of sites and the constraints on resources available for excavation.

region, stretching from southern Scandinavia, through northwest Germany to the Netherlands.[2] This brings with it the danger of adopting a 'melting pot' approach, however unintentionally (Halsall 1995*a*, 1–3). Yet, an appreciation of regional, indeed local, diversity and of the potential for rapid social change in this period is essential. This North Sea zone has been chosen, furthermore, not out of a misguided belief in a 'homogeneous Germanic culture' (ibid.), but because it was in close cultural and economic contact with England and includes the regions from which the Anglo-Saxons believed their forebears to have originated.

The problem of how to strike a balance between considering local sequences and contingencies, and understanding how northwest Europe as a whole was, to some degree, shaped by the same forces, is axiomatic in a study such as this; maintaining an awareness of the small worlds illuminated by regional studies while trying to gain an impression of the 'big picture' is not easy. In the following chapters, case studies from different periods and different regions are sometimes directly compared. Although this inevitably runs the risk of veering into anachronism or neglecting regional differences, it is done in the belief that such a wide-ranging, comparative approach has the greatest potential for illustrating long-term developments, and that one can properly evaluate individual settlements only by locating them within a broad regional as well as a local context.

APPROACHES

The rural communities of northwest Europe during the first few post-Roman centuries have typically been described in historical scholarship as isolated, insular units, scraping out an arduous and primitive 'subsistence' economy, the basis of which, in the words of Georges Duby, lay 'in the struggle that man had to wage against natural forces day by day in order to survive . . .' (Duby 1974, 5; see also Bloch 1961, 60–1). The Marxist paradigm of an ancient 'Germanic mode of production' played a considerable role in shaping these perceptions. Marx, deriving his views mainly from Tacitus' *Germania*, envisaged a primitive communalism based on a 'free' peasantry living in scattered, isolated farmsteads, separated by great tracts of forest. Although these groups needed to assemble periodically for purposes such as defence, the household was seen as essentially self-sufficient (Marx 1964, 78; Layton 1995).

---

[2] It could be argued that a better analogy for post-Roman Britain is provided by Gaul, only the northernmost regions of which are considered here. The archaeological data pertaining to rural settlement in Gaul is, however, less abundant and in many respects not directly comparable to what we find in Anglo-Saxon England. In northern France in particular, settlement excavations have for the most part been small-scale 'rescue' excavations which have uncovered considerable numbers of early medieval buildings, but do little to enable archaeologists to evaluate settlements as a whole (Lorren 1996, 745; but see also Périn and Lorren 1995). Nevertheless, broad differences between settlements north and south of the Rhine are considered.

This view of the 'Dark Ages' is reflected in popular images and has pervaded historical and archaeological writing for decades, colouring our interpretations of early medieval settlements, particularly within the former Roman provinces (Fig. 1.1; see e.g. Chapelot and Fossier 1985, 18–22, 26; Jones 1979; Demolon 1972. But see also Périn 1992, 230). Such images, of course, ultimately have their origins in early written sources, not only Tacitus and Caesar's *de Bello Gallico* (Book VI), but also Germanic law-codes and the histories of Gregory of Tours and Bede. A topos widely found in such sources, for example, is the contrast between the fertile, open, settled plain and the dark, impenetrable, dangerous forests (Lorren and Périn 1997). The authors of these works were not, however, concerned with the countryside as such, and the few images they include of rural life serve merely as a backdrop to the main action. On the rare occasions when rural settlements do make an appearance, it is generally in connection with some ecological disaster such as a ruined harvest or famine, or the theft of or injury to farm animals (ibid.).

Written sources for this period only become truly productive after *c*.750,

De maaltyden en Gasteryen der Germaanen. L.Muller Fecit.

Fig. 1.1. A seventeenth-century image of feasting and hospitality among the early Germans in what appears to be a log cabin, from a Dutch edition of Tacitus' *Germania* (P. C. Hooft, Amsterdam, 1684, pl. 7). Photo: Courtesy of Amsterdam University Library.

when administrative records, especially manorial surveys and charters (mostly recording the transfer of land by monasteries), become reasonably widely available for some of the regions under study, primarily northern Gaul and England. In general, however, written sources offer only meagre scraps for those interested in daily life in the countryside of northwest Europe in this period, when society was overwhelmingly rural. Only rarely can they help archaeologists address the questions raised by the excavations of settlements, although the innovative drawing together of written and archaeological evidence can be very fruitful, as we shall see. Even early medieval law-codes—arguably the most informative documents where rural life is concerned—convey an artificially static impression of customs in a society which was too variable and localized to be described adequately by such fixed 'rules'. The archaeological evidence is, however, rich, varied, and ever-increasing. Excavations and field surveys, particularly over the last two decades, have unearthed an abundance of new information regarding early medieval settlements. In a very real sense, archaeology remains 'the one true frontier of early medieval history' (Herlihy 1985, 30). Indeed, it has brought to light evidence which is leading to a comprehensive re-evaluation of the 'Dark Age' settlements of northwestern Europe and their economies and is helping us to address two fundamental questions:

1. What was the degree of economic integration (i.e. between local/regional and individual/group economies) in the early medieval countryside? Archaeological evidence challenges the historical orthodoxy that early medieval communities were economically isolated and undifferentiated, and indicates that, although these societies were made up of essentially pre-literate 'small communities',[3] their economies and cultural interaction were complex and diverse.

2. How did the changing relationship between land and power which characterizes this period, and which laid the foundations of manorialism, affect rural settlements? In the early Middle Ages, power was based increasingly on the surplus derived from landed resources, a surplus which was extracted by the aristocracy and church using ever more sophisticated means. Can we detect something of how this agricultural exploitation was organized from the remains of settlements and their fields?

THE DEVELOPMENT OF SETTLEMENT ARCHAEOLOGY[4]

The blueprint for the study of the medieval economy drawn up by historians such as Duby (1968, p. xi) urged further investigation of the daily life and

---

[3] Following Giddens's definition, communities 'in which there is only short distance in time–space separation' and where interaction was of necessity face-to-face (Giddens 1979, 206–7).

[4] For a more detailed review of the development of medieval settlement archaeology in Germany, see Fehring 1991, 7–14.

economy of the peasant farmer. Archaeologists, however, have traditionally focused on burials and cemeteries as a guide to early medieval social structure and identity, with an inevitable focus on elites and their opulent grave goods. Interest only began to turn to settlements in the early decades of the twentieth century.

A major watershed was reached with the excavation, conducted by A. E. van Giffen between 1923 and 1934, of a *terp* (a settlement mound made of turves and dung raised in flood-prone coastal regions; such mounds are known as *Wurten* in Germany) at Ezinge in the Frisian marshes northwest of Groningen (Fig. 1.2). This revealed, for the first time outside the Classical world, a village whose development could be traced over more than a millennium, from the middle Iron Age (*c*.500 BC) to the Migration period (*c*. AD 400–600). The excavations at Ezinge, and particularly the discovery there of well-preserved timber farmhouses (Fig. 2.1), helped to set the course of settlement archaeology, with its emphasis on buildings, for the next forty years (Waterbolk 1991*b*; van Giffen 1936).

In Denmark and northwest Germany too, the excavation of 'proto-historic' settlements began in earnest in the 1920s and 1930s (although the first Iron Age houses had been identified much earlier: Näsman and Rasmussen 1998, 5; Waterbolk 1989, 303). It was in the 1950s, however, when several now-famous sites were subjected to large-scale excavation, that settlement archaeology made major advances (Kossack 1984). In 1951 excavations began at Warendorf in Westphalia which uncovered the plan of a Carolingian village and a hitherto unprecedented variety of buildings—not only farmhouses, but also barns, granaries, and outbuildings (see Chap. 3; Winkelmann 1958). Only a few years later, excavation of the *Wurt* village at Feddersen Wierde on the marshes of the Elbe–Weser triangle of Lower Saxony unearthed outstandingly well-preserved buildings (some with walls surviving to a height of over a metre) dating from the Roman Iron Age and Migration period, as well as a unique range of wooden implements, textiles, and other organic artefacts (see Chaps. 2 and 3; Haarnagel 1979*b*). An extraordinarily detailed picture of daily life emerged, further heightening interest in the subject and arguably marking the beginning of the widespread, systematic study of Migration period and early medieval settlements in the region.

This work was followed in the 1960s and 1970s by a number of large-scale excavations of Roman Iron Age and early medieval settlements, beginning with Wijster in Drenthe (1958–61) and including, perhaps most notably, Odoorn, also in Drenthe, Flögeln-Eekhöltjen in Lower Saxony, and Vorbasse in central Jutland (van Es 1967; Waterbolk 1973; Zimmermann 1992*a*; Hvass 1986; these settlements are discussed in Chap. 3). More recent still have been the excavations at Dalem in Lower Saxony, Nørre Snede in central Jutland, and Kootwijk in the central Netherlands (Zimmermann 1991*a*; Hansen 1987; Heidinga 1987). The numbers of square metres excavated convey a sense of the truly epic scale of these projects: at Nørre Snede, 86,000 m^2; at Flögeln, 108,456 m^2; at Vorbasse, over 200,000 m^2 (Hvass 1986).

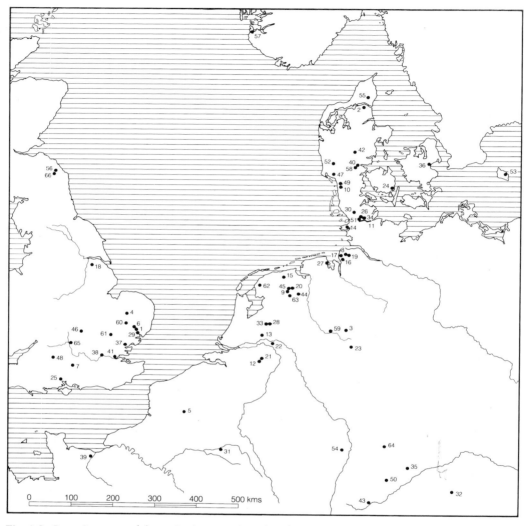

Fig. 1.2. Location map of the main sites mentioned in the text.

Key

1 Barham	18 Flixborough	34 Kosel	51 Schuby
2 Bejsebakken	19 Flögeln	35 Lauchheim	52 Snorup
3 Bielefeld-Sieker	20 Gasselte	36 Lejre	53 Sorte Muld
4 Brandon	21 Geldrop	37 Little Totham	54 Speyer
5 Brebières	22 Gennep	38 Lundenwic (London)	55 Stentinget
6 Coddenham	23 Geseke	39 Mondeville	56 Thirlings
7 Cowdery's Down	24 Gudme-Lundeborg	40 Mørup	57 Ullandhaug
8 Dalem	25 Hamwic	41 Mucking	58 Vorbasse
9 Dalen	(Southampton)	42 Nørre Snede	59 Warendorf
10 Dankirke	26 Hedeby	43 Oberflacht	60 West Stow
11 Danevirke	27 Hessens	44 Odoorn	61 Wicken Bonhunt
12 Dommelen	28 Hoog Buurlo	45 Peelo	62 Wijnaldum
13 Dorestad	29 Ipswich	46 Pennyland	63 Wijster
14 Elisenhof	30 Joldelund	47 Praestestien	64 Wülfingen
15 Ezinge	31 Juvincourt-et-Damary	48 Ramsbury	65 Yarnton
16 Fallward	32 Kirchheim	49 Ribe	66 Yeavering
17 Feddersen Wierde	33 Kootwijk	50 Runde Berg	

The development of settlement archaeology in England was quite different. The first Anglo-Saxon settlement to be recognized as such and subjected to systematic excavation was at Sutton Courtenay, Berkshire, where small-scale excavations were carried out in advance of gravel quarrying on and off during the 1920s and 1930s (Leeds 1947). The unpromising circumstances of that excavation proved to be typical of Anglo-Saxon settlement archaeology for decades to come: it was a 'rescue' excavation which uncovered only small areas of the settlement, with poor structural preservation and virtually non-existent organic preservation. The excavator, E. T. Leeds, excavated a total of thirty-three sunken-featured buildings (Ger. *Grubenhäuser*).[5] He regarded the sunken-featured buildings as dwellings, as did contemporaries such as T. Lethbridge and C. Tebbutt, whose excavations in the 1930s of similar structures at St Neots (Cambs.) led them to envisage conditions of daily life which were, to say the least, rustic:

We have here people living in miserable huts in almost as primitive a condition as can be imagined. They had no regard for cleanliness and were content to throw the remains of a meal into the furthest corner of the hut and leave it there. They were not nervous about ghosts, since they did not mind having a skeleton sticking out of the wall of one of their huts. Pit 1 shows two distinct layers of occupation, and it is possible that when the hut became too stinking and verminous it was either abandoned for a time or a layer of soil spread over the old floor to make it sweeter. . . . It is almost certain that the inhabitants were wretchedly poor serfs. (Lethbridge and Tebbutt 1933, 149)

The perception of life in Anglo-Saxon settlements as primitive in the extreme persisted for decades (e.g. Page 1970, 150). The first ground-level timber buildings of this period (of which only the foundations survive, usually as postholes) were not recognized in England until the 1950s (at Yeavering, Northumberland, and Linford, Essex; Hope-Taylor 1977; Barton 1962), and not until the 1970s had enough buildings of this kind been excavated to enable a clear type of early Anglo-Saxon house to be established. Indeed, as recently as 1972 uncertainty remained as to whether sunken-featured buildings constituted 'the main or most common *dwelling* in such settlements' (Addyman 1972, 302; author's italics).

The scale of excavation in England also remains, for the most part, small by continental standards, although there are exceptions: the excavation at Mucking, Essex, remains one of the largest in Britain, at around 180,000 m² (Hamerow 1993). Catholme, Staffs., where some 37,000 m² were uncovered (Losco-Bradley and Wheeler 1984), Chalton, Hants, with *c.*18,000 m², and West Stow, Suffolk, with *c.*13,000 m² (West 1986), are among the largest settlement excavations for which detailed plans have been published at the time of writing, although recent excavations at West Heslerton (Yorks.), where over 120,000 m² have been uncovered (Powlesland 1990), and Yarnton (Oxon.),

---

[5] See Chap. 2 for a discussion of these structures, often referred to as 'sunken huts', a less clumsy but more contentious term.

where *c*.55,000 m² of the 15 ha investigated contained Anglo-Saxon buildings (Hey, forthcoming), will help to rectify the imbalance. As yet, however, not a single waterlogged settlement of this period has been subjected to investigation on a significant scale.

Showing considerable enterprise, van Giffen funded the excavations at Ezinge through the sale of the phosphate-rich soil from the *terp* as fertilizer (Gerrets 1995). Today, most settlement excavations are undertaken in response to threats from development or quarrying and are funded by a combination of developer and state funding, but a number of the key sites discussed below were excavated as a part of long-term, state-funded research projects to study the development of Iron Age-to-medieval settlement in a given region.[6] In England, however, all the settlements mentioned above (with the exception of West Heslerton and Chalton) were 'rescue' excavations undertaken in advance of development. The particular constraints of such excavations, combined with the more dispersed nature of most early Anglo-Saxon settlements compared with many of their continental counterparts, has resulted in the recovery of few, if any, complete settlement plans (see below, Chap. 3). The greater quantity and range of data available from continental excavations thus has considerable potential to inform and enrich our interpretations of Anglo-Saxon settlements and their buildings.

INTERPRETATIVE FRAMEWORKS

The research agendas and interpretative paradigms within which excavations of early medieval settlements have been conducted have naturally changed over time and vary nationally and even regionally. During the 1950s and 1960s settlements were often investigated as part of wider studies of the historical ecology of a particular region, the most notable example being the long-term investigations of the coastal landscape in Lower Saxony undertaken by the Institut für historische Küstenforschung in Wilhelmshaven (Behre and Schmid 1998). In the course of the 1970s the focus of much research shifted to the development from prehistory to the modern period of settlements and buildings within particular regions and micro-regions, such as the *Siedlungskammer* of Flögeln in Lower Saxony, the province of Drenthe in the northern Netherlands, the Veluwe district of the central Netherlands, and central Jutland (see Chap. 4). This was also when archaeologists began to recognize the considerable degree to which certain features of these settlements (for example, longhouses) were shared across much of northwest Europe (van Regteren Altena 1990, 5). The recognition of these shared phenomena within the 'North Sea Culture' zones stimulated comparative research into settlements south of the Rhine (ibid.).

[6] These include the Settlement and Cultural Landscape Research Programme begun in 1993, funded by the Danish State Research Council for the Humanities (Näsman and Rasmussen 1998); the Central Netherlands Project (Heidinga 1990); and the Flögeln Project (*Die Entwicklungsgeschichte einer Siedlungskammer im Elbe-Weser Dreieck seit dem Neolithikum*), funded in part by the Deutsche Forschungsgemeinschaft (Zimmermann 1992*a*).

In the course of the 1980s and 1990s the emphasis shifted from individual set-tlements and their buildings to their wider cultural landscape. Issues such as set-tlement patterns and territorial development (often seen in relation to state formation) have become increasingly prominent in current research strategies (e.g. Näsman and Rasmussen 1998). For example, the excavations which took place during the 1970s at the Carolingian village of Kootwijk currently form the basis of a much larger study designed to investigate territorial formation in the Veluwe district and central Netherlands as a whole (see Chap. 4).

The kind of archaeological investigation carried out in different regions is also inevitably conditioned by the availability or otherwise of documents relat-ing to early medieval landholding. In very general terms, in Scandinavia and northern Germany, where such sources are lacking, greater emphasis tends to be placed on settlement layout, building typologies, the relationship of settlements to cemeteries, and ecological issues. In southern Germany and the Netherlands, on the other hand, identifying the origins of manorial organization is often a central aim of archaeological fieldwork.

EXCAVATION METHODS

Excavation methods also play a role in determining the kinds of data available for different regions. In the sandy districts of Denmark, northwest Germany, and the Netherlands, for example, a distinctive, cost-efficient method of excavating settlements has been developed which allows for the recovery of complete or near-complete settlement plans.[7] First, the top and plough soils are removed by machine; the outlines of archaeological features thereby revealed (pits, post-holes, ditches, and so forth) are then rapidly 'cleaned' by hand and planned. The dark fills of the settlement features stand out in considerable detail against the light, sandy soils and a certain amount of provisional phasing can already be carried out at this stage, based on the colour of the fills, apparent stratigraphic relationships, etc. (Fig. 1.3). Features are sectioned, but not all are necessarily fully excavated, and excavation usually proceeds by removing layers of, say, 5 or 10 cm (cf Meier 1991; Heidinga 1987, 25). This method, while clearly selective and favouring certain categories of archaeological features—such as buildings—over others, enables large areas to be rapidly recorded with a comparatively small work-force. This has the obvious advantage that most or all of a settlement can be uncovered, including peripheral areas where, for example, evidence of certain kinds of dangerous or noxious processes, such as iron-smelting, is most likely to be found.

Such excavation methods are, however, largely unsuitable for the glacial tills, chalk, and clay soils found over much of England, where excavation is, further-more, carried out stratigraphically according to archaeological layers. At the

[7] This method is set out in detail by Zimmermann (1992*a*, 28 ff.).

Fig. 1.3. Large-scale settlement excavation at Kootwijk, the Netherlands. The stakes mark out postholes belonging to a Carolingian farmhouse. Photo: H. A. Heidinga.

risk of great oversimplification, recording methods tend therefore to be more exhaustive, labour-intensive, and hence, costly. This is not to say that all settlement excavations on the continent are on a large scale, nor that no large-scale excavations have been undertaken in England—indeed, there are several important recent additions to the number of extensively excavated Anglo-Saxon settlements, as already noted—merely that excavation methods lie behind some of the differences apparent in the data sets available for early medieval settlements in England compared to continental northwest Europe.

The extent to which the settlements excavated to date can be considered to be representative of early medieval settlements in general remains a moot point. There are many regions where few or no early medieval settlements have been excavated or even identified, while others—for example, where there is a particularly active local museum or research institute, or on soils where settlements are particularly easy to identify from crop-marks—are very well represented. In Denmark, for example, the vast majority of early medieval settlements excavated to date have been identified on the light soils of central and western Jutland (Hvass 1989, 91). Similarly in England, a high proportion of early Anglo-Saxon settlements have been excavated on the gravel terraces of river valleys (Hamerow 1992). Added to the uneven geographical distribution of the archaeological evidence are significant chronological gaps (see Chap. 4). Until relatively recently, for example, there was a near-complete absence of evidence for sixth- and seventh-century settlements in northwest Germany and Denmark, and settlements of this period in northern France remain dramatically under-represented (Lorren and Périn 1997, 94). It is inevitable, therefore, that many of the generalizations made concerning early medieval settlements are based upon a few well-documented and published sites which may ultimately prove to be unrepresentative of settlements in those regions.

2

Houses and Households:
The Archaeology of Buildings

Buildings are institutions, basic cultural phenomena.

(Rapoport 1979, 2)

As Rapoport suggests, a house is more than merely a shelter against the elements. The built environment and the way space is organized within the house reflect and reinforce social organization. While this is obviously true of the great hall in *Beowulf*, it is equally, if less obviously, true of ordinary houses. If, furthermore, we are to assess the economic conditions and daily life of the early Middle Ages, we need to understand the nature of the buildings in which people lived and worked. Indeed, the study of early medieval settlements in northwest Europe has traditionally been dominated by the study of buildings, chiefly for two reasons: first, on a small number of waterlogged sites, buildings (which were, with few exceptions, constructed entirely of timber) are extraordinarily well preserved, with walls standing in some cases up to a metre or more in height (Fig. 2.1); and second, other categories of artefacts, with the exception of pottery, are usually scarce. In the great majority of settlements, floor layers contemporary with the use of the buildings have been destroyed by later erosion or ploughing, and only the debris which collected or was discarded in pits and ditches survives.

Even where none of the timber superstructure survives, the ground-plans of these buildings, etched into the subsoil as patterns of postholes, reveal that they could be imposing structures. A fifth-century longhouse at Flögeln-Eekhöltjen (Lower Saxony) measured an extraordinary 63.5 m in length (Zimmermann 1992a, 139). A seventh- to tenth-century hall at Lejre (on the island of Zealand) was comparable in floor area (over 550 m^2) to the halls of the Carolingian palaces at Paderborn and Frankfurt, and is estimated to have stood up to 4 metres in height (Fig. 2.2; Christensen 1991; Winkelmann 1971; Stamm 1955). Of similarly lofty dimensions was a Migration period hall recently excavated at Gudme, on Funen, whose main roof-supporting posts were set into massive pits (Figs. 2.3 and 2.4). The fact that these timber buildings have naturally fared less

Fig. 2.1. Excavation of preserved Iron Age timber buildings at Ezinge. Photo: Courtesy of the Groningen Institute of Archaeology.

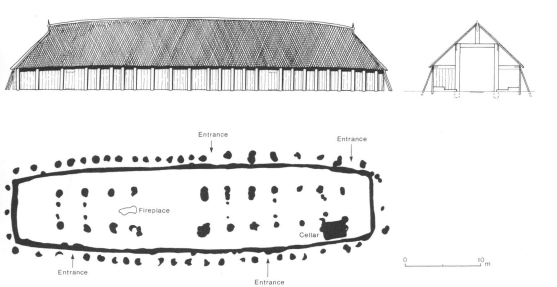

Fig. 2.2. Plan and reconstruction of the 'Great Hall' at Lejre. After Christensen 1991, fig. 14.

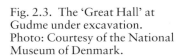

Fig. 2.3. The 'Great Hall' at Gudme under excavation. Photo: Courtesy of the National Museum of Denmark.

well in the archaeological record than their more durable stone counterparts in former imperial territories has often led to gross underestimates of their size, complexity, and quality. Yet beyond the former Roman frontier lay buildings which can truly be described as monumental, whose construction required a highly sophisticated technology and the felling of many acres of woodland.

THE LONGHOUSE

In the region stretching from southern Scandinavia, through northern Germany, south to Westphalia and the lower Rhine, the focal building of most farmsteads,

Fig. 2.4. Reconstruction of the
'Great Hall' at Gudme. After
Sørensen 1994, fig. 9.

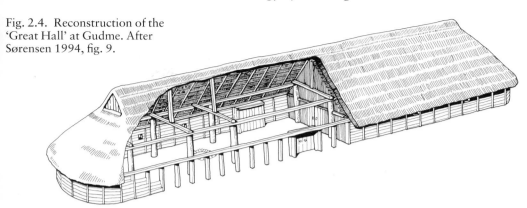

from the Bronze Age to at least the seventh century AD, was the timber longhouse (Fig. 2.5). This generally took the form of an east–west oriented building[1] with living quarters containing a hearth and a variable number of compartments at the west end, a central entrance 'hall' with two opposing doorways, and a byre at the east end; two rows of massive, paired internal posts supported the weight of the roof and divided the interior space into three aisles (Fig. 2.6). Ever since the excavation of the well-preserved waterlogged longhouses of the Frisian *terp* of Ezinge, research into early medieval buildings across northern Europe has focused on these remarkable structures (van Giffen 1936; Waterbolk 1989, 303; 1991*b*).

The Architecture of the Longhouse

Arguably the most significant architectural development of the early Middle Ages was the transition from the longhouse, with its complex arrangement of interior roof-supporting posts and byre, to an open hall in which the interior space was largely free of load-bearing posts and from which farm animals were largely excluded. This evolution, which can be traced throughout most of the region under consideration, reflects, in addition to certain social changes (considered below), changes in the way in which early medieval builders addressed the problem of how to balance the weight and thrust of the roof: by means of internal supports or by placing the load-bearing posts within the walls. The problem of how to build wider structures while freeing the interior space of roof supports was ultimately resolved by introducing transverse joists supported by corresponding pairs of posts. The end-result of this shift from stability derived from rows of internal roof-supporting posts to stability based on posts set within

---

[1] One possible explanation for the prevalence of east–west orientation is that this would maximize the benefit derived from the warmth of the sun on the southern wall, while offering protection against a westerly wind (Hedeager 1992, 196–7).

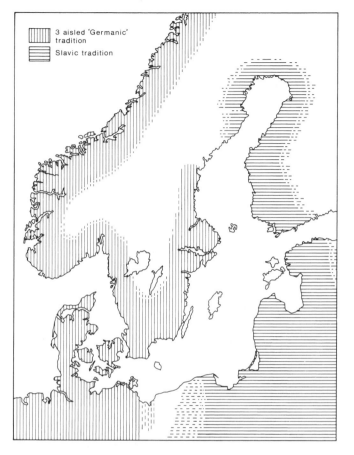

Fig. 2.5. The distribution of the longhouse in northwest Europe. After Ramqvist 1992.

the walls was a truly single-span building, often with slightly bowed long walls, and, in many cases, external struts. This house form emerged by the later seventh and eighth centuries in the Netherlands and northern Germany, where it is known as the 'Warendorf type' house (Fig. 2.7; Reichmann 1982, 170; 1991; Heidinga 1987, 49). It did not appear until the ninth or tenth century in southern Scandinavia, however (Fig. 2.6; Näsman 1987, 461; Waterbolk 1999, 112). Further to the south and in England, as we shall see, buildings followed a rather different development.

These architectural changes took place gradually, and it is possible to see 'hybrids' in which different principles of building construction are combined in the same house, making a simple, evolutionary model of architectural development difficult to sustain. The process has been most closely traced in the Dutch province of Drenthe, where, on the basis of a substantial database of ground-plans of prehistoric and early historic houses, a typological sequence of the Drenthe farmhouse from the Bronze Age to the Middle Ages has been devised

(Waterbolk 1991*a*). The two-dimensional ground-plans of excavated houses have, furthermore, been reconstructed (on paper, at least) in order to understand the economic, technical, and aesthetic concerns of early medieval builders (Huijts 1992).

While local variations and sequences can be identified, the general trend away from internal roof supports and towards the bow-sided form, as the longhouse gradually came to be replaced by large dwelling houses with detached byres, can

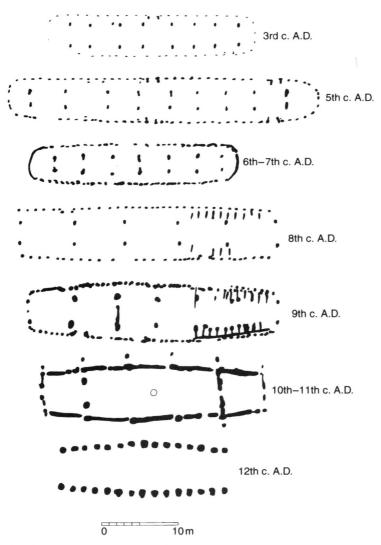

Fig. 2.6. The chronological development of the longhouse in Denmark. After Hvass 1993, fig. 189.

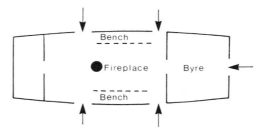

Fig. 2.7. The 'Warendorf type' house. After Heidinga 1987, 49.

be traced across a large region stretching from southern Scandinavia to the central Netherlands (Siemen 1990; Hansen *et al.* 1991; Herschend 1989; Schmidt 1990 and 1994; Waterbolk 1999). The reason for building bow-sided houses remains a matter for speculation (e.g. Hedeager 1992, 196), as does their exact origin, although it has recently been suggested that the emergence and spread of the 'Warendorf type' house were linked to the *wic* (trading centre) of Dorestad (Waterbolk 1999). Their widespread appearance does, however, illustrate the 'international' character of architectural traditions in this period, and how these traditions appear to have 'spread unperturbed by the political and cultural vicissitudes of the moment' (Heidinga 1987, 54).

Analysis of the dimensions of some 120 Iron Age to Migration period longhouses excavated at Flögeln has revealed that their average length gradually increased during the first to fifth centuries AD. This lengthening is partly attributable to a greater number of stalls for cattle, but also to an increase in the average number of rooms per house. The same trend can be observed widely throughout northern Germany, the Netherlands, and Jutland, where exceptionally large longhouses, reaching over 50 metres in length, began to appear in the late Roman Iron Age (i.e. third and fourth centuries AD: Zimmermann 1986, 79; Näsman 1987, 461). What exactly this lengthening reflects—whether the combination of a larger number of different functions under one roof, or a growing number of dependants and increasing levels of production—is considered below. At Flögeln, this increase in the average length of longhouses was followed by a marked decrease in length (but, significantly, not in the number of rooms) in the final, fifth- to sixth-century phase of settlement. A comparison between the longest fourth- to fifth-century house, which measured 63.5 m, and the longest fifth- to sixth-century house, which measured only 39.8 m, highlights this abrupt reversal (Zimmermann 1992*a*, 139). The majority of buildings without stalls also belonged to this latest phase. The fifth-century houses at Peelo (in Drenthe) and Vorbasse (in central Jutland) also exhibited much shorter byres in comparison to their late Roman predecessors (Bardet *et al.* 1983, 20 and fig. 11, House type B; Hvass 1983, 131). The significance of these developments, and their implications for Anglo-Saxon England, where small, byre-less houses were the norm and where not a single continental-style longhouse has been identified, will be considered at the end of this chapter.

Metrological analyses of longhouses reveal a high degree of dimensional coherence around the North Sea littoral. Extraordinarily widespread and long-lived correlations between templates or modules used to lay out buildings from the Iron Age to the Middle Ages are suggested when the ground-plans of buildings from this region, including England, are superimposed (Zimmermann 1988). The buildings show a striking correspondence in terms of the placement of walls, entrances, pairs of roof-supporting posts, subdivisions, and even hearths (Fig. 2.8). Some variability is apparent in the width of longhouses, although even this rarely ranged beyond 5–6 m, a function, perhaps, of the minimum needed to accommodate two rows of stalls and a central aisle (Schmidt 1994, 52). If, furthermore, pairs of roof-carrying posts were tied by a single piece of timber, the width of buildings would have depended in part on the type and quality of the available timber (Zimmermann 1986, 57).

This widespread regularity was presumably based on preferred dimensions (as a comparison of Flögeln Houses 111 and 112, which were not contemporary but which nevertheless correspond almost exactly in layout, suggests; Fig. 2.9; Zimmermann 1992a, Abb. 47),[2] and would have been impossible without a specialized, conservative, carpentry tradition and a high degree of cultural contact. Given the irregularity of the timbers used in these buildings, absolute precision and consistency cannot, of course, be expected, but the similarities are nevertheless striking.

Analysis of the architecture and metrology of longhouses thus reveals that, along much of the continental North Sea littoral, buildings were affected by similar developments during the fifth and sixth centuries: the average length of longhouses decreased markedly and a greater proportion of houses had a shortened byre or none at all. The inner roof-carrying posts of the longhouse, which had previously divided the interior space, were gradually moved outwards and ultimately became integrated with the wallposts to create an open living area. In the course of the seventh to tenth centuries, the aisled structure was largely replaced by a fully framed, often bow-sided, 'single-span' farmhouse with no internal uprights or distinct byre section (Huijts 1992).

This transition can be seen by comparing the plans of the Migration period settlement at Flögeln-Eekhöltjen and the nearby seventh- to eighth-century settlement at Dalem (Figs. 3.19 and 3.6). The latter contained living houses without internal subdivisions instead of the traditional longhouse, as well as separate byres, granaries, and workshops. Phosphate analysis of one of the Dalem houses

---

[2] A wooden rod, probably used as a measuring stick or template, was found during the excavation of a timber causeway at Diepholz, north of Osnabrück (Lower Saxony). This object, which was less than a metre long and probably dates to the late Pre-Roman Iron Age, is, however, more likely to have been used in the construction of smaller objects, perhaps wheeled vehicles, than in the laying out of buildings (Hayen 1979, 91–3).

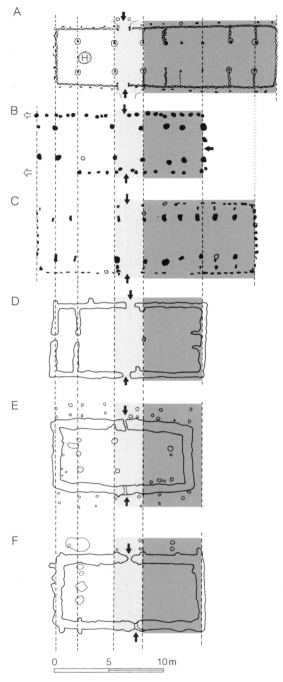

Fig. 2.8. A comparison of fourth- to seventh-century buildings from northern Germany, the Netherlands, and England. (A) Feddersen Wierde House 14. H = hearth; (B) Flögeln House 2; (C) Wijster House XIV; (D) Chalton House AZ I; (E) Thirlings Building A; (F) Thirlings Building L. After Zimmermann 1988, fig. 6, and O'Brien and Miket 1991.

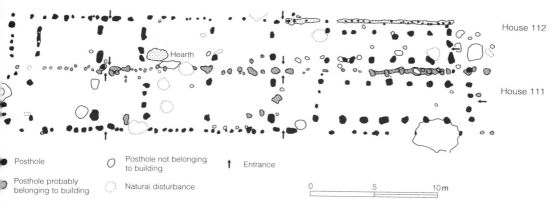

Fig. 2.9. Houses 111 and 112 from Flögeln-Eekhöltjen. After Zimmermann 1992, Abb. 47.

revealed low phosphate-values (in contrast to the Flögeln longhouses), while the small building which lay immediately adjacent to it yielded high values, suggesting use as a byre and reinforcing the impression that by this time buildings were more likely to serve a single function, rather than multiple functions as the longhouse had done (see below; Zimmermann 1986, 76, Abb. 13).[3] A comparison of the sixth- to seventh-century village at Vorbasse with its eighth- to ninth-century successor reveals a similar development (Figs. 3.3 and 3.4).

Exactly why the longhouse with attached byre ceased to be built is poorly understood. It is notable that the southern boundary of the distribution of the longhouse, which runs through central Belgium, the lower Rhine, and Westphalia, corresponds roughly with the southern limits of sandy, Pleistocene soils (Roymans 1996, 53). In the loess regions of the Rhineland and northern France, where arable production was economically more important than cattle rearing, people and cattle had always been accommodated in separate buildings (Roymans 1996, 56). Perhaps the abandonment of the longhouse in regions to the north was therefore related to changes in farming practices. There is evidence to suggest that in the course of the eighth century arable farming became more intensive at the expense of cattle rearing (see Chap. 5).[4] The aisled longhouse was not, however, abandoned everywhere: it remained in use in the coastal marshes, for example, at the *Wurt* settlement of Elisenhof (Eiderstedt) (Bantelmann 1975); indeed, there is evidence that the houses of the Frisian *terpen* (often built primarily of turf rather than timber) in general followed a development which was somewhat different from that further inland (Waterbolk 1991a, 104).

---

[3] Phosphate mapping in this case involved examining soil samples from various parts of the buildings for their phosphate content. High phosphate levels can indicate animal or human occupation, and byres, where manure would collect, thus yield exceptionally high levels.

[4] Since the longhouse continued to be used during warmer climatic cycles in the Iron Age, a warming in climate enabling cattle to be over-wintered outdoors is unlikely to be the cause of its demise (Hedeager 1992, 206 ff.).

The Functions of the Longhouse

Analyses of the architectural design and metrology of early medieval longhouses suggest that their internal space was divided up in consistent ways and that the principles of their construction were among the more conservative elements of early medieval material culture. Since similar house types may occur in widely varying climatic zones, while a wide variety of architectural forms may be found in the same climatic zone, socio-economic factors must play at least as important a role as the environment or technology in influencing the architecture of dwellings (Rapoport 1979). The internal subdivision of the longhouse must therefore have related to symbolic spatial distinctions, for example, between different activity areas, or age or gender groups, as well as reflecting the important relationship between the household and its cattle. The difficulty of detecting such distinctions from such limited evidence is undeniable (Douglas 1972), yet it should not discourage us from examining certain clues which can be brought to bear on the complex and fascinating question of the socio-cultural aspects of the early medieval longhouse.

The conventional interpretation of the functional arrangement of the longhouse envisages a tripartite division—a byre, a 'work room', and a living room (*Stall, Wirtschaftsraum, Wohnraum*)—and is based largely upon Haarnagel's excavation in the 1950s of the well-preserved buildings at the *Wurt* of Feddersen Wierde, in Lower Saxony. Here, the byre sections survived complete with individual stalls, manure, and drainage gullies for slurry. The central room of one longhouse which had burned down contained pottery vessels in which cereal grains had been stored, sorted by type, assumed by the excavator to be in readiness for food preparation (although it could equally have been seed corn). This and other evidence (including the remains of wooden equipment and scraps of textile interpreted as the 'cleaning cloths' of the ever-industrious Germanic *Hausfrau*) led the excavator to interpret these central compartments as rooms for general domestic work and food preparation (Haarnagel, 1979*b*, 119, Abb. 34). The living room, with its central hearth, was, at least in some cases, provided with a clay floor. The best-preserved houses showed that the living rooms were themselves often subdivided, with small side chambers which may have served as sleeping compartments. The remains of wooden furnishings—presumably benches, tables, and so on—also survive from these rooms (Haarnagel 1979*b*, Taf. 40.1). There is, furthermore, very close correspondence observable between the layout of the houses at Feddersen Wierde and other settlements.

The main house types identified a few miles inland at Flögeln-Eekhöltjen have counterparts throughout Germany (including at Feddersen Wierde), the Netherlands, and Denmark: House Type 1 contained a living room, a work room with an entrance zone, and a byre; in Type 2 houses, the byre was placed centrally, between living and work rooms; houses of Type 3 were identical to Type 1, but without a byre, and are interpreted as the houses of craftworkers who did not possess cattle herds (Zimmermann 1992*a*). Elaborations of this tripartite division are common, however, and the number of rooms and location of entrances vary. As longhouses grew in length, particularly during the fourth century, the living areas became increasingly subdivided by walls or screens (as seen, for example, in Flögeln House 91; Zimmermann 1992*a*, Abb. 52). Small compartments which could only be entered from inside the house were often situated in the gable ends. Such a compartment in House 14 contained a wooden trough set into the floor, suggesting that this space served as a domestic workroom; in other cases it could have served as a sleeping room or for storage (Zimmermann 1986, 56). At Nørre Snede, in central Jutland, the main living room was often sandwiched between two small rooms; yet houses in which one of these was absent could be as long as those with both rooms, confirming that these rooms served specific functions, and were not merely a way of providing additional space (Hansen 1987, 176). Likewise, when longhouses became shorter during the fifth and sixth centuries, they remained subdivided, again as seen at Flögeln (i.e. Houses 735 and 756; Zimmermann 1986, Abb. 4 and 6). This is also the period when a greater number and variety of ancillary structures appeared alongside longhouses, heralding, it has been argued, the emergence of the *Vielhausgehöft*—farmsteads with multiple buildings, each serving a separate function (Zimmermann 1986, 57).

Access to rooms furthest from the main entrances in the centre of the house (a third entrance directly into the byre was often situated in the eastern gable end) became more restricted as the number of rooms increased, as this would involve passing through other rooms to reach them. In exceptional cases, particularly from the fourth and fifth centuries, there were several sets of entrances; a house at Baekke (on Jutland), for example, had seven rooms and three sets of entrances (Näsman 1987, 461). At Lejre, which later became a royal centre, the main hall was subdivided into five or six rooms, a layout which altered little even though the hall was rebuilt twice between the late seventh and late ninth centuries (Fig. 2.2, Schmidt 1991). The system of entrances at Lejre was unusual, and presumably reflects its special status: four staggered doorways, two in each long wall, instead of the pairs of directly opposed entrances and gable door usually found. The entrances into the 48.5 m-long building were also exceptionally wide, between 1.5 m and 2.0 m (compared to Feddersen Wierde, where entrance widths ranged from 0.85 to 1.00 m: Haarnagel 1979*b*, 91). Each led into a separate room, which may suggest that these served distinct functions, for example, storage (a pit in the southeastern corner of the house has been interpreted as a cellar), assembly, sleeping, and so on. It certainly indicates that entering and leaving the hall was a complicated business, which could at least partly depend on the status of the visitor (Herschend 1998, 38). The hearth room, which could be entered through a separate entrance, covered at least 100 m², and its exceptional width (approximately 11.5 m) is largely accounted for by the side aisles, which were twice as wide as those found in 'ordinary' houses of the same period. On analogy with other Viking period buildings in Denmark and Iceland, and from accounts contained in Norse sagas, these aisles were probably raised and provided space to accommodate a large number of guests around the hearth (Schmidt 1991). Evidence for benches placed along the walls to either side of the hearth also comes from smaller Carolingian houses in the Netherlands (Fig. 2.7; Heidinga 1987, 49).

Central to the question of the functional layout of the longhouse is the location of the hearth, the focal point of daily life. In many cases, the damage caused by ploughing is such that it is impossible to know where the hearth was sited. Sufficient examples do survive, however, to show that it was normally located in the largest room in the living (usually western) end of the longhouse. This room usually occupied most of the living space (Haarnagel 1979*b*, tables 7–10), and was generally at least the same size as the byre.

Sometimes two hearth rooms were built *ab initio* into one longhouse with a single byre, which raises interesting questions about the composition of the early medieval household. Perhaps the simplest explanation is that such houses represent multiple family households, that is, two 'conjugal family units' linked by kinship or marriage under one roof, with joint ownership of a herd.[5] These would have constituted a single household in economic terms, in that they would have participated jointly in production and consumption, and have been supported by the same 'productive estate' even if they formed separate reproductive units (Goody 1972, 102, 120).

Building II in the settlement of Mølleparken (Jutland), for example, was a longhouse some 35.5 m in length containing two hearth rooms, one at either end, probably with a byre in between; a single entrance was centrally situated in the southern wall of the longhouse (Andersen and Rieck 1984). It lay within an enclosed yard which also contained a much smaller building (approx. 10 m long) without a hearth. Further evidence to suggest that more than one family could occupy a single farmstead is found where several dwellings share the same enclosure or farmyard (Zimmermann 1986, 78; Näsman 1983, 66). Even in such cases, however, there is debate as to whether this represents an ancestral farmstead, with the main house occupied by the 'paterfamilias' and the other house(s) by his children, or (rather less plausibly) a 'chief' and his dependants. It seems likely that, as in most societies, a combination of nuclear, extended (lineally and laterally), and multiple family households coexisted in early medieval Europe (Goody 1972, 122).[6]

The 'syntax' of the longhouse was simple: rooms were strung together, each with a single entrance leading onto the next, and generally only one or two entrance zones leading to the outside. No circuits were possible. The restricted access to rooms furthest from the doorways, particularly those in the gable ends,

[5] Other explanations are, of course, possible, such as a 'summer' and 'winter' living room (Roymans, pers. comm.).

[6] There is a corresponding debate concerning the variable layouts of early medieval cemeteries, and how these might relate to social and family structure (see e.g. Härke 1997).

could relate to a greater need for privacy, or for security of stored goods. A greater number of rooms could have been the result of several functions being combined under one roof, an increased number of dependants per household, or, particularly when there was more than one hearth room, more than one family living under the same roof. Given this simple internal structure, it is difficult to infer the socio-economic aspects of longhouses from their ground-plans alone. It is, furthermore, impossible to identify from such evidence what may have been important distinctions between public and private, male and female, or sacred and profane space. Yet, as the documentary sources discussed later in this chapter confirm, the internal subdivisions indicate spatial transitions which had social significance.

Archaeologists have sought to address the question of functional distinctions within and between houses, even where occupation levels have been entirely destroyed, through the use of phosphate analysis. The most detailed work of this type to elucidate house function has been undertaken at Flögeln. Phosphate mapping of longhouses with multiple rooms at Flögeln revealed that the highest phosphate values were found, not surprisingly, in the byre section and often in the entrance zones, with somewhat lower phosphate values in the central room, and the lowest values occurring in the rooms furthest from the byre. This pattern suggests that the central room acted as the main living and eating area, and the rooms beyond it in the gable end were used for sleeping, storage, or, as the trough in House 14 suggests, domestic work (Zimmermann 1986). This pattern is illustrated by the near-total coverage by phosphate testing of a farmstead which lay in the fourth- to fifth-century settlement (Zimmermann 1986, Tafel 1, Abb. 2). The three longhouses in this yard (Houses 295, 296, 440) (one of which had rested on sill beams or stone footings and was only rendered visible by its four surviving doorposts and the phosphate mapping) were not contemporary, but represent a sequence of rebuildings. The phosphate maps for all three are nevertheless strikingly similar.

Even within byres, phosphate values could vary markedly. Some stalls, particularly in fifth- to sixth-century longhouses, yielded very low values indicating that they had not actually been occupied. It has been argued that this reflects an economic decline also mirrored in the decrease in the overall length of longhouses at this time (Zimmermann 1986, 82). Yet the fact that byres were built on a scale larger than was necessary may well reflect the role of the longhouse in social display, given the importance of cattle as a means of signifying status and wealth in Germania. It may, of course, also be that some 'stalls' were in fact used for storage.

High phosphate levels immediately to the south of a number of the longhouses at Flögeln indicate external activity areas beneath the eaves which, to judge from drip gullies, were between 1.2 and 1.5 m wide (Zimmermann 1992a, 136). The discovery of quantities of carbonized grains in the postholes of some of the longhouses, together with the exceptional depth of some of the inner posts, have led the excavator to suggest that a closed-off roof-space over at least part of the building served as a storage area (Zimmermann 1992a, 137–8). The grain from the postholes consisted primarily of barley and oats, while the percentage of rye, the predominant cereal grain in this region during the Migration period, was very small. Samples taken from hearths, in contrast, show a much higher percentage of rye, and the grain retrieved from storage pits is primarily rye. This suggests distinct storage practices: hulled cereals, that is, oats and barley, were stored, perhaps for fodder, in the roof-space of houses, while rye (a 'naked' grain, suitable for human consumption without further processing) was stored in pits. Direct evidence for the storage of grain in a longhouse comes from a second-century building excavated at Archsum-Melenknop (on the island of Sylt), where several hundredweights of carbonized grain were recovered from the stall area of the longhouse, which must have fallen from the roof-space (Zimmermann 1992a, 138). At the Carolingian village of Kootwijk in the Netherlands, a house which burned down in the first half of the ninth century also contained a large quantity of grain (Groenman van Waateringe and van Wijngaarden-Bakker 1987, 61). A reference in the *Lex Salica* (II, 4) also indicates that hay and corn were sometimes stored in houses (Dölling 1958, 24).

THE EARLY MEDIEVAL HOUSE IN NEIGHBOURING REGIONS

Many of the same essential structural and functional principles of the early medieval house are found over much of northwest Europe, yet much regional variation is apparent as one moves away from the North Sea zone.

Northern Scandinavia

In Norway, the longhouse also gave way ultimately to a building in which the roof was supported on the walls rather than on rows of internal roof supports, although here this process was more gradual than in regions to the south. Indeed, examples of the 'aisled' longhouse survived in Norway into the modern era. Stone and earth wainscotting of some timber longhouses (which could reach a staggering 100 m in length) not only provided insulation, but helped to preserve internal occupation surfaces (Myhre 1982, 203). The distribution of finds within these houses reflects a fairly standardized functional layout, as seen at the settlement of Ullandhaug in southwest Norway. This consisted of two hearth rooms per longhouse (one at either end), a food-preparation room with a cooking pit (often containing querns) adjacent to the western living room, and a byre situated in between the two living zones (Myhre 1982, figs. 7 and 8). Forty-five late Roman Iron Age and Migration period longhouses excavated at Forsandmoen, also in southwest Norway, reveal a similarly uniform layout. In the western end of the houses were two opposed entrances (Fig. 2.10). To the east of this entrance zone was a room with a hearth and often a cooking pit. One or two

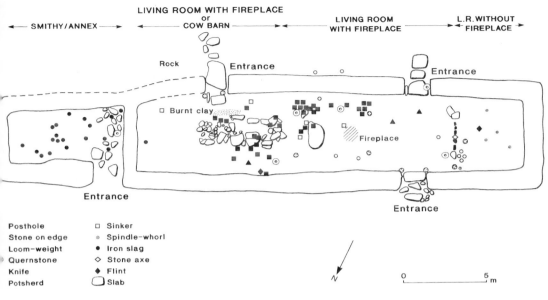

LIVING ROOM WITH FIREPLACE
or
COW BARN

LIVING ROOM WITH FIREPLACE

L.R. WITHOUT FIREPLACE

SMITHY / ANNEX

Rock

Entrance

Entrance

Burnt clay

Fireplace

Entrance

Entrance

Posthole	□ Sinker
Stone on edge	⊙ Spindle-whorl
Loom-weight	● Iron slag
Quernstone	◇ Stone axe
Knife	◆ Flint
Potsherd	◡ Slab

N

0   5 m

Fig. 2.10. A longhouse from Rennesøy, Rogaland, Norway. After Myrhe 1982, fig. 8.

entrances were also located in the eastern end of the living area. Houses over 33 m in length had a second living room, with its own entrance and hearth (Løken 1992*b*). The three-aisled longhouses excavated at the settlement of Gene in northeast Sweden, also yielded preserved ground surfaces, leading the excavator to postulate six rooms corresponding to different activity zones: a work room, living room, entrance hall, byre, storeroom, and kitchen (Ramqvist 1983).

While northern Scandinavian longhouses are distinguished from their southern counterparts by their use of drystone foundations and sill-beams, a comparison of houses from Gene, Forsandmoen, and Vorbasse (central Jutland) shows that the same essential principles of internal layout were followed in both northern and southern Scandinavia (Løken 1992*b*, fig. 5).

Southern Germany

Only comparatively recently have significant numbers of early medieval buildings been excavated in the Alamannic regions of southern Germany, where the building tradition appears to have been more varied and less standardized than in the north. At Lauchheim (Baden-Württemberg: Fig. 3.25), archaeologists have uncovered the remains of a remarkable settlement, comprising over fifty timber buildings arranged in enclosed units, together with small groups of exceptionally rich burials within the settlement as well as a separate cemetery, all dating from the sixth to early eighth century (Stork 1989, 1990, 1991, 1992; see also Chap. 3). The buildings, typically for Frankish and Alamannic regions, were

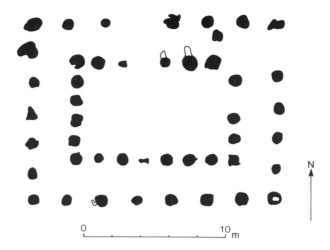

Fig. 2.11. House 'A' from Irlbach, Bavaria. After Böhm 1993, 139.

markedly shorter than their more northerly counterparts, measuring on average only *c.*13–17 × 6 m.[7] Individual posthole as well as post-in-trench or sill-beam construction techniques were used and internal roof-supporting posts were lacking. No contemporary ground surfaces survived at Lauchheim, and the location of entrances is generally difficult to discern from the ground-plans. In at least one case, a single entrance could be identified in the middle of the southern long wall. Phosphate analysis of several of the houses at Lauchheim indicates that at least some of them housed animals as well as people, even though no traces of internal subdivisions survive.

The most extensively excavated settlement in the region of the Baiuvarii in southeast Germany is that of Kirchheim (Ldkr. München; Fig. 3.8), where post-built houses, 12 to 13 m in length, were excavated together with sunken-featured buildings, wells, and presumed storage buildings. Some of these were subdivided into two or more aisles. The *Lex Baiuvariorum*, written down in the mid-eighth century, describes the house of a freeman as having an inner and outer zone ('interioris aedificii'; 'exteriores trabes', *Lex Baiuv.*, cap. X), suggesting that these aisles marked an important spatial transition (Fig. 2.11; Dannheimer 1987, 110).

Northern France

Until the publication in 1972 of some thirty sunken-featured buildings (*fonds de cabane*) of the Merovingian period excavated at Brebières, near Douai (Demolon 1972), virtually nothing was known about the buildings and physical

---

[7] For similar buildings, see also the settlement at Wülfingen, Baden-Württemberg (Schulze 1982).

structure of early medieval settlements in northwestern Gaul, primarily because large-scale excavation was less widely practised in France than in Denmark, Germany, or the Netherlands. Not until the 1980s were a number of settlements subjected to large-scale excavation, providing for the first time a substantial body of data pertaining to early medieval buildings in northern France. The relatively recent discovery of Merovingian ground-level buildings, for example, has led finally to the rejection of the 'hypothèse misérabiliste' that Clovis's contemporaries lived in squalor in sunken-floored hovels (Périn 1992)—an image not dissimilar to that evoked of life in Anglo-Saxon settlements prior to the discovery of ground-level timber buildings in England (see above, Chap. 1).

Excavations at Juvincourt-et-Damary (Aisne) have uncovered the ground plans of at least five such timber buildings dating from the early sixth to early ninth centuries (Bayard 1989). Ground-level buildings such as these were, like those in the Alamannic regions, generally small, with at most one row of internal roof-supporting posts. Their plans are often irregular, with widely spaced wall-posts, essentially straight rather than bow-sided walls, and highly variable ratios of length to width. The reconstruction of House B from Juvincourt demonstrates, nevertheless, that some of these buildings could be substantial (James 1988, pl. 44), in this case with a floor area of around 80 m² and a porched entrance.

From the mid- to late-seventh century, stone was reintroduced as a building material in northern France, at least in the form of drystone footings. Two buildings from Sannerville, near Caen (Buildings 7 and 8), for example, were constructed partly on stone footings, partly of individual earthfast posts (Pilet *et al.* 1992). Building C at Goudelancourt-les-Pierrepont (Aisne) was built with timber posts set into footings consisting of a mixture of chalk, flint, and, curiously, animal bones (Nice 1992, 45).

A number of Merovingian settlements, however, appear to have consisted largely or entirely of sunken-featured buildings (Lorren 1996, 747). These have, in some cases, plausibly been interpreted as dwellings, hence their inclusion here. At St Martin-de-Mondeville, near Caen, the stone buildings of a Gallo-Roman settlement were replaced by timber structures, most of them sunken-floored, around the beginning of the fourth century (Fig. 2.12; Lorren 1989 and pers. comm. 1993). The length of these sunken-floored buildings ranged widely, but could reach 5 m. The sunken floor was sometimes covered with clay or stone; both external and internal hearths were found, and the buildings were accompanied by ovens, granaries, and pits. These buildings (which remained the main building type until the later seventh century, when the inhabitants resumed building in stone) corresponded closely to their stone predecessors in both location and orientation, leading the excavator to suggest continuity of occupation—and presumably of population—from the late Antique to early medieval periods. From the late seventh and early eighth centuries, larger, more substantial buildings whose foundations, at least, were of stone, were constructed at

Fig. 2.12. Mondeville, Calvados: plan of the settlement. After Lorren 1989, fig. 1.

ground level, or with slightly sunken floors, with average dimensions of approximately 7 × 3.5 m. The hearth was no longer directly on the floor, but was constructed on stone slabs in the centre of the buildings (Lorren 1989, 450).

The sunken-featured buildings found at Mondeville and other settlements in northern France differ from the *Grubenhäuser* associated with settlements in northern Germany and Scandinavia, both in the occasional use of stone and in the placement of the posts. This has given rise to a debate about whether these reflect a Germanic presence or influence, or derive instead from an indigenous late Antique tradition, a question which receives further consideration below (Périn 1992, 226–7; Farnoux 1987, 35).

Considerable variety in shape, size, and layout is thus apparent among the buildings of southern Germany and northern France. Although less archaeological information is available for these regions, the general impression is of a less clearly defined and less uniform building tradition than that found north of the Rhine.

SUNKEN-FEATURED BUILDINGS, BARNS, AND OTHER BUILDINGS

Sunken-featured Buildings (Ger: Grubenhaus; Fr: fonds de cabane; Da: grubehus)

All that normally remains of these structures is an oval or rectangular hollow of variable dimensions with (usually) two gable posts, or four corner posts or six (gable plus corner) posts. Only rarely does evidence for an entrance survive; yet wear on the sunken floor of some huts, as well as the appearance of hearths, slots, stakes, and pits in the bottom of the hollow, suggest that this often, if not always, functioned as the floor surface;[8] the sunken floor could in some cases be laid with planks, or provided with a clay or stone surface, but was more usually earthen. Although they are the most numerous early medieval building type to be recorded archaeologically, analysis of sunken-featured buildings has yielded relatively few patterns with regard to their construction, function, or regional trends. While there were sometimes local and regional preferences for two-, four-, or six-post huts, no clear chronological development is apparent. There is, furthermore, no clear correlation between the size and depth of a building and the number of postholes. Thus, although sunken-featured buildings from a particular community may exhibit traits peculiar to it, why one type was chosen in favour of another remains unclear.

The superstructures of two-, four-, and six-post huts were clearly different, and the building materials used also varied widely: wattle and daub, but more commonly planks, turf, and, in France, stone were all used. The two-post huts are often reconstructed as tent-like, with the roof reaching all the way to the ground (Fig. 2.13). Four-post and six-post huts, on the other hand, may have had planked, or wattle-and-daub walls (see West 1985, fig. 285). Their construction would have been relatively speedy, and required far less expenditure of labour and timber than a ground-level building. Estimates of their lifespan vary enormously, from ten to fifty years (Farnoux 1987; Schmidt 1994, 160), naturally depending on how elaborate and substantial a construction is envisaged, but some may simply have functioned as temporary storage facilities, perhaps for a surplus harvest, and been quite short-lived (Chapelot and Fossier 1985, 123).

The greatest number of sunken-featured buildings are found in the North Sea zone, where they emerged in the late Roman Iron Age and continued to be built

---

[8] It has been argued that in England, a wooden floor was normally suspended over the hollow, and that these structures could have been as substantial as ground-level buildings (West 1986; Tipper 2000). This model has not, however, been taken up on the continent, where well-preserved examples provide strong evidence for a sunken floor. For example, a cast taken from a *Grubenhaus* at Bremen-Grambke revealed a series of thin, 'trampled' layers (*Trittschichten*) and suggests that the bottom of the hollow was covered with straw or straw matting (Witte 1992/3). The floors of similar buildings from a Viking period settlement at Sædding (Jutland) are described as having a 'very trampled appearance' (Stoumann 1980, 112). The situation in England could, of course, have been different, and not all sunken-featured buildings need have been sunken-floored, but the published evidence from England so far remains inconclusive.

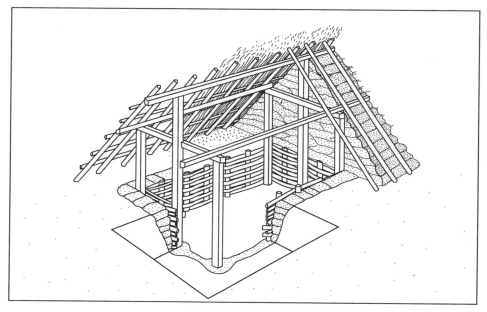

Fig. 2.13. A reconstruction of a sunken-featured building. After Heidinga and Offenburg 1992, 61.

into the Carolingian and Viking periods (their almost total absence on the coastal marshes is almost certainly due to the obvious problems of maintaining a sunken-floored building in wet soils). In the vast majority of cases they were ancillary to ground-level houses (although see the discussion of Mondeville, above). Although sunken-featured buildings are found in late Saxon, Carolingian, and Viking contexts, they largely disappeared from northwest Europe in the course of the tenth century. The reasons for their disappearance are unclear, although the development of cellared buildings, particularly in towns, and the growing use of a variety of storage structures (see below), suggest that technological developments were in part responsible.

Theories regarding the possible functions of sunken-featured buildings depend largely on whether at least some of the finds deposited in them are believed to be associated with their use.[9] The question of whether they could have served as dwellings has long been debated. The excavations at, for example, Mondeville (see above) and Puddlehill, Beds., which have uncovered substantial sunken-featured buildings but few or no ground-level buildings, suggest that this

---

[9] Primary deposits in sunken-featured buildings are rare, though not unheard-of. At the settlement of Bremen-Grambke (Lower Saxony), for example, a pottery vessel was found in the middle of the sunken floor of a building (no. 1299) which appears to have been broken *in situ*, as all the sherds were present and lay with their inner surface exposed (Witte 1994/5).

possibility cannot be ruled out (Lorren 1989; Matthews and Hawkes 1985). Yet these examples represent the exception to the rule; in the overwhelming majority of settlements, sunken-featured buildings are very unlikely to have functioned as dwellings.[10]

Indications of a wide range of activities have been found associated with sunken-featured buildings. At Flögeln, for example, thirteen such buildings contained hearths believed to have been contemporary with their use (although generally not the hearth-pits found in the longhouses; Zimmermann 1991*a*), while a group of sunken-featured buildings at the edge of the fifth- to sixth-century settlement contained significant quantities of non-ferrous metalworking debris; these were, however, secondary deposits, and need not relate to the function of the buildings (Zimmermann 1992*a*, 212). Artefacts related to textile production, such as loomweights and spindlewhorls, are some of the most common finds in sunken-featured buildings across central and northern Europe, including Anglo-Saxon England (Rahtz 1976). This evidence, together with documentary sources (see below), indicate that special buildings were constructed for textile production during the Roman Iron Age and early Middle Ages which were, at least sometimes, sunken-floored.

The discovery of at least six sunken-featured buildings which clearly functioned as weaving sheds at Dalem (Lower Saxony) formed the basis of a wide-ranging survey of such buildings by W. H. Zimmermann (Zimmermann 1982, Abb. 3, 7, 8). The Dalem examples ranged in date from the seventh/eighth centuries to the eleventh/twelfth centuries, were originally dug to a depth of *c*.0.4 m, and had a floor area of up to 17 m². All had a stone oven in one corner, and the posts of at least one of the huts had been renewed several times. The main indication of their function was the large number of clay loomweights which rested on the sunken floors. The most striking example was *Grubenhaus 9*, in which a total of 104 weights lay in two double rows. Many still rested on their edge, where they had dropped from an upright loom when the building burned down, leaving a remarkably detailed record of the position of the loom itself. This would have been a single warp-weighted loom, 4 m wide, set on the floor and leaning against the rafters of the building. Evidence for weaving, and for that matter any craft activity, is of course much less likely to survive in a ground-level building. Sufficient evidence does exist, however, to suggest that weaving also took place in these, although most of this evidence is late, dating to a period when sunken-featured buildings had largely disappeared. One of the best examples, found near Hatzum (Kr. Leer, Germany), dates to the tenth or eleventh century. A building with thick turf walls, approximately 25 m × 10 m, contained

---

[10] In the Slavic regions to the east, large, sunken-floored rectangular buildings clearly did serve as dwellings. These, however, were almost always provided with a stone hearth or oven in one corner and often constituted the primary or only building type in a settlement (Chapelot and Fossier 1985, fig. 38). The fact that most early modern European parallels for sunken-floored dwellings derive from eastern Europe may, thus, not be entirely coincidental (Gojda 1991, 18–21; Chapelot and Fossier 1985, 78–9; Zimmermann 1992*a*, 192 ff.).

an elongated pit in the top of which were a large number of loomweights (Zimmermann 1982, 135 ff.). A broadly contemporary, though less convincing, parallel was found at Goltho, Lincs., where six bone pin-beaters, several spindle-whorls, and heckle teeth were recovered from a ground-level building some 19 m in length (Beresford 1987). A number of buildings which appear to have been used for weaving also contained a shallow rectangular pit oriented longitudi-nally along the floor of the building, situated, where this can be determined, directly under the loom. This feature has been found in buildings from Denmark to northern France, and has been interpreted as a trough for water designed to increase the humidity in the structure and thus facilitate weaving (see below; Zimmermann 1982).

Cross-cultural parallels have also contributed to our understanding of the con-struction and function of sunken-featured buildings. Farnoux has drawn atten-tion to sunken-floored shepherd's cottages in Basse Alsace, the Auvergne, and Switzerland, and to other examples which were seasonally occupied by dairy-workers, who also stored milk and cheese in the huts (1987). In the nineteenth century sunken-floored buildings sometimes served as dwellings of the very poor; in the northern Netherlands, for example, a tent-like dugout hut made largely of turves and measuring 3.1 × 2.8 m housed eight people (Zimmermann 1992*a*, 198 ff.). Sunken-floored dwellings were also known in nineteenth-century Som-erset (Laver 1909). Sunken-floored structures have also been used to house small animals, and as potato and root stores (Fig. 2.14. Farnoux 1987, 33; Chapelot and Fossier 1985, 123; Zimmermann 1992*a*, 192).

Few direct references were made by early medieval writers to sunken-floored buildings. Two passages by ancient authors are, however, relevant and often cited. The first is Pliny's observation with regard to the weaving of linen, that 'in Germany, the women carry on this manufacture in caves dug underground' (*Nat. Hist.* XIX, 2, 2). Ethnographic research and modern parallels in France, suggest that the chief advantage of weaving in a sunken-floored building is the increased humidity, which would prevent fibres, especially flax, becoming brittle (Zimmermann 1982, 133). The second reference is contained in Tacitus' *Germania*, which suggests that sunken-floored buildings served as crop stores (*Germania* XVI). There is also growing archaeological evidence that early medieval sunken-featured buildings were used for grain storage, for example Hut 8 from the Carolingian settlement at Gasselte (NL) (van Zeist and Palfenier-Vegter 1979, 271), but also at West Heslerton, Yorks. (Powlesland 1997, 106). Finally, a passage in Felix's *Life of Saint Guthlac* (cap. XXVIII) seems to refer to a dugout dwelling (dating to the late seventh or early eighth century), though in this case it was dug into a mound or barrow (Colgrave 1956).

The widespread distribution of sunken-featured buildings suggests varied and wide-ranging affinities and origins. These have already been mentioned in connection with settlements in northern France, where they may derive from an indigenous, late Antique tradition, rather than representing an 'intrusive' Germanic element. Yet, although sunken-floored structures are known from the

Fig. 2.14. A dugout hut in Poland (Nowo-Minsk), early twentieth century. Grisebach 1917, 11.

La Tène period in France, they did not appear in significant numbers until the Migration period. The debate concerning their ethnic affinities is far from decided, although socio-economic developments seem more likely than Germanic expansionism to explain their appearance in northwest Gaul (Farnoux 1987, 35).

Free-standing Byres

Small buildings with subdivisions for animal boxes have been identified at Odoorn and Wijster in Drenthe (Waterbolk 1991*a*, Abb. 17). Seven Viking-period examples were also recorded at Vorbasse, one of which was over 13 m long (Hvass 1980, 155, fig. 20). Phosphate analysis at Dalem identified further probable free-standing byres dating to the seventh and eighth centuries (Zimmermann 1986, 76).

Small Buildings of Unknown Function

In many settlements, small ground-level buildings were almost as numerous as longhouses. The ratio at Nørre Snede, for example, was 150 longhouses to 100 smaller buildings. The latter, unlike the longhouses, were sometimes oriented north–south. Their ground-plans are also more variable than those of longhouses in terms of wall construction and the number and placement of entrances and roof-supporting posts. Examples are known both with and without hearths and byres, but nearly all were sited in farmyards near long-houses, although exact contemporaneity is usually impossible to prove. Law-codes (see below) refer to separate workshops, kitchens, and so forth, and it is likely that these are represented by some of these smaller buildings. Yet many are well-built, substantial structures with hearths, suggesting that, where they lay within the same farmyard as one or more longhouses, they were dwellings, perhaps of dependants (see e.g. Houses 30 and 40a from Feddersen Wierde: Haarnagel 1979*b*, 135). Other, apparently 'autonomous' structures have been interpreted as the houses of craft-workers (Haarnagel 1979*b*; Zimmermann 1992*a*).

Granaries

The most common type of Migration period granary found in northwest Europe was raised off the ground, supported by between four and (exceptionally) twenty posts, leaving as its only trace rows of deep postholes. At Feddersen Wierde the bases of some of these posts survived, set into postholes up to a metre deep, and were in some cases reinforced with wooden wedges and crossbars. Modern parallels and medieval illustrations suggest that the granary itself consisted of a heavily daubed wattlework structure set atop a platform which was supported by the posts (Zimmermann 1984, 259). The objective, of course, was to keep provisions dry and safe from vermin, germination, and decay. At Feddersen Wierde, Wijster, and possibly Flögeln, a few granaries were enclosed by a fence (e.g. van Es 1967, 94, fig. 42; Zimmermann 1992*a*, 228).

The rows of deep posts lining one or more edges of fenced farmsteads during the late Roman Iron Age and Migration period in Jutland appear to represent another form of grain store. Isolated examples of such 'lean-to' granaries are also known in northwest Germany and the Netherlands (Zimmermann 1992*a*, 255–9). At Nørre Snede these rows of posts could extend for up to 40 m, running along up to three sides of nearly all but the smallest farmyards (Hansen 1987, 183). If this interpretation is correct, the potential grain-storage capacity of many of these farms was far greater than has previously been imagined.

In central Germany, France, and the 'Celtic' and Slavic regions, however, produce was most often stored in silo pits. Only two such pits, of unspecified date, were found at Feddersen Wierde, as compared to 147 post-built granaries. These pits were exceptionally well preserved, approximately 0.6 m deep, and lined with wickerwork. One still contained several small heaps of hazelnuts which must originally have been stored in leather or cloth sacks (Haarnagel 1979*b*, 159 and Taf. 139, 2).

Haystacks and helms (roofed, open-sided crop stores surviving archaeologically as a roughly circular arrangement of posts, sometimes with a central post) seem to have existed alongside granaries for the storage of winter fodder (Zimmermann 1991*b*; 1992*b*). The fifth-century community at Peelo, in Drenthe, for example, appears to have constructed both four-post granaries and helms (Waterbolk 1991*a*, 80). Most helms, however, date to the Carolingian period or later, for example, at Gasselte (Drenthe), where pentagonal or hexagonal helms replaced the square and rectangular granaries of the earliest phase of the settlement (Waterbolk 1991*a*, Abb. 21). Indeed, from the Migration period onwards the number of post-built granaries found in northwest European settlements dwindled, and few have thus far been dated with certainty to the early Anglo-Saxon period in England (see below, Chap. 3). Clearly grain continued to be stored, but where? The appearance on some continental settlements of post-rows parallel to enclosure fences, mentioned above, coincides broadly with the decline in the number of granaries, strengthening the argument that they represent a new system of grain storage. Sunken-featured buildings could also have served this purpose, on analogy with numerous later medieval and early modern examples of root stores (see above; Zimmermann 1992*a*, 198). It is also likely that provisions were stored in houses, as already noted (see also Chap. 5), and that post-built granaries were in part replaced by barns.

Barns

These buildings (Fig. 2.15), which could be as long as, or even longer than, longhouses, were sometimes divided into two aisles by a single line of roof-supporting posts, but usually lacked any other internal subdivisions. Unlike longhouses, which were almost invariably oriented east–west, barns could also be

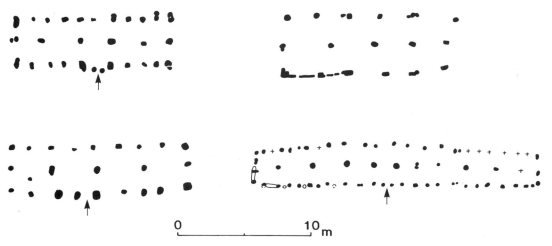

Fig. 2.15. Early medieval barns from Odoorn (1–3, 6), Dalen (2), and Gasselte (7–8). After Waterbolk 1991*a*, Abb. 15.

aligned north–south. Their function has been confirmed by occasional finds of substantial quantities of carbonized grain within them (Zimmermann 1984, 263). Barns could also be sited in fields, presumably for the storage of unthreshed crops (Waterbolk 1991*a*, 74). The most common early type was two-aisled, 8–12 m in length, 4–5 m wide, first appearing in Drenthe in the fifth century. The gable ends are often represented by a single posthole. By the Carolingian period this type was replaced by single-aisled barns with more massive posts, such as those excavated at Gasselte, which were 12–24 m long. Danish examples are less common, and although several small Viking-period buildings interpreted as 'storehouses' have been identified at Vorbasse, their function is by no means certain (Hvass 1980, 147, fig. 9).

BUILDINGS IN WRITTEN SOURCES

The compilers of early medieval law-codes referred to a wide variety of structures, mainly in connection with the fine to be paid by any individual who damaged or destroyed them, usually through arson. The terms used, however, generally refer to buildings only in relation to their function rather than their appearance, leaving the archaeologist to draw tenuous parallels between equivocal descriptions and often equally ambiguous archaeological remains (e.g. Chapelot and Fossier 1985, fig. 17). Given the differences between the buildings found in the regions where these laws applied and those in more northerly parts of Europe, such comparison grows still more problematic. With these caveats in mind, these documents nevertheless offer a unique insight into the roles played by buildings in early medieval society.

The most detailed analysis of the house and farmyard as they appear in Germanic law-codes was published by Dölling in 1958. Her study draws widely from the corpus of the *leges barbarorum*, but particularly illuminating are the *Lex Salica* (whose origins are likely to lie in the reign of Clovis in the early sixth century), the *Lex Baiuvariorum* (*c*.730/40), and the *Leges Alamannorum* (seventh-century in origin).[11] The *LB* is largely based on the *LA*, and indeed its prologue states that the *LB*, the *LA*, and the Frankish laws were all promulgated under a sixth-century Merovingian king (Rivers 1977, 25). It is not surprising, therefore, that strong similarities exist between all three in the terminology used (see Chapelot and Fossier 1985, fig. 17) and in the fines assessed for damage to, or destruction of, different kinds of buildings (Table 2.1).

The laws reveal relatively little about the architecture of buildings *per se*, although the *LB* (X, 7–12) does distinguish between different structural components, based presumably upon functional considerations; the highest compensa-

---

[11] *Lex Salica* (Rivers 1986), hereafter *LS*; *Leges Alamannorum* and *Lex Baiuvariorum* (Rivers 1977), hereafter *LA* and *LB* .

Table 2.1. Fines assessed in the *Lex Baiuvariorum* and *Leges Alamannorum* for damage to or destruction of different kinds of buildings

Building Type	LA (LXXVI)	LB (LX)
Main house	40 s	40 s
Barn, with walls and locked	12 s	12 s
Servant's barn	6 s	
Barn/shed without walls, not locked	6 s	—
Granary		4 s
Master's	12 s	
Servant's	3 s	
Cellar	12 s	—
Servant's dwelling	12 s	—
Bathhouse, bakehouse, or kitchen	3 s	3 s
Sheep- or pig-byre	3 s	—

Note: 's' = 'solidi'.
Source: After Dölling 1958.

tion (12 solidi) is owed, not surprisingly, for damage done to the roof-supporting posts (*firstsul*); the next highest fine (6 s) is specified for the corner posts (*winchilsul*) of the 'inner house' ('interioris aedificii'), while compensation for the 'outer' posts (*spanga*) are payable with only 3 s per post. The distinction made here between 'inner' and 'outer' zones may of course reflect social as well as functional and architectural considerations.

The *LA* (LXXXIX) describes a dwelling in which a newborn child could open its eyes and 'see to the ridge-post (*culmen domus*) of the house and the four walls', evoking an image of a one-roomed building open to the roof. The *LS* (Pact. LVIII, 2) also suggests that the *casa* consisted of a single room with an earthen floor. A building consisting of several rooms is nowhere described. The reasons for this may relate to both geography and chronology. As already noted, houses in Frankish and Alamannic regions were relatively small, with few or no internal subdivisions. Even to the north, longhouses with multiple rooms had, by the seventh and eighth centuries, been largely replaced by houses which were more often single-roomed, surrounded by other buildings with specialized functions.

The Domus

The main residential building is most commonly referred to as the *domus*, although *casa* and *sala* are apparently synonymous. The *domus* was where people lived, ate, and slept, gave birth, and died, and as such served as the emotional centre of the *curtis* or farmstead (*LS* Pact. XLVI; Pact. L, 1; *LA* LXXXIX). The *domus* also provided the setting for the transference of inheritance before witnesses (*LA* LXXXIX, 2; *LS* Pact. XLVI). Loss of honour or authority could, in extreme cases, result in the loss of the *domus*; thus, one guilty of incestuous marriage, patricide, or fratricide lost his claim to hold property (Dölling 1958, 10; *LA* XXXIX, XL).

The social status of those living in the *domus* is rarely specified. The term seems to have referred to any residential building, regardless of the status of the proprietor, whether nobleman (i.e. 'casae dominicae', *LB* I, 13), freeman, or semi-free. In the *LA* and *LB* the *domus*, barn, and granary of a servant or slave are mentioned, indicating that lack of personal freedom did not preclude some proprietorial rights (e.g. *LA* LXXVII, 4, 'spicaria servi'). No mention is made in the *LS*, however, of a *domus* belonging to a servant.

The furnishings of the *domus* are mentioned in several law-codes, usually in relation to their transference or inheritance: tables, benches, chairs or stools, and beds are all mentioned, though never actually described (e.g. *LS* Pact. XLVI, 5). Some spectacular examples of well-preserved early medieval furniture have been recovered from chamber graves, for in high-status burials at least, domestic equipment was often included. An astonishing range of such material—beds, chairs, stools, tables, lighting equipment, and tableware—was excavated from the sixth- to seventh-century Alamannic cemetery at Oberflacht, Baden-Württemberg (Paulsen 1992). Some of the larger pieces of furniture had been cut down in order to fit into the burial chamber, indicating that these were items which had been in daily use, and were not specially manufactured funerary furniture (Paulsen 1992, 55). Several beds were found at Oberflacht representing a variety of types, but the most remarkable examples had canopies fitted in the shape of a gabled roof with an ornamentally carved ridge-post (Paulsen 1992, 41; Fig. 2.16). The bed in Grave 211 even had a shingled roof (Schiek 1992, Taf. 86), providing the most direct evidence so far for the appearance of at least some real roofs. Early medieval manuscripts depict similar furnishings, such as a bedstead with elaborately turned legs and cross-pieces illustrated in the Stuttgart Psalter (Fig. 2.17). The bed was part of the legally defined goods, *Gerade* and *Heergewäte*, with which a woman or man was entitled to be buried, as were pillows, blankets, and linens, traces of which have also been recovered, as has bedding material of reeds, hay, moss, and oak leaves (Paulsen 1992). A tradition of 'bed burial' was also practised in southern Scandinavia, for example at Valsgärde, Sweden (Burial 8), and later, during the Viking period, most notably at Gokstad and Oseberg in southern Norway (Brøgger and Schetelig 1928, fig. 51), as well as in seventh-century England, notably at Swallowcliffe Down, Wilts., and Barrington, Cambs. (Speake 1989; Malim and Hines 1998, 267 ff.).

The recent discovery of similar furniture dating to the fourth and fifth centuries from burials at Fallward, situated on the coastal marshes of Lower Saxony only a few kilometres south of Feddersen Wierde, has shown how widespread and long-lived this tradition was (Schön 1999). Two graves in particular produced well-preserved wooden objects: the grave of a young girl contained a low table made of birch and sycamore, with turned legs and decorated with

Fig. 2.16. Reconstruction of a bed with a gabled 'roof' with ridge-post used as a coffin from Grave 84, Oberflacht. Note the 'double chair' at the foot of the bed. Photo: Courtesy of Staatliche Museen zu Berlin—Preusischer Kulturbesitz: Museum für Vor- und Frühgeschichte.

Fig. 2.17. A bed with turned legs depicted in the Stuttgart Psalter (Bibl. fo. 23, S.30ᵛ: Ps. 24, 13, Württembergische Landesbibliothek).

Fig. 2.18. Table from the boat-grave at Fallward. Photo: Courtesy of Museum Burg Bederkesa, Archäologische Denkmalpflege des Landkreises Cuxhaven.

chip-carved motifs of a kind also seen on metalwork of this period, as well as a three-legged stool; a similar table made of field maple and poplar, and with still more elaborately turned legs, came from the grave of a man buried in a log boat (Fig. 2.18). This grave also contained the most spectacular find of all, an elaborately chip-carved chair made from a single alder trunk, with a footstool displaying a hunting scene and runic inscription. These are admittedly high-status burials, and one cannot conclude from these exceptional finds that such furniture was common, but they do allow us to visualize the kind of furnishings which would have been found in the *domus* of leading families.

Tables, chairs, and chests were also listed as belonging to the *Gerade* and *Heergewäte* (Paulsen 1992, 59). The tables included in burials were for obvious reasons small, and clearly not intended for large feasts. A range of evidence suggests that tables were in fact often portable and could be brought out and assembled for meals (Paulsen 1992, 75).[12] A variety of chairs and stools have been recovered from Alamannic burials, some highly elaborate (including the enigmatic 'double chair' from Oberflacht: Figs. 2.16 and 2.19), others clearly intended for children. Chests are amongst the oldest forms of furniture and were probably a ubiquitous feature of early medieval households, used not only for storage, but also as benches and tables. In medieval iconography a chest is often depicted at the foot of the bedstead, exactly the position in which they were found in the Oberflacht bed burials (Paulsen 1992, 88). Nine wooden candlesticks, each *c.*0.30 m in height, as well as wax candles, were also recovered, remarkably similar to examples still being made over a thousand years later

---

[12] It is interesting to note that Tacitus observed of the Germans, in relation to their eating habits, that 'each has his own seat and table' (*Germania* XXII; Schön 1999, 90).

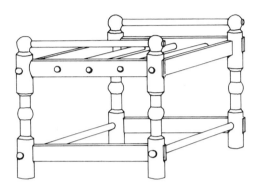

Fig. 2.19. A chair, stool, and table from Oberflacht. After Paulsen 1992, Abb. 48, 50, 72.

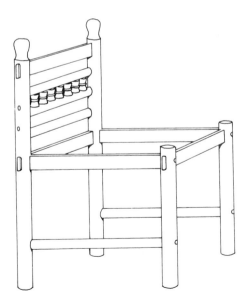

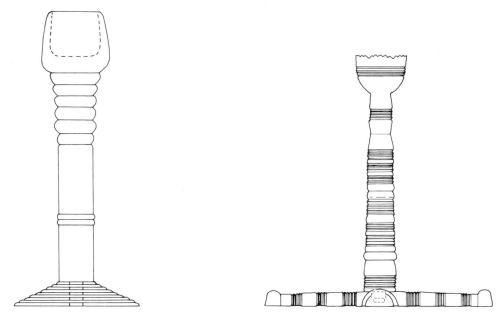

Fig. 2.20. Wooden candlesticks from Oberflacht. Scale approx. 1:4. After Paulsen 1992, Abb. 66 and 67.

(Fig. 2.20; Paulsen and Schach-Dorges 1972, 97). While their appearance in graves reflects their special role in the burial rite, they could also have provided light in a domestic setting.

Other Buildings

Whether the variety of words used to describe non-residential structures such as barns and granaries reflects real architectural and/or functional distinctions is unclear. The hierarchy of fines payable for damage to or destruction of these buildings suggests, however, that there really were different types of barns and granaries and that these terms were not randomly applied. The most obvious distinctions are those between structures which could or could not be locked, and those (especially barns or storehouses) with and without walls (Table 2.1). Those 'without walls', for example the *scof* (*LB* X, 2), were presumably buildings in which the roof reached to the ground, forming a tent-like structure, or were open-sided shelters. The *scuria*, on the other hand, could have walls, and was where hay and corn were stored, according to the *LB* (II, 4: Dölling 1958, 13, 25). This is in contrast to the *LS* (Pact. XVI, 4), where the *scuria* housed *animalia*. The *LS* refers to the *fenile* (*LS* Pact. XVI, 4; from *fenus*) which was presumably specifically for storing hay. On the other hand, while the terms *spicarium* (from *spica*, an ear of corn) and *machalum* (*LS*) clearly refer to granaries, the same fine is assigned to both and no reference is made to the kinds of crop stored in them. Whether they refer to architecturally distinct buildings thus remains a moot point. The relative values of all these ancillary structures was low, however: the fine for destroying a bathhouse, bakehouse or cooking house is specified in the *LB* as only 3 solidi, compared to 40 solidi to be paid in compensation for damage to the ridge-post of a *domus*.

The *LS* (XIII and Pact. XXVII) and *LA* (LXXV) refer to two types of building which seem to have been the preserve of women. These appear in relation to the fine payable for abducting a woman from a locked room or *screona*. Various translators of the *LS* have equated the *screona* with the sunken-featured building, following the recognition of its etymological connection with *écraigne*, the name for dugout buildings used by women for weaving as recently as the eighteenth century (Chapelot and Fossier 1985, 119; Farnoux 1987, 33). The early ninth-century Utrecht Psalter appears to depict women spinning and weaving in just such a building (Fig. 2.21). The term *genicium*, as used in the *LS*, has a similar meaning: 'If the woman managed her master's *cellaria* or *genicium*, one must atone [for the crime committed against her] with 100 s and one penny' ('Si vero ancilla ipsa cellaria aut genicium domini sui tenuerit, C solidos et dinarium pro ipsa conponatur'; C. III, 11; Dölling 1958, 12). 'Cellaria' used in this context may be translated as storehouse (although of course the juxtaposition of

Fig. 2.21. An apparently sunken-floored weaving shed depicted in the Utrecht Psalter. MS32, fo. 84ʳ, University Library, Utrecht.

genicium and *cellaria* need not imply that the former was sunken-floored). The *LA* (LXXV) specifies a similar penalty for abducting a woman from the *genicium*. The *genicium*, and probably the *screona*, thus appear to have comprised separate buildings which functioned specifically as women's work-quarters.

REFLECTIONS ON THE ANGLO-SAXON HOUSE

The archaeological evidence for Anglo-Saxon timber buildings is relatively limited in comparison to that of their continental counterparts, due to the lack of waterlogged settlements with preserved timbers and the relatively small scale (by continental standards) of most settlement excavations in Britain. In the first major survey of the evidence for the Anglo-Saxon house, published in 1958, Radford predicted that ground-level timber farmhouses similar to those at Warendorf would be found in England, were large-scale excavation to be adopted (Radford 1958, 28). Very shortly thereafter ground-level timber buildings were indeed recognized in England, but these were smaller and appeared less complex than the longhouses of continental farmsteads. They averaged around 10 to 12 m in length, lacked cattle byres, and supported the weight of the roof on the walls instead of on internal rows of posts (e.g. Fig. 2.8 D, E, F).[13] Even the larger buildings which began to be built in England at the end of the sixth and early seventh centuries, for example, at Cowdery's Down, Hants (Fig. 3.28; Millett 1984), appear to represent a distinctive architectural form which, while incorporating some continental features, did not closely resemble either the aisled longhouse of the Migration period or the later 'Warendorf type' house.

The progress made in the forty years since Radford described the study of the Anglo-Saxon house as 'one of the most intractable problems in the whole range of early medieval studies' (1958, 27) has been little short of revolutionary, yet key questions concerning the origins of Anglo-Saxon timber buildings, their chronological and regional development, and their functions remain unresolved.

Chronological Development

No detailed building typology comparable with those devised for Dutch, German, and Scandinavian longhouses exists for Anglo-Saxon timber buildings. The tiny number of well-dated buildings must be largely to blame for this, along with the irregularity and incompleteness of many excavated ground-plans. Furthermore, if the buildings of the fifth and sixth centuries represent a process of hybridization of indeginous and continental forms, as seems likely (see below), then this too could also help account for the lack of obvious 'types'.

---

[13] Early Anglo-Saxon buildings fall broadly into two categories: a regular, rectangular structure with paired posts and 'strong' corners (e.g. Mucking PHB 1, Hamerow 1993, fig. 54) and a more irregular structure with 'weak' corners (e.g. Mucking PHB 7, Hamerow 1993, fig. 55).

Some chronological trends in Anglo-Saxon buildings are nevertheless apparent. Recent work by Marshall and Marshall suggests that fifth-century buildings were uniformly small (i.e. less than 12 m in length), aligned east–west, and built using individual posthole construction (Marshall and Marshall 1993; Hamerow 1999*a*, fig. 3). An internal partition, usually at the east end, survives in roughly 25 per cent of buildings, a proportion which remained roughly constant throughout the fifth to seventh centuries (e.g. Fig. 2.8 D, F). This formed a separate compartment which could be entered via an external as well as an internal entrance. The sixth century saw somewhat greater variation in the lengths and proportions of buildings. The use of foundation trenches was introduced towards the end of the century (Fig. 2.8 D, E, F). The first large halls (i.e. with floor areas greater than 150 m²) appeared *c*.600. Very small buildings (i.e. less than 6 m in length) also became more common in the seventh century. Roughly half of seventh-century buildings were constructed using foundation trenches, and for the first time a significant proportion, roughly one-third, were aligned north–south. By the eighth and ninth centuries foundation trenches were used in more than 75 per cent of buildings, and a wider range of proportions came into use as the more coherent building tradition of the earlier period broke down, reflecting in part the emergence of monasteries and high-status secular centres. Of course, difficulties exist with this scheme, not least because of the small number of buildings (fewer than thirty) which can be closely dated.

Function

What little evidence survives for the layout of the Anglo-Saxon house suggests that, in contrast to the longhouse, it consisted essentially of one room, often with a small subdivision at one end. Very few Anglo-Saxon buildings contained traces of contemporary hearths, although this is likely to be due to poor preservation.[14] How we should interpret the one- or two-roomed Anglo-Saxon house is far from clear; indeed, not all timber buildings need have been houses. Cooking, storage, and so on may have been sited in separate buildings, as was the case in northern Germany and the Netherlands by the seventh or eighth centuries and in England by the tenth century, to judge from law-codes and other documents (Dölling 1958, 55 ff.).

Two explanations are generally put forward to account for the lack of a byre in Anglo-Saxon houses. The first is that the milder English winters eliminated the need to stable cattle indoors (Addyman 1972; Rahtz 1976, 61). While this may be part of the explanation (cf. Zimmermann 1999*a*; 1999*b*), it is worth noting that in Iron Age Denmark the longhouse remained in use even during warmer climatic cycles (see above, n. 4). It has also been suggested that cattle were simply less important in the Anglo-Saxon economy. While the proportion of cattle to

---

[14] Fewer than 10 per cent of the buildings at Flögeln, where occupation levels did not survive, yielded traces of hearths, whereas on *Wurten* such as Feddersen Wierde, where occupation levels were preserved, hearths are found in nearly all longhouses (Zimmermann 1992*a*, 147).

sheep does indeed seem to have been lower than in continental Europe, the social value of cattle remained high, and Anglo-Saxon laws show them to have been the most highly valued farm animal (see Chap. 5). A third possibility, that there was strong cultural resistance to the concept of a 'byre-house' by a romanized population (Roymans, pers. comm. 1998) appears anomalous in view of the widespread adoption of continental styles of dress, burial rites, and pottery and the close correlations in dimensions and layout between at least some English and continental buildings (Fig. 2.8). The absence of the longhouse certainly implies a different relationship between the household and the animals which formed its chief source of wealth, but this is unlikely to be the result of a clash between 'romanized' and 'barbarian' ideologies.

Origins

The question of the function of Anglo-Saxon timber buildings thus remains a moot point. We can say rather more about their cultural origins, however, a subject which has generated considerable debate. The continental pedigree of sunken-featured buildings, virtually ubiquitous in Anglo-Saxon settlements from the fifth to eighth centuries, has never been seriously questioned. The type of byre-less house found in England, however, has always been regarded as conspicuous by its absence in continental Europe. This, combined with the absence in England of the longhouse, led the cultural affinities of the former to be debated in a series of papers published in the 1980s which argued, in essence, that the 'Anglo-Saxon' house was in fact Romano-British or, alternatively, a kind of Romano-Saxon hybrid (Dixon 1982, 277; James *et al.* 1985).

Before considering this issue further, it is important to stress that the number of continental examples of byre-less houses without internal roof supports is rapidly increasing, and they can no longer be described as rare (Fig. 2.22; Hamerow 1999*a*). Archaeologists working on the continent, furthermore, no longer dismiss these as 'sheds' and 'outhouses' (*contra* Dixon 1982, 278); instead, they regard them as 'short houses', as at Vorbasse, Wijster (where the Type BII buildings provide close parallels for Anglo-Saxon buildings; van Es 1967, 74 ff.; West 1986, 112), and Nørre Snede, where small houses (some with few or no internal roof-supporting posts) were nearly as numerous as longhouses (Hansen 1987, 180; figs. 7.8, 7.10, 7.11). The need to look to a late Romano-British timber building tradition (which has in any case left little trace) to explain the basic form of the Anglo-Saxon house may thus be unnecessary, and the parallels remain inconclusive (Hamerow 1999*a*).

There is considerable evidence, not only for continental precursors of the Anglo-Saxon house appearing alongside longhouses, but also for the widespread use of continental building templates in England. Zimmermann has demonstrated that the ground-plans of at least some Anglo-Saxon buildings correspond closely to longhouses in terms of the positioning of entrances and subdivisions,

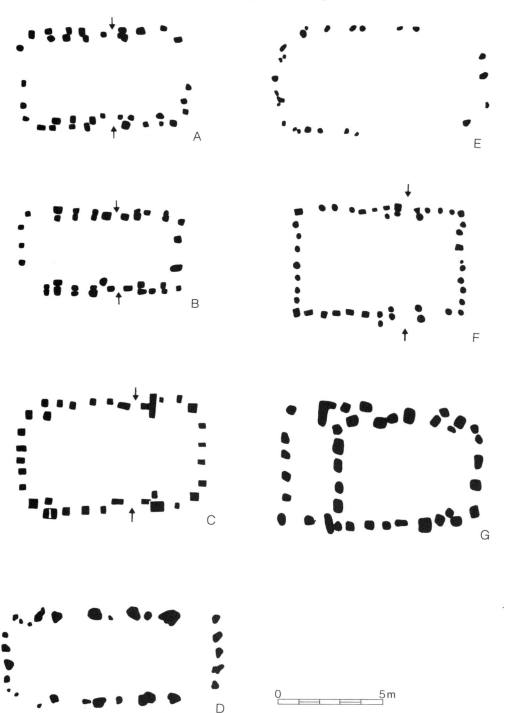

Fig. 2.22. Plans of short houses without internal roof-supporting posts in Germany and the Netherlands. After Hamerow 1999*a*, fig. 5. (A) Peelo, House 35; (B) Peelo, House 51; (C) Wijster, House X; (D) Flögeln, House 149; (E) Flögeln, House 137; (F) Bennekom, House 25; (G) Ede, House 1.

and thus of the organization of internal space, suggesting that continental norms were observed in several regions of early Anglo-Saxon England (Zimmermann 1988, 472; Hamerow 1999*a*). Furthermore, the percentage of continental buildings without rows of internal roof supports and without byres actually increased in the fifth and sixth centuries (Tummuscheit 1995, 111–15, Karte 4; Zimmermann 1988, 472 and 1992, 139) while during the same period, the length of longhouses markedly decreased in many regions, as noted earlier (cf. Zimmermann 1992*a*, 139; Bardet *et al.* 1983, 20 and fig. 11; Hvass 1983, 131).

The early medieval timber buildings found in England should be seen against the background of these wider developments within the North Sea zone, which suggest that Anglo-Saxon buildings of the fifth and sixth centuries fit broadly within a long-lived tradition found across much of northwest Europe. This is not to deny the possibility, indeed the likelihood, that Anglo-Saxon buildings were influenced in various ways by Romano-British traditions. Certain features appearing in the later sixth or seventh centuries, such as double-plank construction and annexes at the gable ends of buildings, are, furthermore, distinctively 'insular', though both appear to have been comparatively rare and there is no clear evidence that they derive from late Roman traditions (James *et al.* 1985, 205).

Conclusion

The apparent absence in England of houses with byres and internal roof-supporting posts remains, nevertheless, a largely unresolved problem. Why, when use of other forms of Germanic material culture (costume and dress ornaments, for example) was reinforced to act as group markers, should the longhouse, for centuries the traditional farmhouse, be given up so readily and so comprehensively when the sunken-featured building was retained? This seeming paradox is still more puzzling in view of cross-cultural studies which suggest that architecture 'becomes so identified with groups, cultures and lifestyles that it is essential in order to feel at home', and that the re-creation by immigrants of their own architectural forms is an important factor in their adjustment to a new environment (Rapoport 1979, 16).

Two explanations for the absence of the longhouse in England and the origins of the Anglo-Saxon house are generally posited. The first is that 'Germanic immigrants [adopted] British buildings . . . but still used their own constructional techniques developed . . . to imitate the fine stone buildings of early times' (James *et al.* 1985, 206). This appears to be ruled out by the close similarities in layout between the Anglo-Saxon house and timber buildings in regions well beyond the imperial frontier. The alternative is that many of the inhabitants of the Anglo-Saxon house were descendants of the Romano-British population who nevertheless sought to emulate the politically and socially ascendant group, in part by adopting their architectural forms as well as their burial rites and costume (ibid.). This is a much more likely scenario. We should, therefore, seek to explain the absence of the longhouse in England through the dual processes of migration and acculturation, and the resultant changes in the composition and economy of the household. The fact that sunken-featured buildings are found throughout early Anglo-Saxon England in a form apparently unchanged from the continent suggests strongly that the key issue behind the absence of the long-house is not ethnic identity. The construction of a longhouse and associated buildings as seen in the enclosed, ancestral farmstead complexes of northwest Europe was a social act as much as a technical one; it required access not only to substantial material capital (i.e. timber) but also to considerable social capital in the form of reciprocal labour obligations.[15] Such an undertaking would have required the voluntary assistance of an extended group beyond the household, possibly even beyond the village, and it seems likely that households in the fifth and sixth centuries simply did not have access to sufficient 'social capital'.

More puzzling, perhaps, than the absence of the longhouse in England is the absence of an English version of the 'Warendorf house'. Earlier in this chapter it was established that the building sequences seen in the Netherlands, Germany, and southern Scandinavia all reflect a general trend towards roof supports set within the walls, with external raking posts and bowed long walls. Variations of the 'Warendorf house' are found all along the North Sea coast and in Denmark. It is all the more striking, then, that they do not make an appearance in England, where rectangular buildings continued to be built as before, although with more varied proportions and wall constructions and with an increased use of post-in-trench and plank-in-trench foundations which allowed for the construction of larger buildings. Relatively few eighth-century Anglo-Saxon building plans have yet been published, however, particularly from the trading settlements known as *wics*, and a closer examination of the buildings of this period is clearly called for. Even so, it is striking that the long-standing links between timber building traditions on the continent and in England appear to have weakened from the later seventh and eighth centuries, precisely when economic, artistic, and political links flourished.

---

[15] By social or symbolic capital I follow Bourdieu's definition of the obligation and prestige which is accumulated, sometimes over generations, by means of services rendered and gifts bestowed (Bourdieu 1990). It is interesting to note in this regard a thirteenth-century law from Zealand, containing several older passages, which specifies that peasants must all participate in the construction of the estate managers' houses (Nissen Jaubert 1998, 222).

3

Settlement Structure and Social Space

A building is a small city; a city is a large building.

(Van Eyck, in Rapoport 1979, 8)

THE SHAPE OF SETTLEMENTS

The way in which a community arranges its living space is only partly due to technical considerations: social relations also play a major role in determining the layout of settlements, as we can see from cross-cultural studies (Rapoport 1980, 9). A correlation exists, for example, between increased economic complexity and complexity and regularity in settlement structure. Thus, while hunter-gatherer settlements tend to have a fairly flexible structure, societies which emphasize concepts of property and territory are more likely to develop fixed 'rules' regarding settlement layout (Fraser 1968). The early Middle Ages saw profound changes in socio-political structures as early states were formed, as well as major developments in food-production strategies and technology. We should, therefore, expect to see these changes reflected, at least indirectly, in the layouts of settlements.

Spatial order in a settlement both reflects and helps to regulate social order and social relations; it provides, quite literally, 'a framework for living' (Chapman 1989; Giddens 1979, 207; Leach 1976, 10). This presents the archaeologist with a daunting prospect, for it is far easier to explain the arrangement of early medieval settlements in terms of function or geometry than in terms of kinship structure, household composition, marriage patterns, and so on, factors which we can at best only glimpse through documentary sources. If, for example, we are to interpret the significance of an exceptionally large house or farmstead accurately, we first need to know whether power was vested in the heads of households or lineages, a council of elders, or in some form of paramount chiefdom. Despite these limitations, settlement layout is an important source of evidence for the social and economic structures of early medieval communities.

The individual household appears to have been the basic unit of agricultural production in northwest Europe from the Roman Iron Age to the Carolingian/Viking periods. The economic importance and, to some degree, independence of the household is underscored by the fact that in most cases each lay within its own enclosure and had its own storage facilities (in contrast, for example, to the shared compounds of the earlier Iron Age, as seen, for example, at Hodde in Denmark: Hvass 1985). Any classification of settlement structure should therefore have as its fundamental criterion the spatial relationship between household units, that is, whether they were contiguous, dispersed, aligned in rows, and so forth. But how are we to define this relationship? The overall 'shape' of a settlement is determined by a great many factors, yet certain basic components which are common to nearly all settlements of this period can be defined:

1. *'units'*, i.e. discrete features such as buildings, pits, and wells;

2. *paths*, linking 'units' or groups of 'units';

3. *boundaries*, enclosing or separating 'units' or groups of 'units'; and less commonly:

4. *central features or unbuilt areas.*

Simply put, the form of a settlement is determined by the way in which these components are articulated.

The only distinction based on size which is made here is that between settlements which consisted essentially of one or two household units, and larger groupings. It may seem odd not to include settlement size as a criterion for determining settlement type. The reason, however, is that we can rarely, if ever, be certain of the precise number of contemporary buildings or households in a given settlement, or even that it has been completely excavated. This complicates the assessment of the overall size of a settlement, particularly as so few communities of this period constructed well-defined boundaries around their settlements. The difficulties of distinguishing between, for example, 'hamlets' and 'villages' are therefore enormous.[1] In any case, the number of contemporary households in these settlements seems from the archaeological evidence to have had a fairly narrow range, usually between five and twenty.

Until recently it could reasonably have been argued, based on the few excavated sites, that each early medieval settlement was unique in character, and that any attempt to classify settlement form was, therefore, spurious. Yet as the number of large-scale excavations grows, certain regularities and recurring

---

[1] See Taylor 1983, 15. To complicate matters further, the word for 'village' refers to different kinds of settlements in different languages (see n. 6 below) and its meaning may vary further according to individual authors and national traditions of research. Thus, in English, French, and German a distinction is made between a 'village' and a 'hamlet', whereas in the Scandinavian languages all rural settlements are simply referred to as *landsbyer* (Nissen Jaubert 1998, 214). While recognizing that early medieval settlements differ in important ways from later medieval planned villages—in social and economic terms as well as physically—the term 'village' is used here to refer to any rural settlement.

features suggest several main settlement 'shapes', using the criteria outlined above. The typology adopted here is loosely based on that proposed for the Dutch province of Drenthe, where the main settlement forms present in the nineteenth century can be traced back to the early Middle Ages (see below; Waterbolk 1991*a*, 56). These forms are as follows:

1. *Row Settlements*: a trackway (or exceptionally a waterway) is the principal organizing element along which farmsteads (usually contiguous) are aligned;

2. *Grouped Settlements* (Peytremann 1992): farmsteads are grouped around a central space or feature, such as a church or green;

3. *Polyfocal Settlements*: several clusters of buildings lie together without a clear articulating structure;

4. *Perpendicular Settlements*: perpendicular trackways divide farmsteads roughly into a 'chequerboard' layout; and

5. *Single Farmsteads*: It should be noted, however, that the physical isolation of a farmstead need not prevent its inhabitants from managing their fields and boundaries in common with a neighbouring settlement (Nissen Jaubert 1998, 222).

Such a system of classification is inevitably unsatisfactory in some respects and some settlements displayed several different forms, or may have incorporated two different forms. Furthermore, deficiencies in the archaeological record impose serious constraints on classifying settlements according to such a formal scheme. First, only rarely can we be certain that most or all of a particular phase of a settlement has been excavated. Second, the poor state of preservation on some sites makes it difficult to establish with certainty the *absence* of relatively shallow features such as trackways and some types of enclosure. Finally, nearly all of the early medieval settlements excavated to date are multi-period, with occupation spanning, in some cases, many centuries. This, and the difficulties involved in phasing settlements with few diagnostic artefacts, little surviving stratigraphy, and repeated rebuilding, means that it is generally not possible to establish which buildings were exactly contemporary and therefore to produce a 'snapshot' of a settlement at a given moment. Assigning buildings to distinct phases is therefore fraught with difficulties, particularly as only longhouses show any clear chronological development. Where phasing has been attempted, it usually follows (explicitly or otherwise) a 'twenty-five year model' which assumes a cycle of rebuilding or 'rejuvenation' of the settlement approximately once every human generation (Heidinga 1987, 32). Despite these obstacles, a number of settlements have been excavated on a sufficiently large scale and phased in enough detail to enable their layout to be characterized with some confidence. In the following section, some of the best-studied examples of these different settlement forms are briefly described.

Row Settlements

Vorbasse (Jutland) Excavations covering approximately 1 km^2 north of the medieval village of Vorbasse have revealed the development of a settlement over more than a millennium (*c.* first century BC to eleventh century AD), at a scale and level of detail virtually unparalleled in northern Europe (Hvass 1986 and 1988*a*; Fig. 3.1). In the fourth century some twenty enclosed farmsteads lay in two well-defined rows running north–south and separated by a wide trackway onto which each farmyard had an entrance. The largest farmstead in terms of area, and number and size of buildings lay slightly apart at the eastern edge of the village.

This structure altered somewhat in the fifth century (Fig. 3.2). The number of

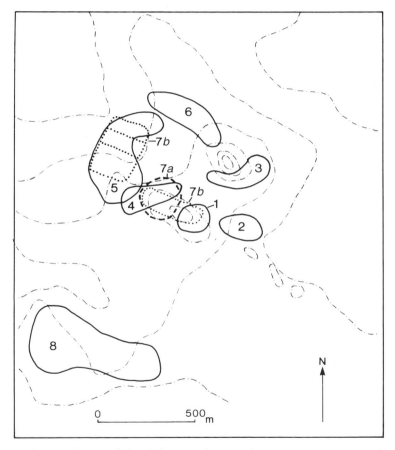

Fig. 3.1. Vorbasse: phases of the shifting settlement. Area 1: 1st century BC; Area 2: 1st century AD; Area 3: 2nd century AD; Area 4: 3rd century AD; Area 5: 4th–5th centuries AD; Area 6: 6th–7th centuries AD; Area 7*a*: 8th–10th centuries AD; Area 7*b*: 11th century AD; Area 8: the village of Vorbasse after the 11th century. After Hvass 1986, Abb. 9.

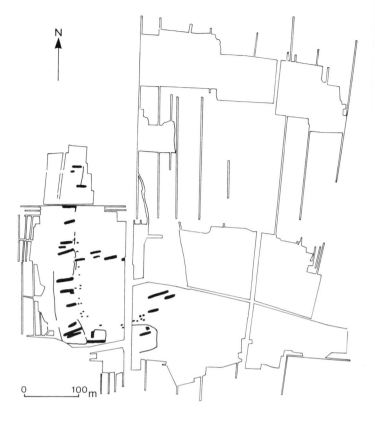

Fig. 3.2. Vorbasse: plan of the
settlement in the fifth century.
After Hvass 1988*a*, fig. 16.

N

0   100 m

farmsteads remained roughly the same, but there were fewer enclosure fences,
although this could be due to poor preservation (Hvass 1986, 534). While most
of the farmsteads were still aligned in a single row, the eastern farmstead and
several others were set apart from the rest, leaving an open central space. The
large eastern farm was rebuilt on the same spot, and still contained the largest
longhouse. One or two sunken-featured buildings lay outside each farmyard
enclosure, at the edge of the central (presumably communal) area. Although not
shown on the interim plans published to date, a further three farms dating to the
fourth and fifth centuries were excavated some 100–200 m to the east of
the main settlement (Hvass 1988*a*, 119).

By the sixth century the settlement had shifted some 200 m north and the
abandoned site of the preceding settlement phase was brought under cultivation
(Hvass 1986, 534). In the sixth and seventh centuries the village consisted of
about ten farmsteads (Fig. 3.3). Although the longhouses were still aligned
east–west, the village now lay along the northern edge of the excavated area and
consisted of an east–west row of contiguous farmsteads, with the result that the
longhouses were aligned end-to-end.

In the eighth century (Fig. 3.4) the settlement shifted some 400 m to the south,

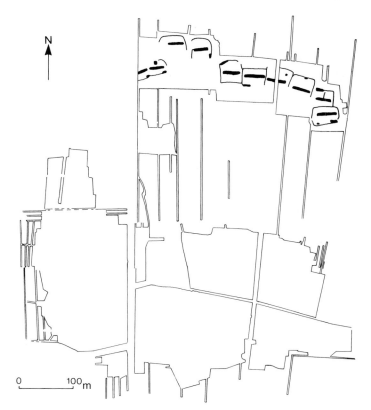

N

0 ___ 100 m

Fig. 3.3. Vorbasse: plan of the settlement in the sixth and seventh centuries. After Hvass 1988*a*, fig. 17.

and major changes can be seen in both the architecture of the buildings and the layout of individual farmyards, although the underlying structure—that of contiguous enclosed farmsteads (now seven in total)—remained unchanged (Hvass 1988*a*, 126–7). The shared boundaries and regular dimensions of the settlement (*c.*240 × 240 m) as well as the trackway which ran east–west through the centre of the village and from which each farmstead could be entered via a gate, suggest a regulated layout. During the late tenth or eleventh century the western part of the settlement consisted of three large farms, the westernmost with a width of 120 m, the other two with a width of 60 m each (Hvass 1980, 162, fig. 26). This careful measurement of individual properties has led the excavator to suggest that these presaged 'medieval paddocks, which regulated common grazing' (Hvass 1988*b*).

Praestestien (Jutland) Another probable row settlement has been partly excavated at Praestestien in southwest Jutland (Fig. 3.5). Excavation of some 30,000 m² revealed a village dating to the fourth to ninth centuries, within which four main phases have been identified (Siemen 1990). In the first phase (Fig.

Fig. 3.4. Vorbasse: the Viking age village. After Hvass 1988*a*, fig. 25.

3.5A, dated to the fourth to sixth centuries), at least six contiguous enclosed farmsteads lay in an east–west running row, with the longhouses situated along the northern edge of each yard, aligned east–west, end to end. Just outside and to the north of these enclosed units were small groups of sunken-featured buildings (not shown on the plan), presumably not all contemporary. During the sixth century the whole settlement moved approximately 150 m to the north (Fig. 3.5B), where it remained for about a century, retaining a similar layout. In the next phase (Fig. 3.5C) the settlement shifted back to the south. During the Viking period the settlement may have taken on a more perpendicular layout (Fig. 3.5D).

Dalem (Lower Saxony) The early medieval settlement at Dalem (Fig. 3.6) lay on an 'island' of sandy soils known as the *Geest*, deposited during the Pleistocene along the coastal regions of the North Sea, on which many of the early settlements in this region were sited. Approximately 20,000 m², roughly two-thirds of the total occupation area, were investigated, revealing at least four enclosed farmsteads dating to the seventh and eighth centuries, lying in a row at the edge of the island (Zimmermann 1991*a*). The individual plots, all of similar size, contained sunken-featured buildings, barns, and granaries arranged around the central house. A cemetery of approximately 100 graves dating to the eighth and

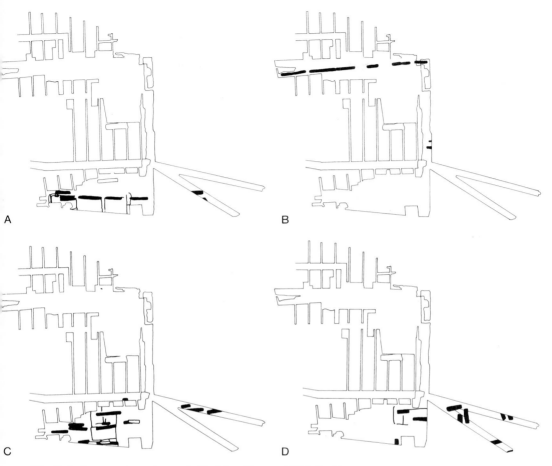

Fig. 3.5. Praestestien: phases A–D. After Siemen 1990, fig. 3.

ninth centuries was situated slightly to the east of the settlement. The rising water table forced the village to shift some 60 m to the west in the tenth century. The number and size of granaries and barns indicates a substantial storage capacity (see Chap. 5).

Bielefeld-Sieker (Nordrhein-Westfalen) Excavation of some 22,000 m² revealed part of a Roman Iron Age and Migration period settlement situated on a flat ridge between two small streams (Fig. 3.7). Eight longhouses, some fifteen smaller buildings, thirteen granaries, and five sunken-featured buildings lay stretched out in a row along the ridge, their layout dictated by the course of the streams (Doms 1990).

Warendorf (Westphalia) Warendorf, situated on a terrace of the River Ems, was one of the first early medieval settlements to be extensively excavated

Fig. 3.6. Dalem: plan of settlement. After Zimmermann 1991*a*, Abb. 2.

(Winkelmann 1958). Some 26,000 m² (an unknown percentage of the total settlement) were investigated, revealing twenty-five houses, forty smaller buildings,
seventy sunken-featured buildings, and twenty 'ephemeral' structures in two
excavation trenches lying some 200 m apart. A north–south running fence lay
*c.*130 m to the west of the settlement, although at least one small building was

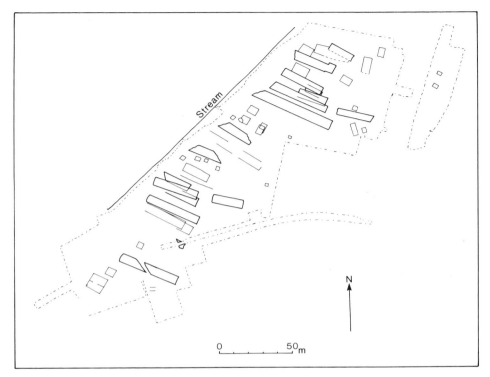

Fig. 3.7. Bielefeld-Sieker: plan of settlement. After Doms 1990, 266.

found immediately beyond this and traces of occupation were found some 200 m further to the west. The settlement is believed to have extended north-eastwards towards the Ems, probably to an old ford leading to a major road.

The layout of the settlement is unclear, and Warendorf may not have been a true 'row' settlement: no enclosures or obvious pathways were identified, and only a small part of the settlement has been phased.[2] There were up to five phases of rebuilding, suggesting a series of around five closely spaced farmsteads in the main trench (Winkelmann 1958, 512). Analysis of the pottery indicates that these rebuildings took place over some 200 years, from the first half of the seventh century until well into the ninth century (Röber 1990). The size of the main residential buildings and the distances between them do, however, show strong dimensional coherence.

Kirchheim (Bavaria) One of the largest excavations of an early medieval settle-ment in southern Germany took place at Kirchheim, near Munich (Fig. 3.8), where some 45,000 m² (approximately half of the settlement, to judge from aerial photographs) of a seventh- to eighth-century village was uncovered, with

---

[2] As no phased plan of the settlement is currently available, Warendorf has not been illustrated.

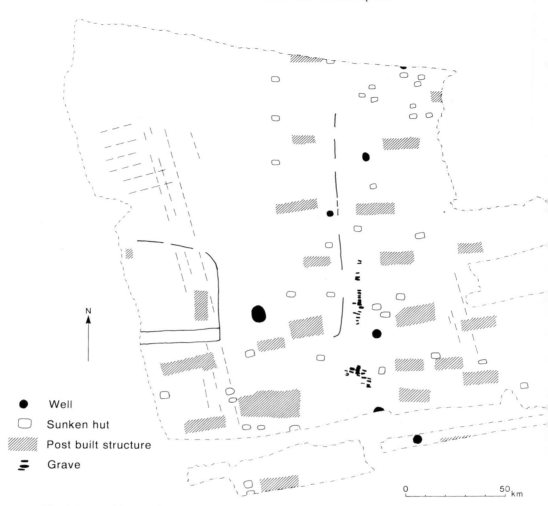

Fig. 3.8. Kirchheim: plan of settlement. After Christlein 1981*b*, Abb. 12.

thirty post-built structures and forty sunken-featured buildings representing around a dozen farmsteads (Christlein 1981*a*; 1981*b*). Most farmsteads appear to have had their own well, and some had a small, presumably family, cemetery of between ten and thirty inhumation graves. Interim plans indicate that the buildings were laid out along a north–south running trackway. The settlement was abandoned by the ninth century, when the community presumably moved to the site of the church from which the village takes its name, some 350 m north-west of the early medieval settlement.

Gasselte (Drenthe) The medieval settlement lies adjacent to the present-day village of Gasselte and was laid out along the western edge of a north–south road

Fig. 3.9. Gasselte: (A) Phase 1; (B) Phase 2. After Waterbolk and Harsema 1979, Plans VI and VII.

(Figs. 3.9 and 3.10). Despite the late date of the buildings—ninth to twelfth centuries—the development and layout of the settlement in relation to its fields is instructive (Waterbolk and Harsema 1979; Waterbolk 1991*a*, 96). In the earliest phase the village consisted of a row, 450 m long, of nine enclosed farmyards separated from one another by narrow pathways; behind these lay a second row of at least two farmsteads. The second phase was laid out in essentially the same way, but consisted of a single, slightly curved row of nine farmsteads, each roughly 40 m wide; the narrow pathways which originally ran between the individual plots had become incorporated into the plots, suggesting that the fields which lay behind were reached via the individual farmsteads (Waterbolk and Harsema 1979, 258). The cadastral map of 1813 shows a striking coincidence between the nineteenth-century field boundaries and the early medieval farmsteads (Fig. 3.10), graphically demonstrating how the layout of the early

Fig. 3.10. Gasselte: the excavated village in relation to the nineteenth-century cadastral map. After Waterbolk 1991*a*, Abb. 34.

medieval settlement was preserved in the field system after the community shifted to a new location and brought the old settlement area under cultivation, a phenomenon which appears to have been widespread in the North Sea zone (see discussion of Vorbasse above, and Kootwijk and Odoorn below; see also Chap. 4).

Perpendicular Settlements

Nørre Snede (Jutland) The settlement of Nørre Snede (Fig. 3.11) lay only some 40 km from Vorbasse in a similar sandy moraine landscape (Hansen 1987). Excavation of an area of *c*.86,000 m² revealed some 400 buildings dating from the beginning of the third century to the seventh century. Five main phases have provisionally been identified (the four latest appear in Fig. 3.11). Viking period and later medieval finds have been recovered from the area of the church and

Fig. 3.11. Nørre Snede: phases A–D. After Hansen 1987, figs. 16–19.

present-day village. It is believed that most, if not all, of the early medieval settlement has been excavated, although at the time of writing only interim plans have been published. A few early medieval graves were excavated, but these must represent only a small percentage of the population.

Nørre Snede, like Vorbasse, consisted largely of contiguous enclosed farmsteads. Although there were trackways running through the settlement, the layout is not straightforwardly 'perpendicular'. This is probably due, at least in part, to the uneven topography of the site, which varied by up to 15 m in elevation. By the fourth century the farmsteads appear to have been grouped around an unbuilt area (Fig. 3.11B). By the seventh century (Fig. 3.11D) the village was laid out around several intersecting trackways, and contained unbuilt areas as well as a number of unenclosed buildings. The largest yards covered approximately 2,500–3,500 m^2, while the smallest covered an area of only $c.375$ m^2. Occupation shifted gradually north and westwards by some 300 m. The number of individual farmsteads in each phase ranged from six to eleven, although not all could be assigned to a particular phase.

Odoorn (Drenthe) Excavations in 1966 established the northern and eastern limits of an early medieval settlement situated on a slightly raised, sandy moraine near a small lake (Figs. 3.12 and 3.13). Seventy-two ground-level buildings, including some twenty longhouses, and sixty-nine sunken-featured buildings were uncovered, dating from the seventh to ninth centuries (Waterbolk 1973 and forthcoming). During the first phase of settlement no obvious system of trackways or enclosures was discernible. In the second phase, however, a square enclosure was built, together with one or more trackways leading through the settlement. During the third and fourth phases (Fig. 3.12A, $c.700$) there is clear evidence of fenced farmsteads and a system of north–south and east–west running trackways. In the course of the fifth phase (Fig. 3.12B) the central precinct was divided into three or four fenced yards or paddocks (at least one of which contained no houses) of roughly equal size, closing off in the process the main north–south trackway as well as other trackways. In the following phase (Fig. 3.12C) all the old trackways were re-established and new enclosures were built along the same boundaries which had been established in Phase 4. These enclosed precincts were no longer residential, however, and contained only barns and a few sunken-featured buildings; unlike the longhouses, some of the barns were oriented north–south, and nearly all adjoined an enclosure fence. This phase represents a period after the community had abandoned the old site and brought it under cultivation, leaving only a few agricultural buildings. Belonging to a still later phase (Fig. 3.12D) were ditches, fences, gullies, and plough marks, indicating the conversion of the old settlement site to arable after the community had shifted north towards the site of the present-day village. As at Gasselte, there is a remarkable correspondence between the field boundaries shown on the cadastral map of 1831 and those of the early medieval enclosures

Fig. 3.12. Odoorn: the main phases. After Waterbolk 1991*a*, Abb. 35–9.

(Fig. 3.13), supporting the interpretation of the enclosed precincts, which first emerged *c.*700 as properties. The re-establishment in Phase 6 (Fig. 3.12C) of the precincts and trackways of Phase 4 (Fig. 3.12A) also points to the continuity of what must have been legally established property boundaries.

A second excavation campaign took place at Odoorn between 1977 and 1981, which extended the site a further 3 ha to the south and uncovered at least another twenty-two longhouses although it is estimated that no more than eight

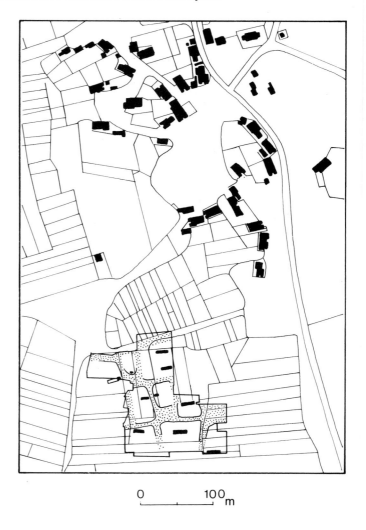

Fig. 3.13. Odoorn: the excavated village in relation to the
nineteenth-century cadastral
map. After Waterbolk 1991*a*,
Abb. 35.

0   100 m

or nine of these stood together at any one time (Waterbolk forthcoming). In this
second area, as yet unpublished, two zones can be identified: a northern zone
which shows a similar layout to that of the adjacent, originally excavated area—
namely, dense occupation and enclosed farmsteads separated by trackways—
and a southern zone which, in contrast, had few overlapping ground-plans and
virtually no enclosures. It is thought that this southern zone was established
around the middle of the sixth century, roughly a century before the more clearly
structured settlement to the north (Lanting 1983; pers. comm. 1993).

Wijster (Drenthe) The settlement at Wijster (Fig. 3.14) was situated on a low,
sandy ridge, adjacent to a small fen. Although the excavations in 1958–61

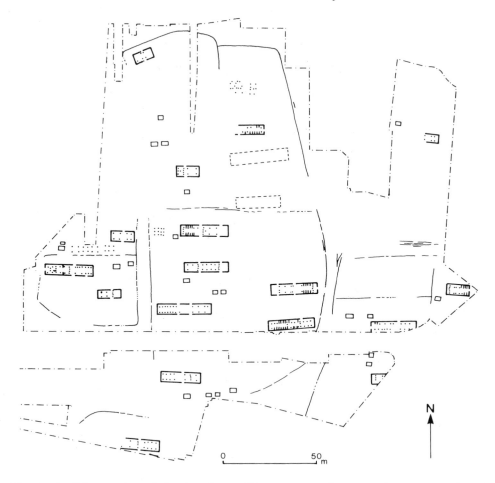

Fig. 3.14. Wijster: plan of the fourth- to fifth-century settlement. After Haarnagel and Schmidt 1984, Abb. 79.

uncovered some 36,300 m², the limits of the settlement were not established (van Es 1967). The earliest occupation of this area, dating to the second century AD, consisted of one to three scattered farmsteads. In the course of the third century a clearly planned layout of trackways, enclosures, and farmsteads replaced the earlier, dispersed units. The latest, that is, fourth- to fifth-century, phase of settlement[3] saw some further reorganization and a more uniform orientation of the main longhouses, although the farmsteads now contained fewer granaries, storage pits, and oven pits than in the preceding phases. The excavated area contained at least fifteen contemporary longhouses, mostly arranged within some

---

[3] A re-evaluation of the pottery and building plans at Wijster suggests, however, that the settlement may have continued into the sixth century (H. T. Waterbolk, pers. comm.).

ten enclosed farmsteads, divided by north–south and east–west running track-ways. Each farmstead contained its own storage facilities (i.e. pits and granaries, sometimes aligned along the edges of enclosures) and water was supplied by a number of wells, which were sometimes, though not always, associated with particular farmsteads. Some burials contemporary with the later phases of the settlement were discovered to the south, in a cemetery which was partly exca-vated in the 1920s.

Kootwijk (Gelderland) Excavations at Kootwijk in the central Netherlands (Figs. 3.15–3.18) revealed two main phases of early medieval occupation (Heidinga 1987): two settlements of the Merovingian period (a small scattered settlement and a large, isolated farm, neither of which was extensively exca-vated), and a Carolingian village established in the early eighth century, which grew rapidly from six or eight farmsteads to around twenty, and was aban-doned by the end of the tenth century. The Carolingian village could not be com-pletely excavated, and an unknown number of apparently scattered farmsteads lay to the south and east of the main village. Kootwijk forms the focus of an important study of early settlement in the Veluwe district (see Chap. 4), but it is the layout of the settlement which concerns us here. The underlying structure was provided by a network of perpendicular trackways running through the village, one of which led directly to a shallow pool at the eastern edge of the settlement. Other main roads ran to the north, south, and west, connecting Kootwijk with unidentified destinations. In addition to these were several smaller trackways 'of strictly local importance' (Heidinga 1987, 25). No zoning is apparent, apart from a few clusters of pits of uncertain function and the con-centration of wells near the pool. The number of wells in the later phases sug-gests that each household probably had access to one or more of these, but only a few were situated on what the excavator has taken to be 'privately owned land' (Heidinga 1987, 27).

This network of roads and trackways divided the fifty-two houses, thirty barns, ten granaries or haystacks, and at least 180 sunken-featured buildings into eight 'precincts', each of which contained one to three houses at any one time. The excavator believes that within these precincts each household had its own plot, even though subdivisions within individual precincts were not readily apparent (Heidinga 1987, 26). Indications that the village consisted of individ-ual properties do, nevertheless, exist. North of Precinct 1, for example (but not shown in Figs. 3.15–3.16), two farmsteads, each measuring *c*.45 × 25 m, repre-sent the bisection of an earlier larger unit. Similar subdivision has been identified in several other precincts. The likelihood that rules of inheritance underlie such subdivision is strengthened by the observation that the outline of the Carolingian 'precincts' became fossilized as parcels of land in the field system which overlay the old settlement once the village had moved elsewhere. A similar phenomenon has been observed at Odoorn and Gasselte (see above). Thus, in

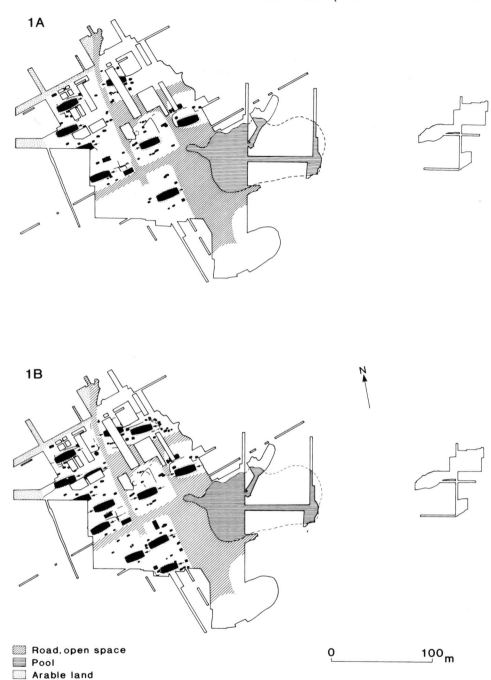

1A

1B

N

▨ Road, open space
▤ Pool
░ Arable land

0 _____ 100 m

Fig. 3.15. Kootwijk: plan of phases 1A and 1B. After Heidinga 1987, figs. II–X.

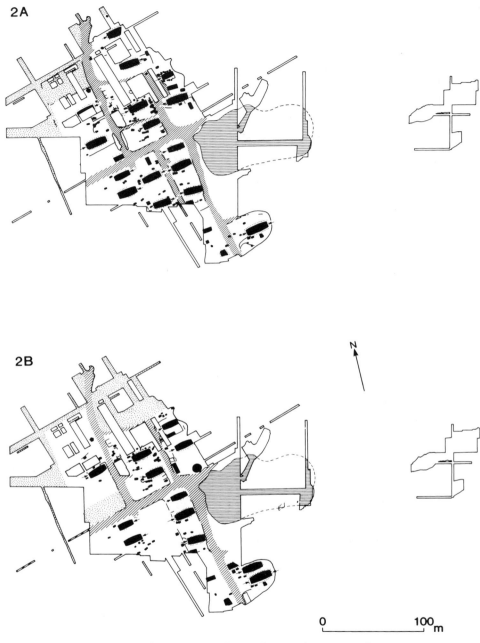

Fig. 3.16. Kootwijk: plan of phases 2A and 2B. After Heidinga 1987, figs. II–X.

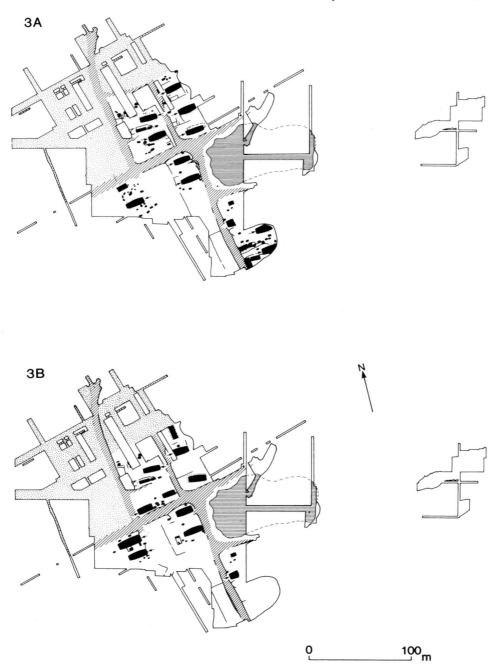

Fig. 3.17. Kootwijk: plan of phases 3A and 3B. After Heidinga 1987, figs. II–X.

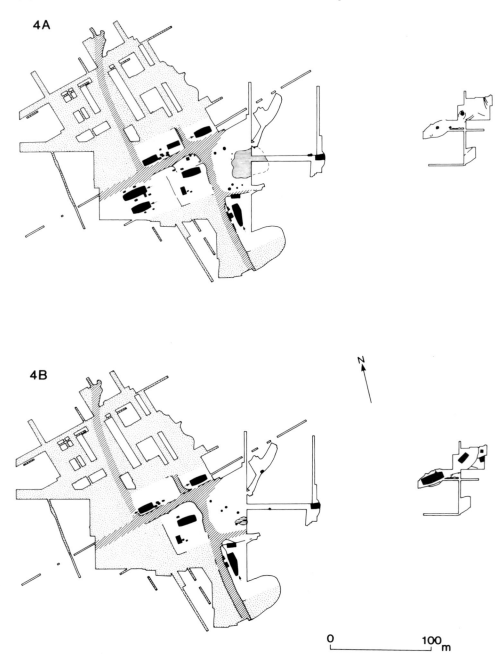

Fig. 3.18. Kootwijk: plan of phases 4A, 4B, and 4C. After Heidinga 1987, figs. II–X.

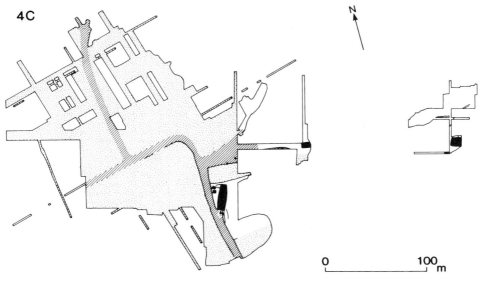

Fig. 3.18. (*Continued*)

Phase 2A two new precincts were established while one of the original precincts was abandoned (Fig. 3.16). This reflects a process which is becoming increasingly well documented among early medieval settlements: that is, as a community expanded onto heath or woodland, demolition took place in those parts of the village which bordered onto the fields, in this case to the north and west of the village; these abandoned settlement plots, with their heightened fertility, were then incorporated into the fields.

As always, exact contemporaneity of structures is difficult to establish, yet it is notable that the distance between residential buildings at Kootwijk varied considerably in Phase 1A: Precinct 1 contained four closely spaced houses, while to the south and east the houses were more widely placed (Fig. 3.15). The excavator attributes this distinction to different 'social backgrounds' (Heidinga 1987, 37). If he is right, the more regular distances between farmhouses in Phases 1B–3A (Figs. 3.15–3.17) represent a significant development; this distance again increased in later phases (Fig. 3.18).

Polyfocal Settlements

Flögeln-Eekhöltjen (Lower Saxony) The settlement of Flögeln-Eekhöltjen (Fig. 3.19) was continuously occupied from the first century BC to the sixth century AD, and lay on the same sandy 'island' as the later settlement of Dalem (see above). Like Dalem, Flögeln was favourably situated between the sandy *Geest* and the coastal marshes, on the main waterway leading to the *Wurten* of the

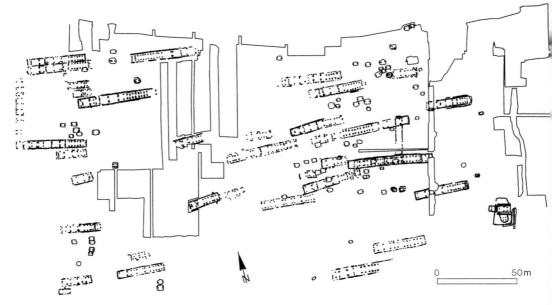

Fig. 3.19(A). Flögeln-Eekhöltjen: fourth–fifth century buildings (enclosures and 'lean-to' granaries not shown). Reproduced with kind permission of Dr W. H. Zimmermann.

Fig. 3.19(B). Flögeln-Eekhöltjen: fifth–sixth century buildings (enclosures and 'lean-to' granaries not shown). Reproduced with kind permission of Dr W. H. Zimmerman.

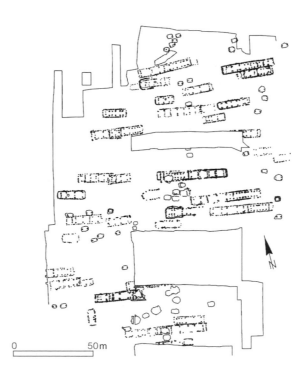

neighbouring marsh, and there is some evidence to suggest that its economic life was closely bound up with communities such as Feddersen Wierde (see Chap. 6). In total, 108,456 m² were excavated. At the time of writing the buildings have been published in full; discussion of the phasing and layout, however, is based on interim statements (Schmid and Zimmermann 1976; Schmid 1982; Zimmermann 1992*a*).

During the fourth to mid fifth centuries, two different layouts appear to have existed side by side. To the west lay a row of three enclosed farmsteads, running north–south. The northernmost of these was a large farmstead believed to be associated with the cremation cemetery of Flögeln-Vossbarg, which lay some 80 m to the south (Schön 1988). In the eastern and northeastern parts of the excavated area lay several unenclosed farmsteads. Few if any granaries could be assigned to the fourth and fifth centuries, although the ratio of sunken-featured buildings to longhouses was approximately 2 : 1, substantially higher than in the preceding phase. A separate craft-working zone, used in particular for iron-working and possibly tanning, lay to the west, downwind from the settlement. This apparent increase in emphasis on non-agrarian production parallels con-temporary developments at the *Wurt* of Feddersen Wierde (see below). In the mid fifth century occupation shifted to the west, retaining a high proportion of sunken-featured buildings and containing a number of byre-less houses. The site appears to have been abandoned during the first half of the sixth century.

Speyer 'Vogelgesang' (Rheinland-Pfalz) Excavations on a terrace of the Rhine (Fig. 3.20) revealed a dense scatter of eighty-one sunken-featured buildings, granaries, and three small ground-level buildings in an area of about 25,000 m² (Bernhard 1981 and 1982). Occupation shifted some 500 m from east to west during a period which spanned the later fifth to eighth/ninth centuries. The latest, western, sector appears to have consisted solely of groups of sunken-featured buildings, although the use of sill-beam construction could explain the lack of timber buildings here and in the region generally.

Grouped Settlements

Feddersen Wierde (Lower Saxony) The *Wurt* settlement of Feddersen Wierde (Fig. 3.21), situated on the coastal marshes between the rivers Elbe and Weser, was subjected to large-scale excavation from 1955 to 1963, and in many ways provided the blueprint for subsequent interpretations of the development of Roman Iron Age and early medieval villages (see Chap. 1; Haarnagel 1979*a*; 1979*b*). The *Wurt* was occupied from the first century BC to the fifth century AD, when it was abandoned due to flooding, to be resettled in the eighth century, although only patchy evidence survives of this later resettlement. Only the third-to fifth-century settlement phases are reviewed here.

In the third century (Horizon 5) some sixteen medium-sized and ten smaller

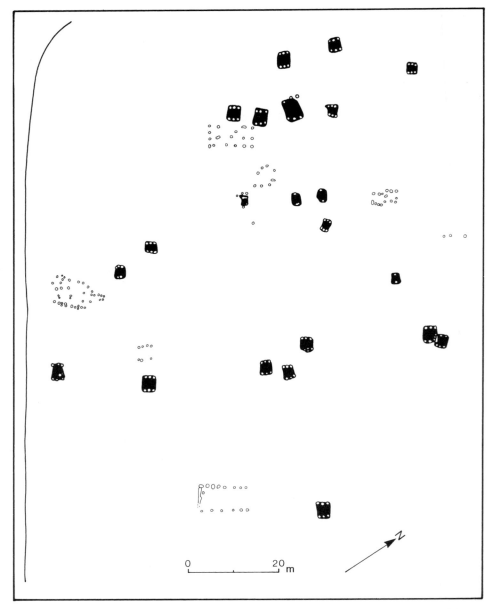

Fig. 3.20. Speyer-Vogelgesang: plan of part of the settlement. After Bernhard 1981, Abb. 8.

farmsteads were identified. These were laid out in a radial fashion, to make the most efficient use of the limited space available on the mound. Houses were aligned along several trackways which led to an open central area. To the east of the main area of settlement, a trackway led to a so-called *Herrenhof* (chief's

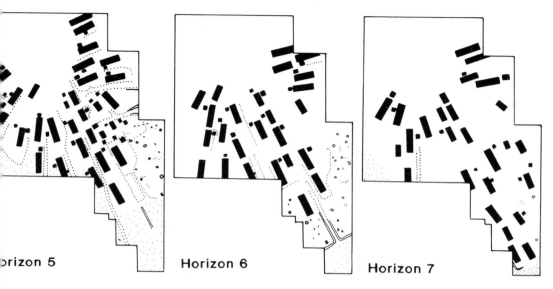

Fig. 3.21. Feddersen Wierde: Horizons 5–7. After Schmid 1984, Abb. 70.

farmstead), a large enclosed complex which had emerged in the second century. This comprised a large longhouse and presumed 'meeting hall', as well as a large craft-working zone to the northeast (with evidence for wood-, bone-, and metal-working) and a storage zone with granaries, interpreted by the excavator as providing food for dependent craftworkers who lived in small houses with little or no provision for stabling cattle. In the fourth century (Horizon 6) there were still twenty-two farmsteads, but these had only around half the number of stalls for cattle as in the third century. The *Herrenhof* remained largely unchanged, however. The overall layout of the later fourth- to fifth-century village (Horizons 7 and 8) was more dispersed and irregular; few of the remaining buildings were enclosed and many were small, again interpreted as the homes of craft-workers. This fundamental change in the composition and layout of the settlement has been attributed to a shift in economic emphasis from agriculture to craft production (cf. Flögeln, above), as a consequence of the increasing salination of the surrounding farmland.

Single Farmsteads

Mørup (Jutland) A single fenced yard (Fig. 3.22), comparable in size (2,600 m²) to the largest yards at Nørre Snede, contained a longhouse, two or three shorter houses, and a row of 'lean-to' granaries. Three smaller houses also lay outside this fenced enclosure (only one of which is shown in Fig. 3.23). The whole complex dates to the sixth and seventh centuries (Näsman 1987, 463). Although

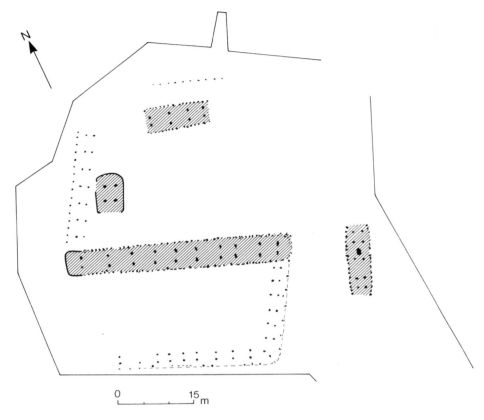

Fig. 3.22. Mørup: plan of the settlement. After D. Mikkelsen, in Hvass 1988*b*, fig. 28.

Mørup is believed to have been excavated in its entirety, one cannot rule out the possibility that a village existed nearby to which Mørup was in some way linked, a situation seen at Vorbasse (see above) and at Bellinge (Zealand) (Nissen Jaubert 1998, 222).

Dalen (Drenthe) A small-scale rescue excavation revealed a seventh- to eighth-century farmstead (Fig. 3.23) consisting of two main longhouses, two smaller buildings, and three sunken-featured buildings, possibly within a fenced enclosure. The excavator believes this to represent an isolated farmstead which was not part of a larger settlement complex (Kooi 1989).

THE EARLY MEDIEVAL FARMSTEAD

The structure of individual farmsteads can be examined using many of the same criteria used to characterize the layout of entire settlements. To gain an accurate

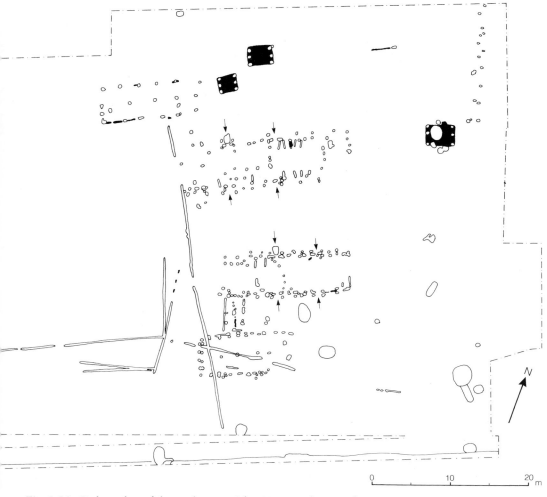

Fig. 3.23. Dalen: plan of the settlement. After Kooi *et al.* 1989, fig. 2.

picture of an individual farmyard at any one time, however, is exceptionally difficult, for although longhouses can be roughly dated according to their ground-
plans, fences and smaller buildings usually cannot. The phase maps produced by
archaeologists therefore 'show the houses at a certain *moment*, but surrounded
by [other structures] from a certain *period* . . . Every sunken hut, fence [*etc.*] has
its own history that is partly dissociated from that of the main building, and that
certainly did not develop to fit in with the phasing system of the archaeologist'
(Heidinga 1987, 32).

Archaeological data of exceptionally high quality, as well as detailed, phased
site-plans, are therefore needed if we are to ascertain whether the main

farmhouse was rebuilt on the same site or whether it shifted, whether there were zones for different activities, how many entrances led into a farmstead and where these were located, and how all these and other features changed over time. Recent analysis of the settlement of Nørre Snede has shown that contemporary farmsteads could develop in quite different ways, with one, for example, undergoing well-defined phases of rebuilding in which buildings were moved to entirely new positions, while another's layout remained unchanged despite repeated rebuildings (Holst 1997, 117–18). What such differences mean in social terms, however (with regard, for example, to patterns of marriage and inheritance), is far from clear. Since very few excavated settlements have reached such an advanced stage of analysis, answers to such questions must await future investigation. These limitations notwithstanding, there is ample evidence to suggest that individual farmsteads were arranged according to certain norms or 'rules'. Such patterns are most clearly seen in settlements with a large number of contemporary farmsteads, and for this reason the following discussion is restricted to a relatively small number of sites.

The Migration period farmsteads at Vorbasse and Nørre Snede had in general at least two entrances: a small 'pedestrian' entrance (on average around 1 m wide), and a larger entrance (around 2–3 m wide) for wheeled vehicles which presumably led on to trackways (Hvass 1986, 531; 1988a, fig. 13). During the fourth to seventh centuries most farmyards were heavily built up along the inner edge of the enclosure fence with lean-to granaries; in many cases buildings (apparently houses, though not necessarily longhouses) were also incorporated into the enclosure, in such a way that access to the farmyard could also be gained via a building. In the third and fourth centuries fewer than half of the farmsteads at Nørre Snede and Vorbasse could be entered in this way. By the sixth and seventh centuries, however, nearly all the farmsteads at Nørre Snede, and most of those at Vorbasse, could be entered via a building. The central area of the yard was left relatively open.

A Migration period farmstead at Nørre Snede may serve as a reasonably typical example of this kind of layout (Fig. 3.24). It covered an area of about 50 × 40 m and contained structures which had been rebuilt on roughly the same spot up to five times, indicating that individual property boundaries remained fairly stable over several generations. The longhouse lay along the northern edge of the yard, forming part of the enclosure fence. Two smaller houses, one of which was also built into the enclosure fence, lay to the south. The yard also contained five four-post granaries (as many as four of which could have been contemporary), as well as 'lean-to' granaries lining two sides of the enclosure (T. E. Hansen, pers. comm.).

In the eighth and ninth centuries a more uniform farmstead layout began to appear, as seen most clearly at Vorbasse. The main houses (all *c*.30 m long) were now located within the farmyards rather than being incorporated into the enclosure fence. Smaller houses and granaries lay around the edges of the yards. Groups of sunken-featured buildings were positioned between the main

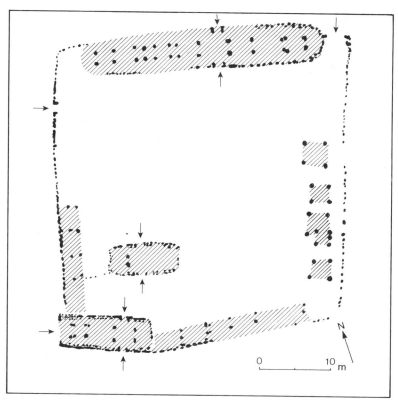

Fig. 3.24. Nørre Snede: a farmstead. After Hansen 1987, fig. 11.

longhouse and the road, and now lay within the yard, in contrast to the preceding period (see Fig. 3.4).

Although these regularities in the layout of the farmsteads at Vorbasse have been attributed to a 'division of activities' (Hvass 1985, 216), direct evidence of activity zones is in fact relatively scarce. During the fourth century groups of iron-smelting pits lay behind and just outside of two enclosed farmsteads. In the fifth century sunken-featured buildings, at least some of which appear to have been associated with craft activities, lay in small groups associated with individual farmsteads, but immediately outside their enclosures, in the space between the two main rows of buildings. As noted above, a similar pattern is seen in the early Viking period, when the sunken-featured buildings also lay between the main house and the road, but were situated within the farmyard.

The publication of Wijster provides some of the most detailed descriptions of Migration period farmsteads in the Netherlands (van Es 1967). The longhouses lay more or less centrally within individual enclosures, with a gable end directed towards a north–south running trackway; in one or two cases the gable end of a house was incorporated into an enclosure fence, so that the house could be entered directly from the trackway. In the mid- to late fourth century (Phase 3B), a number of longhouses had sunken-featured buildings adjacent to their 'living rooms', although most storage facilities lay along the edges of the yard. Most, though not all, farmsteads contained a well. By the late fourth and early fifth centuries (Phase 3C) the few remaining granaries were adjacent to longhouses and the number of storage pits had dwindled markedly.

At Odoorn the longhouses also lay more or less centrally within the farmyard. In the latest phase, however (Fig. 3.12C), barns were in several cases built into the enclosure fence, like the Migration period houses of central Jutland, although with the important difference that it seems unlikely that the enclosure could actually be entered through a building.

At Gasselte the main ninth-century farmhouses lay oriented centrally within the farmyard, with barns and sheds positioned around the edges, groups of sunken-featured buildings lying to the east of the main house, and a north–south aligned barn at the back of the yard, away from the road (Fig. 3.9A). Nearly every farmyard had its own well, but granaries were relatively scarce, suggesting that barns and the roof-space in houses were used for storage (see Chap. 5). Although several rebuildings took place, these adhered 'to strict rules with respect to the location and grouping of buildings' (Waterbolk and Harsema 1979, 254), as reflected in the relatively uniform layout of each farmstead, the western boundaries of which were defined by a ditched enclosure.

In northwest Germany Feddersen Wierde has produced perhaps the largest number of clearly defined farmsteads thus far. There, the long axis of the longhouses was invariably aligned with a trackway. Most longhouses had a granary directly adjacent to the hearth room, until the final phase of the settlement, when the number of granaries declined sharply. In contrast, the seventh- to eighth-century farmsteads at Dalem (not unlike those at Gasselte a century or two later) were arranged with the farmhouse more or less centrally positioned, with one or two ancillary buildings (usually a granary or sunken-featured building) adjacent to it. Set some distance away from the main house were barns, granaries, and sunken-featured buildings. The sunken-featured buildings, several of which have been identified as textile workshops (see Chap. 2), lay to the west of the main house.

From this diverse body of evidence a general picture of the development of the early medieval farmstead can be painted, albeit with broad strokes. First, the orientation of buildings suggests that the cardinal points played an important role in determining layout, an observation which finds support in certain early medieval law-codes (see below). Until the eighth and ninth centuries residential buildings, indeed nearly all buildings, were oriented approximately east–west (see Chap. 2). From the Carolingian period, however, a growing number of buildings, especially barns and sheds, were aligned north–south. Although the incorporation of buildings into one side of the enclosure fence was a widespread phenomenon, it emerged at different times in different regions. In Denmark, residential as well as other buildings were frequently incorporated into the enclosure, particularly from the sixth century onwards, and the farmyard could be entered through these buildings. In the Netherlands, on the other hand, only barns appear to have been built into the enclosure, and only from the ninth century. From the evidence currently available, it appears that this practice was absent in northern Germany.

Zones for craft activities, particularly metalworking, often appear to have been situated outside the farmyard. For example, the ironworking pits at Vorbasse lay outside the fenced enclosures, although they may nevertheless have been associated with particular farmsteads. The distancing of certain industrial activities involving fire or foul smells (iron-smelting, tanning, and flax retting) from the habitation area must have been for largely practical reasons.[4] Storage facilities, particularly in the form of lean-to granaries, were often displayed around the edge of the farmyard, although a single granary was often adjacent to the longhouse, as seen most clearly at Feddersen Wierde.

DOCUMENTARY EVIDENCE FOR SETTLEMENT AND FARMSTEAD STRUCTURE

What little documentary evidence exists regarding the layout of early medieval settlements is primarily to be found in law-codes.[5] This evidence, however, is indirect, and nowhere is a settlement or farmyard described *per se*. There is, furthermore, some ambiguity in terminology, most significantly in the use of the words *curtis* and *villa*: while the former refers specifically to the enclosed yard within which the house was situated, and *villa* is normally used to refer to a whole village, *villa* can also refer to an individual farm (Schwind 1977, 453; Schmidt-Wiegand 1977, 423).[6] Despite these limitations, a number of inferences regarding the layout of the *curtis* can be drawn from the laws.

The emphasis in the law-codes is overwhelmingly on the rights associated with the individual *curtis* rather than with the settlement as a whole. Intrusion without permission into another's *curtis* was strictly forbidden (*LA* Pact. XXI, 3; Dölling 1958, 27), and not surprisingly, the enclosure (most commonly *sepis* or *concisa*) was central to the legal concept of the *curtis*. It is described as a timber fence of chest height, substantial enough to impale any unfortunate animal which tried to break into or out of the *curtis* (*LA* Pact. XXX). Although a major function of the fence appears to have been to control the movement of farm

---

[4] Although see Chap. 6 for a discussion of the magical associations with metalworking.

[5] Gregory of Tours, for example, tells us very little regarding the layout of villages, apart from references to streets and open areas and a description of a fire which spread from house to house and from shed to shed, suggesting closely spaced units (Lorren and Périn 1997, 94; *De virtutibus & miraculis S. Martini* IV, 17, 18; *de gloria confessorum* XXI).

[6] It is interesting to note that the word 'villa' became 'village' in French and English, but *Weiler* (i.e. 'hamlet') in German (Nissen Jaubert 1998, 222).

animals (Dölling 1958, 21), it was more than merely a physical barrier, as suggested by *LB* (XII, 9, 10): it acted to define the legal extent of the *curtis*. Thus, if the owner of a newly built house wished to secure his property before the enclosure had been built, he stood by the house at midday and hurled an axe to the south, east, and west, thereby defining the legal extent of the *curtis*. The northernmost limit is defined as lying no further than the shadow cast by the *domus*.

The social status of the occupants of the *curtis* could vary, and the level of compensation for theft from or damage to a *curtis* was dependent on the status of the owner. In *LB* distinctions are made between the *curtis* of a nobleman (the *curtis ducis* or *curtis nobilium*, described as a *domus publica*, perhaps referring to its role as a public meeting place) and that of a freeman (*curtis liberi*) (e.g. *LB* II, 12; see also *LA* XXX). No indication is given of the relative sizes of the *curtis*.

Despite the obvious importance of the *curtis* as a legal concept, many excavated settlements show no clear evidence of enclosed farmsteads. At Kootwijk, for example (see above), each 'precinct' contained several residential buildings. The excavator has speculated that this was 'because of close family ties or hierarchical relations between neighbours', and further, 'it is probable that the precincts formed the original "territories" of social units within the settlement that were later divided up' (Heidinga 1987, 26). Excavations at a number of settlements, such as Warendorf and Speyer-'Vogelgesang', have uncovered well-preserved ground-plans of buildings, but no signs of enclosures. It may be that hedges were used; if, however, the absence of enclosures at these sites is genuine and not just the result of incomplete preservation, this would imply a different relationship between households as well as considerable vulnerability to incursions from both humans and animals.

SETTLEMENT STRUCTURE, SOCIAL STRUCTURE

The settlement forms identified at the beginning of this chapter do not correspond, at least directly, to regional traditions or chronological developments; examples of most can be found throughout the fifth to ninth centuries and across much of northwest Europe. That said, some forms do seem to have predominated in certain regions at certain times, although the number of extensively excavated examples of each type is still far too small to provide a statistically valid sample. Perpendicular villages, for example, emerge most clearly after the seventh century, and most examples so far come from the Netherlands. Waterbolk and Harsema (1979, 264, following Slicher van Bath) suggest that row villages first appeared in the Netherlands in the tenth century; yet they were already present in Denmark in the Migration period (e.g. Vorbasse), and date from the seventh and eighth centuries in southern Germany (e.g. Kirchheim). The clearest examples of grouped villages are the *Wurten*, although the farmsteads at Vorbasse appear to have been grouped around a central open area in the fifth century. Polyfocal settlements, on the other hand, become somewhat less prominent in the archaeological record from the eighth century onwards, when planned layouts were more widely adopted.[7]

Although settlement forms thus did not 'evolve' in a linear fashion, a generally less flexible, increasingly normative use of space is apparent in the layout of both individual farmsteads and of whole settlements from the eighth century onwards. We see a particularly striking example of this in the greater dimensional coherence of the buildings, boundaries, and layout of Viking period Vorbasse compared to its predecessors. Similarly, in parts of the Netherlands the mostly small, dispersed hamlets of the fourth and fifth centuries were in many cases replaced by villages arranged along perpendicular trackways (as at Kootwijk) or along a road (as at Gasselte), layouts which persisted into the modern period (Waterbolk 1991*a*, 104).

The greater uniformity and planning apparent in the layout of some settlements during this period must be linked, at least indirectly, to the appearance on the scene of powerful landlords seeking to augment their revenues. Attempts to intensify production through, for example, systems of crop rotation and use of the mould-board plough (see below, Chap. 5) would have required strict communal management of resources which could, in turn, have contributed to a more regulated village layout. Thus at Vorbasse it is possible to demonstrate that the farmsteads of the last Viking period phase, before the village shifted to its present location, are essentially the same size as the tofts recorded in eighteenth-century cadastral surveys which were proportional to the fields at the farms' disposal; the introduction of such a system would thus have contributed to a more regulated settlement layout (Nissen Jaubert 1998, 216; see Chap. 3).

Ethnographic analogies suggest that increasingly planned and uniform settlement layouts also reflect increasingly controlled and circumscribed social roles and daily activities (Brück 2000, 287; see below, Chap. 7). It is clear, however, that a range of different settlement forms was present in most regions at any one time, and this leads us back to the observation that village layout did not develop according to a simple chronological progression or conform to regional traditions. Although the archaeological remains of early medieval settlements are unlikely to yield direct evidence of the underlying determinants of settlement structure—patterns of inheritance and landholding, kinship structures, and so on—close analysis of settlement plans can at least suggest some of these causes. It appears, for example, that the distance between residential buildings in row settlements was more regular than in other forms; this is particularly striking at Gasselte and Dalem. Another remarkable feature of row villages and, to a lesser extent, of perpendicular villages is the stability in the number of households over many generations, even when a community moved to a new site. The length of

---

[7] There are exceptions, however, such as the settlement of Peelo in Drenthe, where a dispersed layout was maintained at least into the eighth century (Kooi 1995).

the rows and the number of farmsteads generally varied little, and only occasionally is there evidence for the subdivision of old plots or the addition of new plots. The main row of buildings at Vorbasse, for example, consisted of some eight farmsteads during the fourth and fifth centuries; the overall size of the village may have declined somewhat during the sixth and seventh centuries, but the main row still contained ten farmsteads; the eighth- to tenth-century village contained seven or eight farmsteads. At Gasselte the length of the row and the number of farmsteads—eight or nine—remained unchanged throughout the ninth to twelfth centuries. It would be premature to propose generalities on the basis of such a small number of examples, though if the patterns tentatively identified here are substantiated by further excavation, we will be closer to understanding the different socio-spatial strategies employed by early medieval communities in village planning. For example, evidence for subdivision of farmsteads or rapid growth in the number of farms could indicate some form of partible inheritance, while long-term stability in the number of farms presumably reflects other rules, such as primogeniture, governing the inheritance of properties as well as constraints on newcomers settling in a village.

Developments in settlement structure are also apparent at the level of the individual farmstead. In his wide-ranging study of social structure in early historic Europe, Steuer identifies two key transitions in farmstead structure which took place in Germanic regions during the late Roman Iron Age and Migration period (Steuer 1982). The first is the emergence of the multiple farmstead (*Mehrbetriebsgehöft*). This consisted of several (in exceptional cases, up to five or six) contemporary longhouses, as well as smaller buildings, sharing a single enclosure. The largest of these complexes resembled small hamlets in themselves, and could easily have accommodated twenty to thirty people (cf. the central farmstead at Wijster: Fig. 3.14). Second is the increase in the size and number of rooms in longhouses, which often incorporated multiple entrances and hearths, and which could suggest the presence of more than one resident group (see Chap. 2).

These developments did not, of course, take place everywhere simultaneously or in the same sequence. Farmsteads with several contemporary and/or highly subdivided longhouses emerged on the North Frisian island of Sylt as early as the second century. At Vorbasse these developments came about in the third or fourth centuries. At Flögeln multiple farmsteads emerged before longhouses became highly subdivided, while at Vorbasse the sequence was reversed (Steuer 1982, 273). Both developments, however, are usually interpreted as responses to the same demographic situation: increased population. If this is correct, then the changes in the structure of farmsteads and in houses may represent new strategies for articulating larger social groups. What seems clear, however, is that in the course of the fifth century longhouses became shorter, sunken-featured buildings more numerous, and granaries more scarce in much of the region under consideration here. Enclosed ancestral farmsteads gave way in many cases to unenclosed, loosely structured farmsteads (Schmid 1982, 92). The fact that so few fifth-century settlements had enclosed farmsteads makes it difficult to determine whether multiple farms survived into this period.

What caused this breakdown in the fifth century of the planned layouts seen in so many settlements of the preceding century is far from clear. Explanations are frequently couched in terms of climatic change and demographic pressures culminating in an agricultural crisis, particularly in Germany and the Netherlands (see Chap. 4). This putative crisis resulted in a shift in emphasis from arable farming to craft production, reflected in the dwindling numbers of granaries and stalls for cattle as well as the increased numbers of sunken-featured buildings. As will be seen in the following chapter, the same factors are believed to be responsible for the widespread disruption and thinning out of settlement seen in certain regions, a trend which began in the fifth century and was not reversed for over 200 years.

SETTLEMENT STRUCTURE AND STATUS

Interpretations of early medieval settlements often betray an urge to square the archaeological record with the kind of society evoked by early medieval documents. This consisted in essence of a class of landowners, belonging either to the military aristocracy or clergy, a free and semi-free peasantry who had the right to exploit parcels of land, and slaves. Questions of status and the identification of lordship thus loom large in attempts to explain the physical layout of settlements. Yet, just as the equation drawn between certain 'quality groups' of grave assemblages with legally defined ranks is now regarded as simplistic (Samson 1987), so too the assumption that legal status or disparities in wealth necessarily found expression in the size of the *domus* or *curtis* must be questioned. The number of stalls in the longhouse, in particular, is often regarded as a measure of both wealth and status (cf. Winkelmann 1958, 516). It is possible, however, that only a selection of the herd was stabled, for example, only dairy cattle. Furthermore, there is a strong correlation between the length of the byre and the size of the living room(s) (Steuer 1982, Abb. 19). The clear implication is that larger longhouses were designed to accommodate larger, non-nuclear households (for example, the 'classic' patriarchal family of husband and wife, two married sons, their wives and children). It may be, of course, that only leading families could expand in this way, as only they had access to the wealth necessary to support a larger household. In practical terms, large households would have been difficult to maintain due to high mortality and the complications of holding them together in the face of 'centrifugal forces' such as conflict between in-laws (Goody 1972, 103); they may, nevertheless, reflect contemporary mores of how best to maintain and control reproductive units. The proposition that large houses reflect rich or high-status households is, however, difficult to sustain archaeologically; the excavator of Kootwijk has observed that there was no discernible difference in the proportion of imported pottery (one likely measure of wealth) found in large and small houses (Heidinga 1987, 39). At Feddersen Wierde, however, a concentration of imports and craft debris was identified around the *Herrenhof* while at Vorbasse, the largest farm seems to have been a focus for ironworking (see Chap. 6).

A simple equation cannot, therefore, be drawn between the size of farmyards, or the size and number of buildings they contained, and the wealth or social status of the household. Evidence for ranking has also been sought in the architecture of the longhouse. In the 1930s the small chamber found at the western end of some longhouses was interpreted as the site of a 'high seat' (a *Germanischer Hochsitz*; Steuer 1982, 280).[8] No direct evidence exists to support this interpretation, however, and Steuer's suggestion (sparked by the discovery of a silver pin and other objects in the foundation trench of such a room in one of the Flögeln longhouses: Steuer 1982, 280) that only one longhouse per multiple farm possessed such a chamber, therefore indicating 'special' status, has since been refuted (Zimmermann 1992a, 103, 133).

The designation of exceptionally large farmsteads with large buildings, such as those found at Feddersen Wierde and Vorbasse, as *Herrenhöfen*, or 'lords' farmsteads', carries with it certain assumptions about the nature of relations between the occupants of these complexes and the rest of the community, particularly the postulated dependants. The planned layouts of these and other settlements has, for example, been seen as evidence of co-ordinated manipulation of settlement space by a pre-eminent group. The related thesis, that the more orderly village structure which emerged in the Carolingian and Viking periods is linked to the rise of centralized political authorities, is by no means universally accepted, however, and the counter-argument has been made that 'local native farmers must also be considered capable of establishing order in their home environment' (Heidinga 1987, 44).

The most substantial and intensively studied evidence for the existence of an early *Herrenhof* comes from Feddersen Wierde. The settlement incorporated numerous communal projects, such as paths, bridges, a central unbuilt space, and of course the *Wurt* itself. The enclosed *Herrenhof* was set slightly apart from the rest of the settlement, adjacent to, and dominating, the main trackway leading in and out of the village; craft debris and Roman imports were, furthermore, concentrated in a zone around it, and a large building without cattle stalls, possibly a meeting hall, was constructed adjacent to it in the third century. Smaller houses were believed by the excavator to be the homes of craftworkers, and those without granaries were assumed to have housed families who were to some degree dependent on the *Großbauern*, and above all, the *Herrenhof*, for provisions (Haarnagel 1979a, 94). On the combined strength of this evidence, a hierarchical social structure comprising a leading family, free farmers, craftworkers, and dependants was proposed by the excavator (ibid. 95).

---

[8] For a more recent, if somewhat uncritical, consideration of this issue see Herschend 1998, 25 ff.

Large farmsteads found in subsequent excavations elsewhere were characterized in a similar vein. At Vorbasse the largest farmstead lay at the eastern end of
the village for at least 200 years, from the third to fifth centuries. It comprised a
yard of some 4,000 m² (the next largest was 2,700 m²) containing the longest
house of the settlement as well as several other buildings. The excavator has
argued that it 'must be characterized as the most high-ranking farm of the
village' (Hvass 1988*a*, 114).[9] The excavator of Wijster also believed that the
regular layout of the settlement 'suggests a certain amount of central authority',
but he found 'no convincing proof of the existence of a *Herrensitz*, [although]
the different size of the farmhouses probably reflects differences in wealth
between their owners' (van Es 1967, 408).

Steuer has offered an alternative interpretation of these supposed 'lordly' residences, suggesting that some, at least, represent households whose economy
was oriented primarily towards craft and trade, and that some may even have
functioned as trading stations (Steuer 1982, 282–3; see below Chap. 6). If so,
this could explain the survival of the so-called *Herrenhof* at Feddersen Wierde,
despite the worsening agricultural conditions of the fifth century which led to the
decline of the other farmsteads on the *Wurt*. According to this view, the concentration of iron-smithing debris around the *Herrenhof*[10] would suggest a strong
link between those overseeing the importation of iron ore (for which there was
no local source) and those who worked it into tools. This, however, assumes that
craft production was in the hands of 'entrepreneurs', an image which does not sit
easily with our sources, which indicate instead that craft and trade at this early
period were firmly embedded in social relations.

It is important to note, however, that most settlements of this period, including
those with a clearly planned layout, did *not* include a farmstead of exceptional
size. Documentary evidence and the burials of the late Roman Iron Age and
Migration period suggest a further paradox: power was highly unstable at the
time when these supposed *Herrenhöfe* emerged, and was based on the personal
charisma and ability of the individual to provide for followers, particularly for
a war band, rather than on dynastic connections (Steuer 1982, 112, 278 ff.;
Hedeager 1992). This would appear to be inconsistent with the existence of
leading families who maintained their pre-eminent position over many generations[11] although this apparent contradiction could be explained if the instability
lay primarily at a higher (i.e. supra-settlement) socio-political level.

The archaeological evidence for the existence of 'aristocratic' settlement

---

[9] If this did represent a 'chiefly' farm, it is interesting to note that by the eighth century at the latest,
and perhaps already by the sixth, there was no longer a pre-eminent farmstead, at least in terms of size,
suggesting that the 'leading family' now lived elsewhere.

[10] Although the concentration of metalworking debris around the *Herrenhof* is now known to have
been less marked than originally thought (Schuster and de Rijk 2001).

[11] Similarly, current interpretations of Anglo-Saxon burials containing exceptional burial wealth in the
form of grave goods see these as the burials of heads of households, rather than of 'leaders' or 'aristocrats',
at least until the seventh century (cf. Welch 1992, 51; Härke 1997, 147).

complexes is rather more substantial for the seventh and eighth centuries.[12] A striking example of this comes from Lauchheim (Baden-Württemberg), where a large row-cemetery of some 700 graves and an associated settlement dating from the late sixth to eighth centuries have been excavated in tandem (Stork 1991 and 1992). The settlement contained over fifty timber structures (at least some of which were arranged in enclosed farmsteads), lay about 200 m from the cemetery on a lower terrace of the River Jagst, and was defined along its southern edge by a ditch running 195 m east–west. At the eastern edge of the village lay the largest enclosed farmstead (*c*.60 × 50 m: Fig. 3.25). This complex contained at least ten structures (not all contemporary), at least one of which was large by the standards of the rest of the settlement (i.e. some 14 m in length), as well as four probable granaries. A group of six inhumation graves, five male and one female, lay along the southern edge of the farmyard. These were extraordinarily richly equipped, the men with weapons and riding gear, the woman with gold jewellery inlaid with semi-precious stones, glass, and enamel. Grave 27, the most spectacular of this group, contained weaponry, no fewer than five gold-foil crosses (originally sewn onto a shroud), and some 270 wooden objects and furnishings. Most, probably all, of these graves date from the late seventh or early eighth century. They clearly do not represent a nuclear family group. It is perhaps more likely that they were leading members of the family which owned, or was

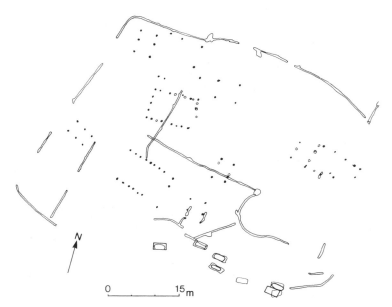

Fig. 3.25. Lauchheim: the 'manor farm'. After Stork 1992, fig. 164.

---

[12] Although see the discussion of Gudme and related Scandinavian settlements in Chap. 6.

granted, the estate at Lauchheim, and who became royal agents, administering the king's scattered estates on his behalf. Certainly the foundation of the nearby monastery of Ellwangen in 764 is testimony to the presence of such an aristocratic group half a century later. In this case, the term 'farmstead' applied to this enclosed group of buildings may be a misnomer, and 'manor farm' or even 'estate centre' might be a more accurate description (Damminger 1998).

Any clear distinction which may have existed between the residences of the heads of households or lineages and those of their followers and dependants seems, for the most part, to have been lost due to the vagaries of the archaeological record, although as we shall see in Chapter 6, separate, high-status rural centres have been identified for this period. Most of the questions concerning what the different sizes and compositions of farmsteads meant in social terms remain to be satisfactorily addressed. It seems likely that what we see dimly reflected are distinctions not only between nuclear and extended families, but also between socio-economic sub-groups; to define such groups with confidence, however, will require more than isolated archaeological examples.

SETTLEMENT STRUCTURE IN ANGLO-SAXON ENGLAND

In many ways, the settlements of early Anglo-Saxon England look, prima facie, very different from their continental counterparts. This impression is gained not only from the absence in England of the imposing longhouse, but also from the lack of enclosed farmsteads and clearly planned layouts (e.g. row, perpendicular, or grouped settlements), at least during the fifth and sixth centuries. Indeed, some of these early settlements are so dispersed that some archaeologists have hesitated to call them 'villages' at all. This perception has discouraged the comparative study of Anglo-Saxon settlements, as has the fact that fewer than a dozen of the hundreds of Anglo-Saxon settlements so far investigated have been excavated (and published) on a scale and under conditions which allow for a detailed analysis of their layout and development over time. A further complicating factor is that the relatively small-scale excavations which are normally carried out in Britain are, by their very nature, unlikely to reveal even one-quarter of a shifting settlement on the scale of Flögeln or Vorbasse (see Chap. 1). Despite these limitations, the similarities and differences between early medieval settlements in England and on the continent can be usefully explored. Just as the links between the Anglo-Saxon house and the continental longhouse (which have been considered in Chapter 2) can be shown to be closer than has generally been believed, so too, differences in the layouts of fifth- and sixth-century settlements in southern and eastern England and their continental counterparts may be less marked than they at first appear.

The earliest post-Roman settlements in England are generally characterized by a lack of clearly defined edges, planned layouts, and boundaries or other signs of delineation, such as enclosed groups of buildings. Evidence for functional zones is also scarce, although part of the settlement at West Heslerton in Yorkshire which contained only sunken-featured buildings has been interpreted as a storage and craft-working zone (Powlesland 1997). The overall impression gained from most fifth- and sixth-century settlements is of a fairly dispersed spread of structures, although most ground-level buildings shared a broadly east–west alignment. Evidence of enclosures around buildings (as distinct from enclosures which may have served as animal pens or paddocks) is scarce, perhaps even absent, before *c*.600. The best-known published examples of this kind of settlement are Mucking, Essex, and West Stow, Suffolk (Jones and Jones 1975; Hamerow 1993; West 1986). Mucking, which overlooks the Thames estuary, is the most extensively excavated early Anglo-Saxon settlement to be published to date (Fig. 3.26). Some 18 ha of land were investigated by archaeologists in the 1960s and 1970s, in the course of which over fifty timber buildings and over 200 sunken-featured buildings were uncovered. Not all of these buildings were occupied at the same time, however. The focus of the settlement shifted over a large area in the course of 250–300 years, as buildings were abandoned and replaced, and it seems likely that, on average, only around ten household units stood at any one time. West Stow, though excavated on a much smaller scale, appears to reflect a similar process, and there is growing evidence to suggest that such shifting settlement was widespread in fifth- and sixth-century England, as it was in northwest Europe (Hamerow 1991 and 1992).[13]

The layouts of early Anglo-Saxon settlements and those in the continental North Sea regions thus seem to differ in important ways. Yet when we consider the far-reaching changes which affected so many continental settlements during the fifth and sixth centuries (see above), the links with England seem less tenuous. The fifth and sixth centuries saw a decrease in the length of longhouses and an increase in the number of byre-less houses, particularly in coastal regions; a decrease in post-built granaries and an increase in the number of sunken-featured buildings; and more dispersed layouts compared to the often planned settlements of the late Roman Iron Age. It is worth noting that a significant number of continental settlements dating to the fifth and sixth centuries have been identified which, with their high ratio of sunken-featured buildings to ground-level buildings and dispersed layouts, would not look out of place in early Anglo-Saxon England; in northwest Germany these have been dubbed 'Loxstedt type' settlements, after a settlement to the south of Bremerhaven whose fourth- to sixth-century phase contained thirteen longhouses and ninety-nine sunken-featured buildings, but no enclosures or clear signs of planning (Fig. 3.27; Zimmermann 1995*a*, 269; Zimmermann, 2001).[14]

---

[13] See discussion of settlement shift in Chap. 4.
[14] Another example of this type of settlement was excavated at Bremen-Grambke (Witte 1994/5).

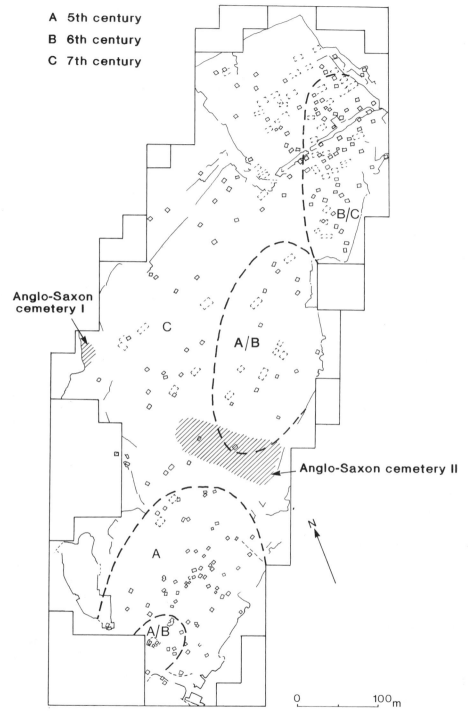

A 5th century
B 6th century
C 7th century

Anglo-Saxon
cemetery I

Anglo-Saxon cemetery II

B/C

C

A/B

A

A/B

N

0   100 m

Fig. 3.26. Mucking: the spatial development of the Anglo-Saxon settlement. After Hamerow 1993, fig. 195.

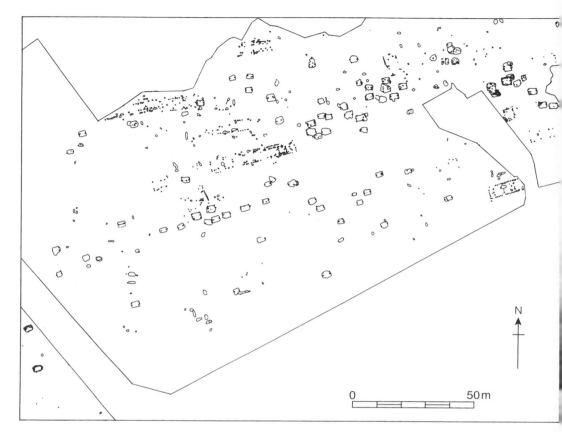

Fig. 3.27. Loxstedt: plan showing most of the fourth- to sixth-century settlement. After Zimmermann, forthcoming.

In Denmark, large enclosed farmsteads which were rebuilt on the same spot over several generations, as identified at Vorbasse and Nørre Snede, have been plausibly interpreted as ancestral farms and seen as signalling the emergence of land-controlling groups (Hedeager 1992). If so, their absence in small, mixed 'Anglo-Saxon' communities of migrants and Britons whose extended household structure would have undergone dramatic changes in the face of migration and assimilation, not to mention the economic implosion which accompanied the end of Roman rule in Britain, should occasion no surprise; neither should the inability of these communities to command the concentration of labour and resources needed to erect longhouse complexes; nor, indeed, should the lack of clearly planned layouts.[15] In short, the organization of productive and

---

[15] The role of the British population in shaping the settlements of early 'Anglo-Saxon' England should not be overlooked, though as yet it remains impossible to define. The presence of Britons in 'Anglo-Saxon' communities is beyond question, and this undoubtedly affected the socio-spatial strategies adopted.

resource-controlling units within northwest European, 'Anglo-Saxon', and post-Roman British societies was undergoing profound changes during the fifth and sixth centuries.

While traces of enclosures are found at some early Anglo-Saxon settlements, for example, at Bishopstone, Sussex (Bell 1978), essentially permanent enclosures surrounding planned arrangements of buildings—which can perhaps be called 'properties'—and even trackways, are not apparent much before *c*.600.[16] It was during the seventh and eighth centuries that settlements became more firmly inscribed onto the Anglo-Saxon landscape. Some of the earliest examples of this kind of settlement are Yeavering, Northumb. (a royal vill of the seventh-century King Edwin: Hope-Taylor 1977), and Cowdery's Down (Fig. 3.28) and Chalton, both in Hants (Millett and James 1984; Addyman and Leigh 1973). Despite the geographical distance which separates them, these settlements displayed planned layouts containing strikingly similar arrangements of units, including alignments of two or more buildings, and rectangular fenced enclosures within which buildings (access to which was thus controlled) were arranged in a perpendicular fashion, with a larger building adjoining or leading into the enclosure.

This was also the period when the first exceptionally large buildings—sometimes referred to as 'great halls'—appeared. Herschend has argued that the position of the 'great hall' in England is comparable to that on some continental settlements, notably Wijster, where the gable end of some houses was incorporated into an enclosure:

In both cases the hall constitutes an interface between the private, fenced farm and the outside. In Wijster, where the eastern short end with its entrance facing the street forms a part of the fence around the farm, this interface is something new to a society where farms were normally designed as a group of houses within a fenced area. Here the hall breaks the barrier and becomes a concrete symbol of the meeting between the farm and his guests. (Herschend 1998, 20)

This 'fence-breaking' role, he suggests, indicates that the idea of the 'hall' was imported into Britain and shows parallel developments with its continental

There is no need, however, to explain the marked differences between settlements such as Mucking and Vorbasse primarily in 'ethnic' terms, particularly in light of the fact that most other aspects of the material culture of England in the fifth and sixth centuries—at least that which is archaeologically visible—clearly followed continental models (see above, pp. 48 ff.)

[16] Catholme in Staffordshire, at the western fringes of early Anglo-Saxon cultural influence, appears to be exceptional in this regard. The settlement comprised some half-dozen farmsteads which appear to have been laid out along trackways as early as the sixth century, with groups of buildings lying within ditched enclosures which were maintained over many years, demarcating ancestral farmsteads (Hamerow, forthcoming). Catholme's distinctive layout, together with its location, have led to the suggestion that it represents a post-Roman British community (Losco-Bradley and Wheeler 1984). Catholme's buildings, however, and the few artefacts associated with them (as well as a nearby cemetery), fit at least as readily within an 'Anglo-Saxon' cultural tradition as a late Romano-British one. It has also been argued that the settlement of West Heslerton in the Vale of Pickering was planned at an early date (Powlesland 1997, 110).

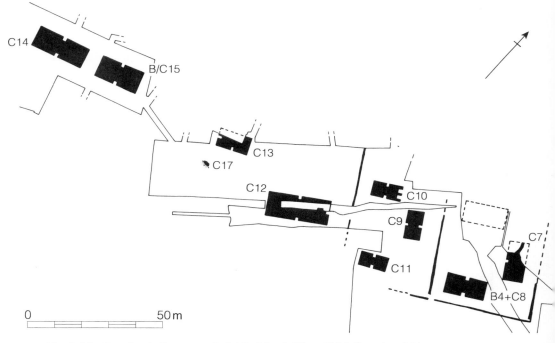

Fig. 3.28. Cowdery's Down: period 4C. After Millett 1984, figs. 6 and 31.

counterparts (Herschend 1998, 20). While this is undoubtedly true in broad terms, it overlooks certain important differences, namely, that at Cowdery's Down the largest hall was not enclosed and in fact lay some distance from the enclosed buildings; that in England, the role of the hall as 'fence breaker' so far appears to be restricted to a very few, probably high-status, settlements such as Cowdery's Down, Yeavering, and Chalton; and that in Denmark, and possibly the Netherlands, it appears that minor buildings as well as 'halls' acted as 'fence breakers'.

What is not in doubt, however, is that settlements which possessed 'great halls', with their lavish consumption of timber and labour, should be interpreted as the homesteads of leading people—landlords who established separate settlements and whose ostentatious dwellings were displayed within a distinctive layout. In the case of Yeavering and Cowdery's Down, their carefully planned layouts and use of enclosures reflect a desire to impress and restrict access to special buildings and zones. The use of enclosures was not, however, restricted to high-status settlements. The settlements at Pennyland (Bucks.), Riby Cross-Roads (Lincs.) and Thirlings (Northumb.) contained neither large buildings, carefully planned layouts, nor particularly rich material culture (although none has been completely excavated), yet by the late sixth or early seventh centuries all were provided with track- or droveways and fenced enclosures defining pad-docks and, in most if not all cases, enclosing buildings (Williams 1993; Steedman 1995; O'Brien and Miket 1991). These and other examples point to an increased emphasis on defining and regulating space within settlements during the mid-Saxon period.

4

Land and Power: Settlements in their Territorial Context

As settlements became more clearly bounded and fixed in the landscape, so too did territories based on landed production, which became increasingly intensive and politically controlled (as we shall see in Chapter 5). These territories became formalized when leaders were able to exercise authority within them by protecting clients through juridical and/or military means, and by extracting surplus from, and controlling access to, landed resources. The identification of communities and individuals with a particular territory or region, whether this was defined by shared markets, dialect, military allegiances, or other commonalities, must also have grown in importance in this period, as ties of ethnicity and kinship began to give ground to bonds of clientship and rank. The formalization of territories was of course key to the formation of early kingdoms. What can archaeology tell us about the effects of territorialization and estate formation on rural communities?

Certain regular features govern territorial formation in pre-industrial societies. In particular, universal 'push–pull' factors underlie the territorial structure and settlement pattern of agrarian communities. Briefly stated, every community needs to establish a territory in order to keep neighbouring communities at a distance and preserve its resources ('push' factors), but the necessity of maintaining certain social ties between communities, such as marriage, trade, and shared defence ('pull' factors), will act to minimize the distance between them (Heidinga 1987, 157). For example, the distribution of settlement in the Veluwe district of the central Netherlands shows that the northeast and the southwest regions were largely empty in the seventh century, even though their soils were suitable for farming and they were occupied both before and after this period. They lay outside the core area of the seventh-century resettlement of the Veluwe, however, and it appears that communities chose not to spread out thinly across the entire territory, but rather to remain relatively close to one another (Heidinga 1987, 162).

In the Netherlands, Germany, and England, early territories could, under certain circumstances, be remarkably stable and survive to be detected in much later boundaries (e.g. Waterbolk 1982 and 1991*a*; Cunliffe 1973; Janssen

1976).[1] In view of this stability and the behavioural 'rules' which appear to govern territorial formation, some archaeologists have attempted to reconstruct proto-historic territories. Several presuppositions underlie such reconstruction. The first is that the 'push–pull' factors already mentioned invariably operate between neighbouring communities. Assuming that these factors roughly balance each other out, the boundary between two territorial centres should lie approximately halfway between them. Following this reasoning, the 'Thiessen Model' of land use has been widely used to help reconstruct early medieval territories (Smith 1976, 7).[2] According to this model, polygons—which are meant to approximate ancient territories—are formed by drawing lines connecting neighbouring settlements of comparable status and bisecting them with perpendicular lines, the latter representing the notional boundary between the two territories (Fig. 4.1). The differing sizes and shapes of the resulting 'territories' should reflect variations in the needs for, and availability of, resources, soil fertility, and so on.[3] According to this model, when an unoccupied landscape is initially colonized and population pressure is low, territories should approximate roughly equally sized polygons; as internal expansion takes place, these territories tend to be partitioned into units of unequal size (Jankuhn 1979, 30; Myhre 1978, 244; 1987).

There is empirical evidence to suggest that the organization of early territories in many regions did conform broadly to this model (see e.g. Heidinga 1987, 159, n. 11), and hypothetical territories constructed using Thiessen polygons correspond well in some cases with later documented boundaries, as in the Veluwe (Fig. 4.1) and Drenthe (Waterbolk 1991a). Drenthe was a relatively impoverished region in the early Middle Ages due to a rising water table, podsol formation, and a consequent decline in habitable arable land, and was therefore of marginal economic importance. This impoverishment was conducive to the survival of early settlement and territorial patterns, and analysis of the distribution of settlements, field systems, and cemeteries suggests that the origins of many medieval territories lie in the late Iron Age and Roman periods. Indeed, when Thiessen polygons are drawn based on concentrations of finds of early medieval and even Roman date, they correlate closely with historically documented boundaries, such as those recorded in nineteenth-century cadastral maps (Waterbolk 1982, 99; 1991a, 52). To reconstruct early territories in this way, however, requires a high degree of confidence that the majority of early medieval

---

[1] It would be incorrect, however, to see pre-tenth-century territories as embryonic parishes, even though there is sometimes a correspondance between them. While early medieval territories often formed the 'building-blocks' of later administrative units, parishes served a different function and were imposed at a much later date (Hamerow 1991; Heidinga 1987, 158).

[2] For early medieval examples, see: Waterbolk 1982; Myhre 1987; Theuws 1986; and Heidinga 1987, figs. 71–3; for Anglo-Saxon England, see Arnold and Wardle 1981.

[3] The Thiessen Polygon Model has been much criticized as being too functionally driven; it does not, furthermore, take into account factors such as intervisibility of sites, for example. Its success is also to an extent dependent upon the terrain of the area under study. Myhre's study of southwest Norway, for example, works well because it operated in a highly partitioned terrain with natural boundaries (1978).

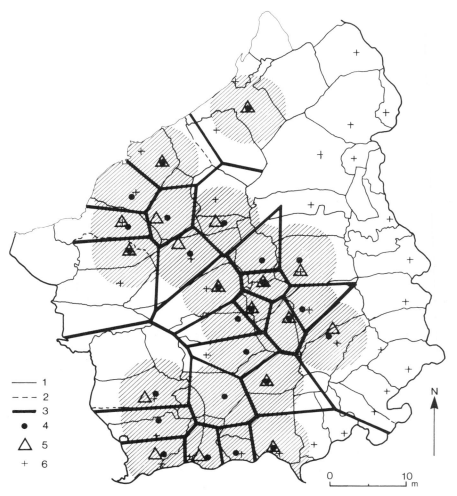

Fig. 4.1. Territorial model of the Veluwe based on centres known or presumed to have existed in the seventh century. 1: territorial boundary, historical; 2: territorial boundary, conjectural; 3: Thiessen Polygon; 4: centre of Thiessen Polygon; 5: settlement or cemetery; 6: pre-thirteenth-century church. After Heidinga 1987, fig. 73.

settlements in a given region have been identified and that they are all broadly contemporary—a tall order, even when archaeology (often the final arbiter in dating settlements), documentary sources, and place-names can be combined.

Along with the Thiessen Model, the concept of the 'nuclear region' (cf. 'adaptive areas'; Waterbolk 1995, 33) underlies many attempts to reconstruct early territories. The idea is based largely upon the analysis of 'site catchments' (Vita-Finzi and Higgs, 1970), an approach which has been used since the 1970s as a means of reconstructing early territories by analysing how natural resources were exploited by individual settlements. The theory is based on the premise that a settlement will normally be sited near the centre of a territory which is notionally divided into concentric zones in order to make the most efficient use of time and energy; those zones which lie nearest the settlement are exploited most intensively (e.g. cultivated fields), those furthest away, least intensively (e.g. pasture). The size of these 'exploitation territories' for agrarian settlements tends to approximate a circle with a radius approximately equivalent to half an hour's walk. In generally level terrain, this means a territorial diameter of approximately 5 km, an interval which recurs in a wide range of agrarian societies (Bintliff 1994, 209).[4] The rationale behind this model is that a larger territory would result in inefficient use of resources due to the long time required to reach distant fields, although where there is an essential resource lying at a greater distance from a settlement, the territory will tend to be elongated in order to incorporate that resource (Heidinga 1987, 159; Bintliff 1994, 207–8).

Theories of territorial formation which are based on the idea of 'site catchments' tend, however, to overemphasize environmental determinants at the expense of the political and cultural dimensions of territorial formation. They assume that a community's decision to settle at a particular location was based primarily on the resource potential of the surrounding area, and that each settlement possessed an essentially independent economic status. Allowance must be made, however, for more complex arrangements, such as resource sharing, economic specialization, or the deliberate siting of settlements at the margins of territories. It appears, for example, that Merovingian *villae* did not consist of clearly defined territories, but rather of scattered estates whose boundaries were generally so ill-defined that landowners were unsure about the exact extent of their properties (Halsall 1995a, 192). While the premise that, on the whole, territories are formed and exploited in an economical way holds good, ideas of what is 'economical' vary.

Of course, no single model can be put forward to explain the origins of early medieval territories, and while parallel developments between regions can be pointed to, local contingencies resulted in considerable regional variation, particularly between former Roman areas and those which lay outside the Empire. Furthermore, unlike the study of buildings and settlements, for which a generally accepted methodology exists, a number of different conceptual approaches have been taken to the study of territorial formation, some emphasizing environmental and geographical factors, others stressing socio-political relations. The approach adopted to some extent determines the kind of fieldwork undertaken, as is apparent from the two case studies presented later in this chapter. In part for this reason, this chapter offers neither a general overview of such studies (many of which are, in any case, at an interim stage) nor a radical reinterpretation of their results. Instead, what follows is an examination of several general features of rural settlement which conditioned the formation of territories in this period,

---

[4] No general agreement exists, however, on the exact walking time involved; Heidinga, for example, suggests approximately one hour, or 3–5 km from the settlement (Heidinga 1987, 159).

namely, settlement mobility, the distribution of early medieval settlements in relation to preceding settlement patterns, and population levels. Finally, two case studies are presented which, while representing different analytical approaches, demonstrate how archaeological and documentary evidence can be brought together to shed light upon the development of early medieval settlements within their regional context.

SETTLEMENT MOBILITY

The normal pattern of rural settlement in the Migration period was dispersed; nucleation as a widespread phenomenon began only at the end of the period under study. These dispersed settlements were, furthermore, for the most part mobile, as had been the case during much of prehistory. Such settlement mobility, which was a characteristic feature of the early Middle Ages across much of northern and western Europe, could take two forms: the gradual shifting of a settlement within its territorial boundaries, or the relocation of a settlement as a whole.

Shifting settlements (dubbed *Wandersiedlungen*, or 'wandering settlements') are a well-documented phenomenon of the prehistoric and early historic periods (Nissen Jaubert 1999).[5] In the pre-Roman period settlements shifted frequently around extensive ('Celtic') field systems as different parts of these systems were exploited; by the early medieval period settlements shifted somewhat less frequently within more intensively cultivated fields (see Chap. 5; Waterbolk 1995, 30). In Denmark, for example, settlements shifted every one or two generations during the Bronze Age and early Iron Age; from the Roman Iron Age onwards they remained on the same spot for a longer period, but not until the eleventh or twelfth centuries did they become more or less fixed at sites where many remain to the present day (Näsman 1987, 464; Hvass 1989, 92). Several examples of such so-called 'wandering' settlements have been described in Chapter 3, such as Kootwijk, which gradually expanded onto heath or woodland while older farmsteads, which bordered onto the fields, were demolished and incorporated into the fields.

The process of shifting settlement has been traced on a regional scale in the Dutch province of Drenthe. Territorial boundaries had been broadly established by the Migration period, yet settlements did not remain in the same place within those territories (Waterbolk 1982). Indeed, over a period of centuries settlements could shift over considerable distances. Settlement mobility has also been recog-

---

[5] The term *Wandersiedlung* is somewhat loosely defined. The Danish equivalent refers primarily to early Iron Age settlements which shifted every generation or so, whereas the later phases of settlements such as Vorbasse and Nørre Snede, where farmsteads were rebuilt several times on the same plot, are regarded as essentially stable. In Germany, however, the term is applied more widely (Nissen Jaubert 1999). I use the term without making assumptions regarding whether shifts were gradual, or consisted of abrupt, co-ordinated relocations, a distinction which can in any case only rarely be made with certainty.

nized as a widespread phenomenon in Jutland, seen most strikingly at Vorbasse, and in northwest Germany, for example at Flögeln (see Chap. 3).

Villages did not, of course, shift independently of their fields and cemeteries, although burial frequently continued to take place in ancestral burial grounds even when settlements moved, and many cemeteries remained in continuous use from the late Roman period until the inception of churchyard burial some three or more centuries later. The positions of villages and their fields were obviously more closely interdependent, and settlements usually lay close to the edge of their arable lands (see e.g. Waterbolk 1982, 103; Heidinga 1987).

Why farms were abandoned and rebuilt on a new site remains a matter of considerable debate. Ethnographic studies suggest causes such as the death of the head of a household and the establishment of a new farmstead by a new generation, which might explain the apparently cyclical rebuilding at many settlements every twenty-five years or so (Heidinga 1987, 32; Gerretsen 1999). It is also beneficial for practical reasons to move the farmyard to a new site periodically so that humans and farm animals avoid being unduly afflicted by parasites and to bring the old farmyard, with its enhanced fertility, under the plough.

In parts of northern Germany and the Netherlands settlement mobility continued until at least the tenth century, and in Denmark until the twelfth (Näsman 1987, 464; Willroth 1990, 11; Waterbolk 1982, 134; Reichmann 1982). What brought settlement shift to an end is no more certain than what caused it in the first place; the fact that settlements shifted less frequently over time suggests that it probably involved the introduction of new systems of farming which required more intensive use of human labour and natural resources (such as 'turf manuring'; see Chap. 5), together with more controlled allocation of land for settlement and cultivation and the need to extract greater surpluses from it. Growing constraints on settlement mobility must, in short, have been linked to the formation of estates and the construction of village churches (Steuer 1989, 118). It is interesting to note, in this connection, that settlement shift is less apparent in Frankish and Alamannic regions, where there seems to have been greater stability (Damminger 1998, 57). Why this should be so remains a matter for speculation, although it seems likely that the answer lies in different, more intensive, farming regimes as well as some underlying continuity in the structures of landholding.

This gradual shifting can be difficult to distinguish archaeologically from the relocation of entire settlements, a phenomenon which persisted throughout the Middle Ages. In some cases the cause of such relocation is clear; at Kootwijk, for example, the drying-up of the community's water supply forced the relocation of the settlement in the early eleventh century (Heidinga 1987, 102 ff.). In other cases socio-economic developments may have lain behind such relocation, forces which, paradoxically, were similar to those which brought an end to 'wandering' settlements. In the southern Swedish region of Scania, for example, a survey of seventy-eight early medieval settlements suggests that roughly half moved very little over time and lie near their later medieval successors. The others, however, shifted considerable distances to new sites. The author of the study argues that this dislocation, resulting in a phase of settlement abandonment between *c.* AD 900–1050, was connected with the introduction of new field systems and forms of landholding, that is, with the creation of estates (Callmer 1987). An episode of settlement relocation has also been identified in Drenthe in the ninth century. New row settlements were also established at around this time, houses became larger, and the storage capacity of some farmyards increased tenfold, pointing to changes in agricultural technology, such as the introduction of strip fields, two- or three-field rotation, and the use of *Plaggen* (turf-enriched) soils (Waterbolk 1982, 134; see Chap. 5). It is, however, often difficult to be certain that we are not mistaking settlement shift for settlement desertion, as excavation rarely takes place on a scale large enough to exclude the possibility that the 'missing' phase of a settlement lies undetected in a neighbouring field.

SETTLEMENT PATTERNS AND DEMOGRAPHY

A phenomenon apparent in most of the former western provinces of the Roman Empire is a marked reduction in the density of early medieval settlement in comparison to the Roman period. Several possible explanations for this have been put forward: first, that there was a dramatic decline in population in the late Roman or immediately post-Roman period. Another possibility is that the smaller number of early medieval settlements is due to extensive continuity of occupation, so that these settlements lie concealed beneath modern villages. In the region around Metz, for example, roughly one-fifth of rural Merovingian cemeteries lie beneath modern villages (Halsall 1995*a*, 184). If such continuity of settlement was widespread, then a significant element of the early medieval settlement pattern in northern Gaul lies hidden beneath present-day settlements.[6] In the absence of the kind of large-scale excavation needed to establish the stability or otherwise of Merovingian settlements, however, it would be rash to assume that settlements sited away from modern settlements were in any sense 'failed', a term loaded with economic implications (ibid.). A third possibility is that the small number of Merovingian settlements which have been identified, compared to Roman settlements, is due to the less durable material culture of the period, which is therefore less likely to survive and be recognized by archaeologists. A consensus in favour of this last explanation is now forming, based on a growing number of archaeological surveys in Gaul and other former western provinces (Halsall 1995*b*; Haselgrove and Scull 1995; Christie 1995).

A good example of an apparent demographic 'slump' is provided by the late

---

[6] This argument has sometimes been made for early Anglo-Saxon settlements, but is now widely refuted (Hall, 1988; Hamerow 1991, 16–17).

Roman/Frankish cemetery at Krefeld-Gellep, which lay near a late Roman forti-fication on the lower Rhine and where over 4,000 graves have been excavated (Pirling 1986). Approximately 640 of the datable graves belong to the fourth century, fifty to the fifth century, and 600 to the sixth century (Bloemers and Thijssen 1990, 145). The small number of fifth-century burials is presumably due, at least in part, to a lack of grave goods or the reuse in these graves of late Roman objects, as well as to the perishable nature of fifth-century material culture, all factors which make burials of this period hard to recognize. The dif-ficulty of identifying fifth-century populations in the northernmost regions of Gaul, as in Britain, could also be due to the inhabitants of both town and coun-tryside adopting a more self-sufficient economic strategy involving a dispersed, mobile, and archaeologically fugitive pattern of settlement following the col-lapse of Roman rule; the fact that the collapse also brought to an end state sup-plies of durable goods such as pottery and military gear, as well as coinage, contributes to the difficulty of identifying and dating such settlements (ibid.).

The greatest range of evidence for this demographic decline and subsequent expansion comes from Frankish areas where a relative abundance of excavated Roman settlements, Merovingian cemeteries, and early medieval charters is now complemented by the recognition of a growing number of early medieval settle-ments. After a dramatic contraction of settlement in the fourth and fifth centuries in northern Gaul—indicated not only by a reduced number of cemeteries, but also in some areas by reafforestation in the early Middle Ages (Zadora-Rio 1989)—the number of cemeteries increased substantially in the seventh century, in some regions doubling in number from the sixth. Several hypotheses have been put forward to explain this dramatic increase. The first simply sees popula-tion growth and settlement expansion as the key factors, the latter promoted by the foundation of hundreds of rural monasteries (Périn 1992, 230). In a paper published in 1971, Donat and Ullrich calculated average population sizes for a number of Merovingian cemeteries spanning the sixth and seventh centuries. While the accuracy of these calculations as absolute measures of population size is debatable, the overall pattern seems to point to population growth during these two centuries: each cemetery (and by implication the living community) was smaller than its average size at the beginning of use and larger than its average size at the end of use. A second trend apparent from this study is that the smallest cemeteries (representing, it is assumed, the smallest settlements) were in use for the shortest periods of time, whereas the largest populations were seen in those cemeteries which continued in use for at least two centuries. The average population represented in at least some cemeteries, according to the authors' cal-culations, nearly trebled between the sixth and seventh centuries (Donat and Ullrich 1971, 249 and table 4).

Population growth is thus likely to have been a factor in the increased number of burials and the establishment of so many new burial grounds. Yet the rise in the number of recognizably Frankish burials, particularly in the sixth century, is simply too steep to be due to a natural population increase. It is far more likely to reflect growing numbers of local groups coming under Frankish overlordship and adopting the more readily datable modes of burial favoured by the Frankish aristocracy (James 1979). Another hypothesis put forward to explain the growth in the number of cemeteries during the seventh century is that 'social changes . . . [led] to a reduced need to demonstrate social status to a wide audience at a funeral' (Halsall 1995*a*, 184 ff.); as a consequence, single large cemeteries which served several settlements were replaced by a larger number of smaller cemeteries, established to serve individual settlements.[7]

In northern Germany and southern Denmark archaeologists have for many years recognized a marked gap in the evidence for settlement dating from the later fifth to seventh centuries; here too the question of depopulation at the end of the late Roman Iron Age arises. The famous passage in Bede's *Ecclesiastical History of the English Church and People* (I, 15), which names the continental homelands from which the peoples of England originate, notes how the region of *Angulus* (whence, he tells us, came the Anglian peoples) still lay deserted in his day, namely, the first half of the eighth century; the implication is that this desertion was a result of mass emigration to Britain. Bede's testimony seemed to be confirmed archaeologically by the scarcity of evidence for settlements and burials dating to the later fifth to seventh centuries in large parts of the North Sea zone. This hiatus in settlement was apparent, however, not only where one might expect it, namely, along the coastal marshes (where settlements such as Feddersen Wierde were demonstrably flooded out as a result of rising sea levels) and in the region of *Angulus* (corresponding broadly to modern Schleswig-Holstein), but seemed to extend right across northern Germany, the Netherlands, Denmark, and beyond, even to southwest Norway. Thus, settlements such as Vorbasse, Flögeln, and Wijster appeared to contain no buildings or finds post-dating the mid-fifth century and were assumed to have been abandoned by *c*.AD 450 (Zimmermann 1974, 69; 1982; Schmid 1977, 40; Hvass 1979, 107; Myhre 1978, 239; 1982, 208). This fifth- to seventh-century settlement gap has usually been explained in terms of depopulation brought about by a plague, an agricultural crisis triggered by worsening climatic conditions, and/or large-scale emigration.

In the 1980s, however, it became increasingly clear that the settlement gap in most of these regions was more apparent than real and was in fact the result of changes in material culture, burial practices, and building types which made the recognition of sixth- and seventh-century settlements difficult. On the island of Bornholm, for example, a change in burial rite to unfurnished cremations (sometimes not even contained in urns) in small cemeteries or as single burials accounts

---

[7] This would, however, run counter to Donat and Ullrich's observation that the largest cemeteries continued in use for the longest period of time. In any case, Wormald's *caveat* is worth recalling here: 'when historians fall back on rising population as the explanation of historical developments, you can be quite sure that they have no idea what the real explanation is' (Wormald 1994).

for the small numbers of fifth-century burials which have been identifed there (Jørgensen 1991, 178). In other cases, settlement mobility accounted for the 'missing' phases of settlements, as at Vorbasse, where excavation eventually uncovered sixth-, seventh-, and eighth-century farmsteads (Hvass 1989, 92; see Chap. 3). In the Netherlands, the sixth century has become visible through the excavation of settlements such as Odoorn; in the Elbe–Weser triangle, finds dating to the first half of the sixth century have now been recovered at Flögeln-Eekhöltjen, only a few miles inland from Feddersen Wierde (Zimmermann 1992).

A certain revisionist zeal has followed these discoveries, leading some archae-ologists to reject the idea of large-scale emigration altogether and to dismiss Bede's account as merely part of an 'origin myth' (Higham 1992). Yet in parts of northwest Germany, along the Frisian coast, and above all in Schleswig-Holstein, there is now persuasive evidence for a marked reduction of settlement.

Schleswig-Holstein

Rural settlement in Schleswig-Holstein, the heartland of the Angles, has been subjected to intensive study, particularly in the east, between the River Schlei and the Flensburg Förde, thanks to the interest in the region sparked by the excava-tion of the trading town of Hedeby (Müller-Wille *et al.* 1988). The evidence for depopulation in this region during the Migration period is striking. Indications of activity during the fifth to seventh centuries are exceedingly scarce, consisting primarily of a few hoards and gold bracteates found mostly near trade routes (Dörfler 1990, 41; Willroth 1990, 11). While significant numbers of settlements dating from the later eighth century onwards are known, there remains an almost complete lack of evidence for settlement in the preceding two centuries, despite the persistent efforts of archaeologists to find it.

The near-total excavation of several cemeteries has allowed this decline in population, which began at the end of the fourth century, to be traced in some detail (Willroth 1990, Abb. 2; Fig. 4.2). First, the number of known sites decreases dramatically: some forty-one settlements and fifty-four cemeteries dating to the late Roman Iron Age (*c.*AD 170–350) have been identified in eastern Schleswig, while only eight settlements and twenty-two cemeteries are known from the middle of the fourth century to the sixth century (Willroth 1990, 9). What is more, only two of the large ancestral cemeteries of the region—Sörup and Süderbrarup—remained in use beyond the mid-fifth century; the others were abandoned. The evidence suggests that these burial grounds did not all go out of use at the same time, and that the decline was a drawnout process and not the result of a single event, such as the sudden departure of a large sector of the population (Willroth 1990, 10). Gebühr has argued that this concentration of burials into a few, large cemeteries at the end of the Roman Iron Age reflects a concentration of the dwindling population into fewer, larger settlements, although the paucity of excavated settlements makes it impossible to confirm this hypothesis (Gebühr 1998). This putative reduction and concentration of the population is explained by Gebühr as a response to increased piracy and military disturbances, a thesis supported by the retreat of settlements from exposed coastal areas in the same period, although climatic and ecological changes, such as over-cultivation, may also have played a role (ibid. 55).

This settlement 'gap' can be seen at the village of Kosel in eastern Schleswig-Holstein, whose settlement history has been examined in particular detail (see Chap. 6 for a discussion of this site). Pollen cores taken at twelve locations within the Kosel micro-region, bounded to the south by the Danevirke—the massive defensive rampart which stretches some 30 km across the 'neck' of Jutland—to the west by the River Schlei and to the north by a small lake, yielded profiles which indicate a clear hiatus in settlement: 'Anthropogenic indicators . . . distinctly diminish [during the sixth to eighth centuries]; the forest re-extends and takes over the abandoned areas' (Müller-Wille *et al.* 1988, 56). The results, it seems, could not be more conclusive (Fig. 4.3).[8]

Comparison with contemporary developments on the island of Funen, however, suggests that we need to be cautious about inferring depopulation from such evidence alone. Until recently the fifth to seventh centuries on Funen were represented almost entirely by hoards; as in Schleswig-Holstein, cemeteries and settlements appeared to be absent (Willroth 1990, 11). This image of a largely empty landscape has had to be radically revised in light of the recent spectacular discovery on Funen of a large, rich settlement complex and trading centre at Gudme-Lundeborg, whose economic heyday lay in the fifth and sixth centuries (see Chap. 6).[9] It remains possible, therefore, that wide-reaching changes in material culture during the fifth to seventh centuries rendered many settlements in Schleswig-Holstein archaeologically invisible. Nevertheless, the combined weight of archaeological, palynological, and place-name evidence for depopulation in Schleswig-Holstein is hard to counter: not only is there an absence of settlements and burials, but the number of hoards from eastern Schleswig from this period is far smaller than on either Funen or Jutland, and place-name evidence as well as the pollen diagrams point to a substantial decline in settlement from the fourth century (see Abb. 2 in Dörfler 1990; Müller-Wille *et al.* 1988; Willroth 1990, 11).

Southeastern Schleswig was gradually resettled in the course of the eighth century, when it became the border region between the Danes and the Saxons.

---

[8] A concentration of settlement such as that postulated by Gebühr would help to account for the changes in the pollen profiles seen in this region which indicate reafforestation. This could be explained as the result of numerous small settlements being replaced by fewer large settlements with more intensive farming systems and consequently larger areas of 'waste' between them, or with a greater proportion of pasture and woodland compared to arable (cf. eastern Denmark and southwest Norway in the Viking period; Hedeager 1992, 212 ff.; Myhre 1978).

[9] Indeed, it is interesting to speculate, as Gebühr has done (1998, 55), whether a Gudme-type settlement might be revealed, were the settlement associated with the exceptionally large cemetery of Süderbrarup, near the rich Thorsbjerg votive deposits, to be discovered and excavated.

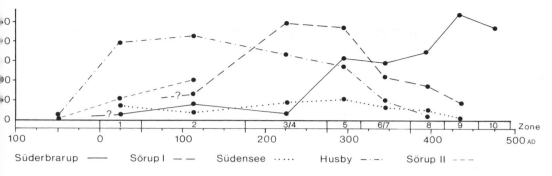

Fig. 4.2. Graph showing average population sizes estimated for the Anglian cemeteries of Husby, Sörup I and II, Sörup-Südensee, and Süderbrarup. After Willroth 1990, Abb. 2.

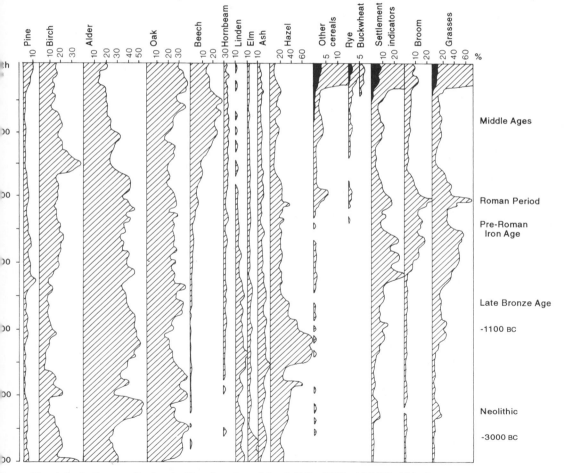

Fig. 4.3. Pollen profile for the Kosel region. After Müller-Wille 1994/5, Abb. 9.

This process can be detected archaeologically and is partly documented in written sources of the ninth century. The *Annales regni Francorum* record that in 804 the Danish king Godfred arrived in Sliesthorp (presumably Hedeby) with his fleet and mounted soldiers (Kurze and Pertz 1895). Four years later he returned, bringing with him merchants from the trading station at *Reric*, and establishing them in Sliesthorp. The *Annales* record that Godfred stayed there for several days while he arranged for the construction of the Danevirke. Archaeology has shown, however, that Godfred was not in fact the originator of this vast project. The earliest construction phases of the Danevirke are now known to date to *c*.640–50 (Jansen 1999, 122). Given the evidence for significant depopulation during the sixth and, especially, seventh centuries in the immediate hinterland of the Danevirke,[10] the implication is that levies were brought from some distance to undertake this colossal construction project, as may have been the case with Offa's Dyke, built at around the same time (Hill 1985).[11] Of course, the construction of a great territorial marker such as the Danevirke implies a period of competition and territorial formation, depopulation notwithstanding.

Northwest Germany

Archaeological and pollen evidence also indicates a thinning out of settlement along the north Frisian coast during the fifth to seventh centuries, which was widespread, if not as dramatic as in Schleswig-Holstein. A maximalist interpretation of this evidence has led some archaeologists to infer 'the abandonment of nearly all settlements in large regions of the north German plain' (Reichstein 1987, 377; author's translation), although in view of the still limited state of research, there are grounds for being rather more cautious. Flögeln in Lower Saxony provides an instructive case study. Pollen samples taken from both the centre and edges of the habitation zone of Flögeln, a sandy 'island' of approximately 25.5 km^2 (see Chap. 3), indicate a gap in settlement during the sixth and seventh centuries followed by a resumption of cereal cultivation from the eighth century onwards, when the settlement of Dalem was founded less than 2 km from the Iron Age and Migration period settlement of Flögeln-Eekhöltjen (Behre and Kučan 1986, 95, Encl. 13). A widespread revival of settlement in the north German coastal region as a whole is apparent from the late seventh and eighth centuries, as the excavation of a series of settlements founded during this period has demonstrated; on the Ems and Weser marshes old *Wurten* such as Feddersen Wierde and Jemgum were resettled, and new *Wurten* such as Hessens were built; new settlements were established further inland on the

[10] The settlement of Kosel, for example, a mere 3 km north of the Danevirke, appears to have lain abandoned from the sixth to the eighth centuries. See Chap. 6.

[11] Even if the immediate hinterland of the Danevirke were only sparsely populated, however, an earthwork built across the 'neck' of the Jutlandic peninsula could have been a means of protecting populations in central and northern Jutland (Gebühr 1998, 44).

Geest, as at Midlum, and on the north Frisian coast itself, as at Elisenhof (Reichstein 1987, 376).[12]

The Rhine Frontier

Until the early fifth century the settlements and burials of partly romanized Germanic groups are readily visible in the archaeological record near the Rhine frontier at settlements such as Wijster (see Chap. 2) and cemeteries such as Rhenen (Heidinga 1994, 202; Ypey 1973). After this time, however, these groups become archaeologically all but invisible, thanks to a paucity of diagnostic and datable artefacts, leading archaeologists to postulate depopulation and possibly mass emigration (cf. van Es 1967, 565–6; see above). Since the 1980s, however, several post-Roman settlements sited near old Roman centres have been identified in what was formerly northern Germania Inferior. As yet, we do not know what the indigenous settlements of this region looked like—in any case, the line between Frank and Gallo-Roman during the fifth century in this 'no man's land' was ill-defined—and the term 'Frankish' to describe these settlements should therefore be used advisedly. They consisted primarily of sunken-featured buildings with a few small timber buildings; the longhouses prevalent further to the north are lacking, although the material culture of these communities is otherwise distinctively Germanic: 'If there were any Gallo-Romans left they must have disguised themselves as Franks' (Heidinga 1994, 203).

These post-Roman settlements are typified by Voerendaal (Prov. Limburg, NL) and Neerharen-Rekem (Prov. Limburg, Belgium), both of which were located on the lands of former Gallo-Roman *villae* (Willems 1989). At Voerendaal, occupation of the villa had ceased by the mid-fourth century. Soon thereafter, a group of sunken-featured buildings and small timber buildings was constructed around one of the villa's stone farm buildings which remained standing. Such settlements presumably represent communities who used the semi-derelict villa buildings while farming the villa lands (Heidinga 1994, 203; Bult and Hallewas 1990, 75).

Voerendaal and Neerharen-Rekem may prove to be typical of the earliest post-Roman settlements in Germania Inferior. But what of the high-status settlements which would have been home to the powerful retinues of the rulers who inhabited this cradle of Frankish power? (Heidinga 1994, 204). This was, after all, where a partly romanized Frankish chiefdom buried its leaders in great splendour, as demonstrated by the extraordinary gold-rich burial of Childeric I, the father of Clovis (James 1988, 58–64). Excavations at Gennep (N. Limburg, NL) have uncovered such a settlement, sited at the chronological and geographical interface between the late Roman and Germanic worlds.

Gennep lies near the Meuse–Niess confluence (Figs. 6.9, 6.10) and is discussed

---

[12] A similar pattern has also recently been identified in Ostfriesland (Bärenfänger 1998, 45).

in more detail in Chap. 6 in connection with the evidence for trade and craft production that excavations there have yielded. Briefly, the settlement was established around the end of the fourth century when it consisted primarily of scattered groups of sunken-featured buildings with a few other timber structures; the artefacts from this phase indicate extensive reuse of Roman building material (Heidinga 1994, 205). In this early phase, Gennep must have resembled Voerendaal and Neerharen-Rekem. The settlement became more substantial in the course of the fifth century, with large timber halls (without byres), a rich material culture, and evidence of intensive craft production, including the working of precious metals and the manufacture of Roman official metalwork. In view of the strategic importance of the Meuse–Niess confluence, the excavator has suggested that the community, for which farming appears not to have been the primary economic activity, was associated with a Gallo-Roman military stronghold (Heidinga 1994, 205).

SETTLEMENT HISTORIES: TWO CASE STUDIES

Along with micro-regional studies of settlement mobility and changing population levels, a number of large-scale regional projects have been undertaken whose primary aim has been to examine territorial formation in relation to early medieval settlements, as well as the connection between estate formation and wider social, political, and demographic developments. The two case studies presented here (both of which remain work in progress at the time of writing) have been selected not only for their intrinsic importance, but also because they exemplify how archaeological and documentary evidence can be brought together to investigate the relationship between rural settlements and territorial formation.

Northern Austrasia: The Veluwe

The ten-year excavations (1971–81) around the village of Kootwijk in the Veluwe district of the central Netherlands form the core of an even larger project led by H. A. Heidinga, the aim of which is nothing less than to understand the 'social, cultural and economic context of [early medieval] Kootwijk on a regional and supra-regional scale' (Heidinga 1990, 9). Thanks to this ambitious study, the process of territorial formation in the Veluwe can be traced in some detail.

The development of the Carolingian village of Kootwijk has been summarized in Chapter 3. Understanding its territorial context is one of the main objectives of the Veluwe Project. The Veluwe in the early Middle Ages was effectively an island of habitable sandy soils, largely surrounded by peat bogs, low-lying, poorly drained soils, and water courses, as were most habitable regions in the Netherlands. Strong links must have developed between clusters of such 'islands' through shared cultural, defensive, and political structures, as well as through intermarriage. Indeed, these islands of settlement, which Heidinga has termed 'nuclear regions', formed the building-blocks of the larger territories referred to in Carolingian sources. The earliest reference to the Veluwe appears in a document of 795, and by the ninth century it was referred to as a *pagus* (meaning 'district' and implying fixed boundaries: Heidinga 1987, 154–5). The boundaries of these nuclear regions and rules pertaining to the use of forest and waste associated with particular properties were written down by the late eighth century although a recognition of territorial boundaries presumably existed before they were written down (ibid. 157).

Based on a close examination of both written sources and the distribution of archaeological finds, a hypothetical reconstruction of these early territories has been proposed for the Veluwe (ibid. 161 ff.).[13] Because early medieval settlement in the Netherlands was restricted to 'islands' of habitable soils, and since the distribution of archaeological finds dating to between 450–750 are concentrated on these islands, nuclear regions are relatively easy to identify (ibid. 175). On the basis of the proximity of these nuclear regions and the presence of communication routes linking them, Heidinga has sought to identify those which together formed the districts named in the Carolingian sources. He has argued that the Veluwe belonged to a cluster of nuclear regions which formed a 'Central Netherlands' territory, surrounded by peat bogs except to the south, where it was connected via the Meuse to the Frankish heartland. This area became a frontier zone during the power struggle which took place during the seventh and early eighth centuries between the Franks to the south and the Saxons and Frisians to the north, until the Franks under Charles Martel ultimately gained control over the Great Rivers delta, including the Veluwe, in 719 (ibid. 178 ff.). Thereafter, the central Netherlands became integrated into the economic and political structure of the Frankish empire, as loyal local elites were rewarded with estates confiscated from those who had backed the wrong side (ibid. 181). By the time of the laws of Charlemagne, compiled at the beginning of the ninth century, the Veluwe appears as a *ducatus*, that is, a territory under the authority of a *dux*; significantly, these laws pertained to territorial units rather than to a particular group of people, unlike earlier law-codes such as the *Lex Salica* or *Lex Frisionum* (ibid. 182).

Another aspect of the formation of territorial identities is the relationship of farming communities to central places. Villages such as Kootwijk operated at the periphery of elite centres which were sited closer to the great rivers, the Rhine and Meuse (Heidinga 1990). One such centre lay at Rhenen (Prov. Utrecht), some 30 km to the south of Kootwijk on a ridge overlooking the lower Rhine, a site ideal for controlling east–west trade. Rhenen is the site of the largest early

[13] Based on a reconstruction of the number of early medieval territories in the Veluwe (25), and the number of farms contained in each territory (10–15, each assumed to house five to seven people), Heidinga suggests a population of around 2,000 during the seventh century (Heidinga 1987, 171). Even allowing for a substantial margin of error, this calculation clearly indicates that the Veluwe was, in comparison to the Frankish heartland, thinly populated, unable to mobilize large numbers of fighting men, and therefore a fairly marginal region politically.

medieval ring-fort in the Netherlands, and there are other signs that it was an early central place: fifth-century votive deposits; two large late Roman/early medieval cemeteries, at least one of which contained high-status burials; and Merovingian charters pointing to a concentration of large estates in the area.

This approach to the reconstruction of 'nuclear regions' and early territories in the Veluwe may provide a model which can be applied more widely. However, in order to examine the impact on rural communities of estate formation and the emergence of a landowning nobility more closely, good-quality cemetery evidence is necessary, and this is lacking at Kootwijk. Settlements and their associated cemeteries have, however, been excavated in the Kempen region in the southern Netherlands, and these provide important evidence for the effect of new structures of landholding and power relations upon rural communities.

Northern Austrasia: The Kempen Region

A project initiated in 1981 by F. Theuws combines historical and archaeological methods to examine how the culturally diverse region of northern Austrasia (bounded by the Ardennes forest to the south, the Rhine to the north and east, and the *Silva Carbonaria* to the west) became integrated to form the power-base of the Carolingian dynasty (Theuws 1986; 1990, 55; 1991; 1994). The project focuses on the development of the *villa* as the basic unit of early medieval agrarian production. In northern Gaul, the Merovingian *villa* shows little or no direct continuity with late Roman villa organization, but appears instead to have been introduced in the later seventh century, during a period of extensive land clearance (Theuws 1991, 313).

As part of this wider investigation Theuws has made a detailed study of the Kempen region in the southern Netherlands (N. Brabant), a small district measuring only some 40 × 20 km, southwest of Endhoven and west of the River Dommel (Theuws 1986). Prior to the eighth century this was a thinly populated area near the northeastern margins of Austrasia, yet certain changes in rural settlement which took place around the beginning of the eighth century in the Kempen region, as in the Veluwe, signalled a major reorganization of the socio-political and physical structures of landholding (Theuws 1990, 41; 1994, 195).

Early medieval settlements in the Kempen were sited on sandy plateaux between stream valleys, each plateau supporting roughly one 'burial community' as represented by a cemetery (Theuws 1990, 60). The earliest burials in the five early medieval cemeteries which have been excavated date to the second half of the sixth century, the period when the Meuse–Scheldt region was recolonized. There is little evidence of royal authority in the Kempen before the eighth century, but written sources indicate that, in the course of that century, the region became integrated into the sphere of Austrasian authority, the core area of which lay well to the south, in the middle Meuse valley, to judge from the distribution of rich burials and settlement density (ibid. 48 and Theuws 1986, 122).

This process can, Theuws argues, be traced archaeologically. Several new types of settlement were established in the Kempen in the later seventh or early eighth century, the first of which Theuws has dubbed 'local centres' (Theuws 1994, 195 ff.). Only a few have so far been investigated archaeologically, but their existence throughout the Kempen is indicated by the cemeteries and churches that were left isolated in the landscape after these centres were abandoned in the twelfth and thirteenth centuries. Those which have been excavated were found to have been associated with groups of rich burials dating to the later seventh century, suggesting that their foundation was connected with elite groups (Theuws 1986; 1994, 196).

One of these centres, at Dommelen, has been excavated in its entirety. Dommelen was founded in the mid- to late seventh century, when it apparently consisted only of a single timber building and a well. It grew in the first half of the eighth century to between nine and twelve buildings, laid out in two clusters, which were accompanied by two contemporary groups of burials (Fig. 4.4; Theuws 1991). The southern group contained twelve relatively rich chamber graves, including a pair of founder graves dating to *c*.675, the male buried with weapons and a *triens* (a bronze coin), the female with jewellery including a gold disc brooch and silver earrings (Theuws 1991, 367). A short distance to the north lay a group of seventeen ordinary coffined burials, which contained almost no grave goods (Theuws 1986; 1990, 60). The rapid growth of the community cannot, in Theuws's view, have been due to a natural population increase but must have been the result of the arrival of dependants from elsewhere, perhaps in connection with new land clearance in the area; it was, perhaps, these dependants who were laid to rest in the northern cemetery. In the ninth century the bipartite settlement layout was replaced by a single row of widely spaced buildings, although what this indicates in terms of social organization is unclear (Theuws 1991, 369).

Excavations at Geldrop appear to support this interpretation. Here, each farm was accompanied from the mid- to late seventh century by a small group of burials, including some rich female graves and a male chamber grave with weapons. Some of the women wore earrings originating from a region to the south, suggesting, Theuws has argued (1998), the movement of high-ranking groups to the area (although the possibility that it is merely an indicator of exogamy should not be ruled out). But why were only a few members of the family buried next to the farms?[14] The current hypothesis is that 'founders', as well as a few of their descendants, were buried within the new settlement as a means of establishing the claims of these newcomers to the land. The other members of these families would have been buried either in the old ancestral cemeteries of the sixth century, or in churchyards built at the centres of new estates.

---

[14] Groups of burials found in Frankish settlements such as these suggest that the link between the abandonment of row-grave cemeteries and the appearance of churchyards is less clear-cut than has sometimes been assumed (Zadora-Rio 2000); it may in fact have been a rather drawn-out process, as it was in England.

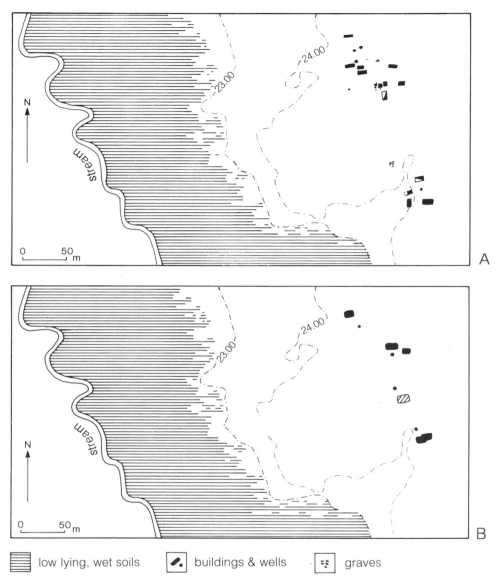

low lying, wet soils   buildings & wells   graves

Fig. 4.4. Dommelen: (A) plan of the settlement, *c*.700–50; (B) plan of the settlement, *c*.800/25–875/900 (intermediate phase, *c*.750–800, not shown). The hatched building was probably already in place during the latter part of the previous phase. After Theuws 1991, figs. 16 and 18.

In summary, new local centres such as Dommelen and Geldrop were established in the Kempen in the mid- to late seventh century by elite groups. The thesis that they lay within large estates is supported by the fact that burial of the dead took place within these settlements in newly established burial grounds with rich founder graves, not in the large ancestral cemeteries of the Merovingian period in which the heads of lineages would previously have been interred. These local centres often consisted of little more than a single building, without sunken-featured buildings, barns, or granaries, a further indication that they were not themselves farms but instead formed part of a larger agricultural network (Theuws 1991, 367, 370).

A second type of settlement appeared in the eighth and ninth centuries, identified by Theuws as 'small colonisation settlements'. Archaeological information regarding these remains limited, but they appear to have been isolated, generally consisting of only a building and a well, and to have remained in use for only one or two generations. They were, he suggests, connected with the expansion of settlement onto newly cleared land (ibid. 375).

The existence of a third type of settlement established in the eighth century, 'settlements of supra-local importance', has been inferred by Theuws based on the absence of burials postdating *c.*750 from the first two settlement types. Burial, he argues, must have taken place in churchyards associated with settlements that have yet to be found. The very limited functions carried out at the first two types of settlement, furthermore, imply that most agricultural activities, for example, grain storage, must have been carried out in manorial centres. None of these centres, however, has as yet been excavated (ibid. 375).

The establishment of these new types of settlement and associated changes in burial practice indicate a breaking-up and reorganization of traditional burial communities in the Kempen region, and the increasing role of social class rather than kinship alone as a unifying feature (Theuws 1994, 196). Indeed, it reflects the earliest stages in the development of a manorial system in which landownership rather than kinship formed the basis of power and status, and in which the rights of local farmers to resources became increasingly constrained. The donation by high-ranking individuals of estates in the Kempen to religious institutions (particularly to Willibrord's monastery at Echternach) in the eighth century reflects this trend towards centralized landholding (Theuws 1986, 132). This is particularly clear for the Kempen region thanks to the fortuitous survival of charters, but it is likely to have been a widespread phenomenon. Bequests of estates to monasteries would thus have had a stabilizing and 'de-tribalizing' effect on Frankish society by concentrating landownership in the hands of religious institutions. Manorialization transformed the elite from warleaders, who maintained their retinues and formed alliances largely through gifts of 'treasure', into 'proprietors and administrators of land', whose wealth was based primarily on their ability to extract surplus from dependants tied to landed estates (Theuws 1990, 44; 1991, 352–3; 1994, 198). While this is perhaps an overly polarized characterization, the two objectives must have been closely linked: manorial organization, apart from its potential economic benefits, was also a means of establishing a stable social order. Indeed, it was actively promoted by churchmen, who were themselves involved in the manorial reorganization of church properties—in the process enhancing royal and ecclesiastical power (Theuws 1991, 313; 1994, 198).

By comparing the distribution of known Carolingian settlement sites in the Kempen with the extent of estates under single ownership recorded in charters, Theuws has shown that nearly all the settlements fall within these estates, although it is impossible to know from archaeological evidence alone whether a particular settlement was a *mansus* or a *sala*. To seek this kind of direct correlation, however, is perhaps unrealistic, since the charters describe the administrative and organizational features of manors, while excavation reveals their physical structure (Theuws 1991, 395). What we can see from the archaeological evidence is that, by the late seventh century, the 'burial community' on each sandy plateau in the Kempen represented five to eight families, a number that compares favourably with the numbers of *casatae* (small domestic units with perhaps a plot of land and some stock) and unfree *mancipia* mentioned in the charters (ibid. fig. 28, 364).

According to this (essentially Marxist) model, the integration of the Kempen into the network of Austrasian authority was based largely on the outcome of internal competition between regional elites for wealth and power (Theuws 1990, 42–3). Competition between these elites (who, thanks to their rich burials, are archaeologically the most visible group) led them to cultivate inter- and intra-regional contacts which acted as catalysts to centralization. Thus, in the Veluwe and Kempen regions, the decades around 700, when the Pippinids established their authority in Austrasia, saw both internal integration and an expansion onto new landscapes linked to the introduction of a new agricultural and social system based on *villae* (Theuws 1991, 318). This integration was achieved through the incorporation of local elites into a larger Austrasian network centred on Pippin II, whose support of major religious institutions, especially Echternach, and the donation of estates to these institutions by members of the local elite, bound the latter up into a wider web of authority. In this way, local elites came to derive power and status through belonging to this larger network and enjoying the patronage of the Pippinids which enabled them to 'get a firmer grip on the local population' (ibid. 337). These developments are reflected archaeologically in changing settlement patterns, particularly the establishment of new local centres such as Dommelen and Geldrop by these elites, the abandonment of Merovingian cemeteries in favour of new burial grounds, and the founding of colonization settlements (ibid. 391).

ANGLO-SAXON ENGLAND

While no regional surveys to investigate the development of early medieval settlement in England have been undertaken on a scale comparable to the Kempen and Veluwe Projects, surveys such as the Raunds Area Project in Northamptonshire (Dix 1986/7), the Shapwick Project in Somerset (Aston and Gerrard 1999), the Meon Landscape Project in Hampshire (Hughes 1988), and the East Anglian Kingdom Survey (Newman 1989; 1996) have effectively combined archaeological fieldwork and documentary research to trace the origins and development of early medieval settlement patterns and associated land use.[15] In addition, the growing number of extensively excavated settlements are yielding important evidence of the impact on settlements and settlement patterns of the fundamental changes in landholding and production strategies which took place during this period.

Soils, Surplus, and Settlement Shift

As in northwest Europe, most early Anglo-Saxon settlements appear periodically to have shifted location (Hamerow 1991). This can be seen most clearly at Mucking, where large-scale excavation of the settlement enabled a shift from south to north in the course of the fifth to (at least) the early eighth century, to be traced (Hamerow 1993; see Chap. 3). A study of the distribution of pottery and other finds suggested that this shifting was gradual, occurring as buildings were rebuilt on new sites, as seen at Flögeln, Vorbasse, Kootwijk, and numerous other continental settlements (see above, Chap. 3). The excavator of West Heslerton in Yorkshire, however, has argued for a different model: although the early and mid-Saxon phases of the settlement were centred on different parts of the site, he interprets this as representing a single, planned relocation, rather than a gradual process (Powlesland, pers. comm. 2000). The lack of closely datable house-types in England makes it difficult to distinguish between these two types of 'shift', but even if the mechanics of settlement shift remain open to debate, such mobility was clearly widespread in early Anglo-Saxon England, most obviously in the south and east. Indeed, in densely settled regions such as the Thames valley, this shifting has left large swathes of the landscape littered with the remains of Anglo-Saxon settlements.

The recognition of settlement mobility has implications for wider issues regarding settlement patterns. It has long been recognized, for example, that the early Anglo-Saxon village was not, in most cases, the direct ancestor of the medieval village. Thus, while fifth- to seventh-century settlements were primarily sited on light, easily cultivated soils, such as those on river gravels (Hamerow 1992), a shift onto heavier, more productive soils had occurred by the time of Domesday Book. The date and underlying causes of this shift have been the subject of considerable debate.

A widespread displacement of settlement—a 'mid-Saxon shift'—has been postulated to explain why most excavated early Anglo-Saxon settlements appear to

---

[15] There have been few attempts to reconstruct Anglo-Saxon territories based on archaeological evidence, although there are exceptions, notably Cunliffe's work around Chalton, Hants (Cunliffe 1972; 1973).

have been abandoned by the end of the seventh century.[16] Arnold and Wardle (1981) were the first to propose a detailed explanatory model, drawing extensively on archaeological evidence, which involved a shift of settlement from light soils, often in elevated locations, to richer soils, often in valleys in the seventh to early eighth centuries; this shift did not merely involve the 'relocation of settlements within a defined land unit, but . . . the reorganization of such territorial units', and was attributed to changes in 'land use requirements' (ibid. 148). Their theory was based in large part on the apparently widespread abandonment by *c*.700 of most settlements which had been established in the fifth and sixth centuries, and the appearance of others apparently founded around the same time. In 1991 I argued that much of the evidence for these abandonments and foundations was inconclusive, and could be the result of excavating only small areas of shifting settlements such as Mucking, thereby uncovering only the 'early Anglo-Saxon' or 'mid-Anglo-Saxon' phase of occupation. I also suggested that the shift onto heavier soils was a somewhat later phenomenon, dating to the late eighth and ninth centuries (Hamerow 1991, 12 ff., 16), and corresponding with a stabilization of settlement that in turn was linked to new forms of landholding and the more intensive farming systems associated with them. This was largely on the grounds that, in regions where detailed surveys have been undertaken, such as Northamptonshire, comparatively few medieval villages overlie early or mid-Anglo-Saxon settlements, indicating that a shift or reorganization occurred after this period (Hall 1988, 100–3).[17]

More recently, Moreland has reaffirmed Arnold and Wardle's model of 'a major dislocation in settlement patterns in England by the end of the seventh century', citing the East Anglian Kingdom Survey as providing key evidence for an early and rapid reorganization (2000, 86–7). This pioneering survey identified numerous surface scatters of Ipswich Ware—a mass-produced pottery traditionally dated to *c*.650–850, manufactured in Ipswich and distributed widely within East Anglia—in the vicinity of parish churches and separate from scatters of early Anglo-Saxon pottery (ibid. 83; Newman 1989; 1992).[18] The dating of Ipswich Ware has, however, recently been revised, and its production is now seen as unlikely to commence before *c*.720 (Blinkhorn 1999, 8–9); it is, furthermore, generally not possible to distinguish between Ipswich Ware produced in the eighth century and that produced in the ninth. The shift and expansion onto

---

[16] The seventh and eighth centuries saw an increase in the total number of settlements as well as an expansion into new regions, such as the Fenlands, and onto heavier soils, as in northwest Essex and southeast Suffolk (Williamson 1988, 162–4; Newman 1989). It is worth noting that the identification of settlements in this period is greatly facilitated by the appearance of hard-fired, mass-produced pottery wares which largely, though not entirely, replaced the more friable pottery of the early period. Settlements in regions where such wares were not widely in use, such as the upper Thames Valley, are very difficult to identify from surface surveys (Vince 1984).

[17] There are, of course, exceptions, such as Wharram Percy, Yorks., and Eynsham Abbey, Oxon., although continuity of occupation on the same spot from the early or mid-Anglo-Saxon period onwards appears to be a feature of high-status centres (Beresford and Hurst 1990, 77, 82–4; Keevil, forthcoming).

[18] A similar pattern has been identified in Norfolk (Andrew 1992, 14–15).

heavier soils seems therefore to have been a *process* which began sometime in the eighth century, lasted at least a century, and proceeded at different rates in different regions.[19]

There can be little doubt that the shift to heavier soils was a response to the need to intensify production in order to meet the demands of new secular and ecclesiastical landlords for surplus, and to provision the populations of the newly established emporia (Moreland 2000). It is therefore tempting to see the 'mid-Saxon shift' as contemporary with other changes in rural settlement which can be dated with more certainty to the seventh and eighth centuries, and which have already been reviewed in Chapter 3: the appearance of planned settlements, high-status centres, and complexes of enclosures (pointing to new systems of farming), as well as the widespread circulation of exotic goods. These changes clearly do mark a fundamental reorganization and intensification of rural production at a period when settlements became more firmly fixed within their territories; yet, while the roots of the shift to more productive soils undoubtedly lie in the eighth century, it is likely to have been a gradual process rather than a single event.

A further element in this reorganization was the breaking-up of traditional patterns of burial. As on the continent, ancestral cemeteries with which settlements had been closely linked for centuries were gradually given up in the course of the seventh century. This general dislocation of burial, along with the abandonment of the rite of burial with (often datable) grave goods, occurred in England long before churchyard burial became well established (Blair 1994, 72–3). This greatly complicates the identification of eighth- and ninth-century burials, of which far fewer have been identified than for the pre-Christian period. Single burials and small burial groups became more common in the mid-Anglo-Saxon period (Scull 2001, 73); in a few cases these have been found within settlements, although there is no evidence to suggest that these were 'founders' or other individuals of high status.[20] It is interesting to speculate whether the establishment in the seventh and eighth centuries of so-called 'Final Phase' cemeteries, which were long assumed to represent a transitional stage between pagan and Christian burials (a view now largely discredited. Boddington 1990), in fact have more to do with the formation of estates than with religious conversion.

An obvious question which presents itself is whether a degree of continuity can be detected in the way in which rural settlements and their territories were articulated in Roman Britain and Anglo-Saxon England. We know that some early Anglo-Saxon settlements occupied the same sites as Romano-British farms,

---

[19] *Contra* Hamerow 1991, where, as already noted, I saw this as a late eighth- or ninth-century phenomenon—associated with the breaking-up of multiple estates.

[20] Isolated or small groups of burials within settlements have been found at Yarnton (Hey, forthcoming), Ipswich (Scull 2001), and possibly Puddlehill, Beds. (Matthews and Hawkes 1985). A small seventh-century cemetery of 24 graves has recently been excavated at Bloodmoor Hill, Suffolk, within a contemporary settlement (Mortimer 2000).

for example at Barton Court Farm, Oxon., and Orton Hall Farm, Cambs. (Miles 1984; MacKreth 1996). In northern Gaul, furthermore, 'as long as the old structure of the region [e.g. roads] was not completely erased and the exploitation methods had not changed essentially, a new territorial organization developed approximately along the same lines' (Heidinga 1987, 166). No such clear-cut conclusion can be drawn for post-Roman Britain, however, although it does appear that, in some regions, larger territorial units followed the political geography of Roman Britain. It has, for example, long been recognized that some of the earliest Anglo-Saxon kingdoms, such as Kent, Bernicia, Deira, and Lindsey, correspond broadly with Romano-British tribes and/or districts. A range of primarily linguistic and place-name evidence also exists for the survival of Roman, and indeed pre-Roman, territories or districts into the Anglo-Saxon period (e.g. Barnwell 1996 and Balkwill 1993). Indeed, the continued use of old boundaries, geographical divisions, and meeting-places is intrinsically likely, although it need not imply that these boundaries were politically maintained. Ultimately, however, it remains exceedingly difficult to define the limits of a late Romano-British villa or an eighth-century estate, let alone establish whether they were identical.

CONCLUSION

It is striking that many parts of northwest Europe, including England, saw a major reorganization and stabilization of rural settlement during the later seventh and, especially, eighth centuries. These changes reflect an intensification of production, but also new systems of distribution which altered the socio-economic structure of rural communities in important ways, as reflected archaeologically in the evidence for increased access to imported goods, new burial patterns, and new farming strategies (see Chaps. 5 and 6). Families and individuals must have become increasingly aware of their place within ever larger territories and of the importance to their communities of distant centres. New administrative structures would have superseded, and in some cases even dismantled, older tribal loyalties—as, for example, ancestral burial grounds were replaced by new, smaller cemeteries in northern Austrasia and parts of England in the seventh and eighth centuries. How this would have affected daily life, and how the establishment of *villae* and estates shaped local identity, are questions that must remain firmly in view, even if archaeology does not have at its disposal the means of resolving them. New strategies of agrarian and non-agrarian production accompanied, indeed were central to, these changes, and these are the subjects of the following chapters.

5

The Forces of Production:
Crop and Animal Husbandry

INTRODUCTION

In a world in which virtually everyone was a farmer, farming was not an 'occupation': the early medieval *leod* who, on the one hand, was in military service to the king, could also have fields to till. It is perhaps for this reason that, although the *Lex Salica* deals extensively with farming matters, it contains no term for 'farmer'. The daily life and world view of early medieval communities were undoubtedly shaped in fundamental ways by the agricultural cycle, yet it is difficult to treat farming activities *per se*, precisely because there is so little description of everyday activities. Further complicating matters, ancient field systems are notoriously difficult to identify and date, and although animal bones and plant remains survive in relative abundance from this period, agricultural tools are very rarely preserved. Even excavating settlements is unlikely to tell us much about systems of farming. A web of economic and environmental factors underlies the developments in farming practices apparent during the second half of the first millennium AD, and agrarian production remains among the most intractable, yet crucially important, subjects in early medieval studies.

This chapter begins with a broad overview of what is known about the agrarian practices of individual communities from archaeological and written sources, and concludes with a consideration of the implications of this evidence for wider social and economic issues.[1] For example, in those regions lying within the former western Empire, how much continuity was there with the late Roman rural economy? When did at least some farms begin regularly to produce a substantial, tradeable, surplus? Finally, how did the intensification of cereal production apparent throughout the North Sea zone relate to changes in the nature of lordship and land tenure?

---

[1] The potential role of 'wild' food sources such as game, fish, fruits, and nuts in the early medieval diet are therefore not considered in detail here.

ANIMAL HUSBANDRY REGIMES

Sources of Evidence

Early medieval law-codes and charters generally have more to say about animal rearing than about crop husbandry and some of this information is remarkably detailed; the *Lex Salica*, for example, refers to some ten different categories of pig! (Wickham 1985). Some Carolingian charters, furthermore, refer to the relative values of different animals; those for the estates of Werden, for example, state that a cow was worth 8 denarii, as much as a ewe with a lamb, and so on (Wulf 1991). Yet the emphasis placed on livestock in these sources should not be seen as a reflection solely of the economic value of animals (for, as will be argued below, cereal crops played at least as important an economic role), but also of their social value (Wickham 1985, 404). In any case, isolated references to farm animals do not tell us much about animal husbandry practices (ibid.). Analyses of animal bones from excavated settlements—which constitute the primary archaeological evidence for animal husbandry—are therefore of crucial importance. These can give us a good idea of the relative proportions of domestic species, from which the contribution of each to the diet and general economy of a community can be assessed. Sex ratios and the ages at which animals were slaughtered also shed light on a settlement's economy by telling us, for example, whether animals were reared primarily for meat, traction, or dairying. Even the size of animals can reveal something about standards of animal husbandry and how these changed over time. The chief problem with drawing conclusions based on faunal remains is that large parts of northwest Europe are covered with acidic, sandy soils in which bone is preserved very poorly, if at all.[2] All too often, bone assemblages from rural settlements survive in such a reduced state that they cannot be considered to be representative. Despite these limitations, however, the economic importance of different domestic species, as well as certain important trends in animal husbandry, can be recognized.

The Economic and Social Value of Domestic Animals

Domestic animals account for the overwhelming majority—usually well over 90 per cent—of the animal bones recovered from early medieval settlements, suggesting that hunting played a very limited role in supplementing diet. There are, however, exceptions. At Gennep, for example (see Chaps. 4 and 6), red deer accounts for some 20 per cent of the animal-bone assemblage, a reflection in all likelihood of the community's high status as an essentially 'consumer' community with military connections. More typical, however, is Feddersen Wierde,

---

[2] Bone from settlements on the coastal marshes is, in contrast, generally well preserved. Thus, whereas some 100,000 animal bones were recovered at Feddersen Wierde, only a few boxes of bones were recovered from Flögeln (K.-E. Behre, pers. comm.).

where 98 per cent of the faunal remains derived from domestic animals (Reichstein 1991). Similarly, at the Migration period settlement at Gielde, Lower Saxony, of some 11,000 animal bones recovered, only 2.2 per cent derived from game animals such as deer and aurochs (Häßler 1991, 294). By the end of our period, hunting would in any case have been increasingly an aristocratic pursuit and privilege.[3]

The strategies adopted for rearing livestock were naturally shaped by the environment and the economy of individual communities, but they were also socially conditioned. This tends to be overlooked in studies which focus solely on the economic importance of different domestic species as sources of food and secondary products such as leather or wool. Like site-catchment analysis, such 'optimization' models of farming emphasize the availability of resources needed to support particular agricultural regimes, and assume that farming was driven entirely by economically 'rational' considerations;[4] yet the social dimensions which helped to shape farming strategies in this period also require consideration (Zimmermann-Holt 1996). By the eighth century agricultural produce was widely exchanged as a commodity, yet this had not always been the case, and livestock in particular played an important role in gift exchange, and thus in cementing social relations, particularly in the Migration period. Different types of produce, furthermore, had different social values. Goods which need to be consumed soon after they are exchanged, such as some dairy products and meat, for example, tend to be of lower social value than those which have a longer usefulness, above all live animals (ibid.). Thus, the relative proportions of species represented in animal-bone assemblages reflect more than merely the local availability of resources such as water and pasture, or whether a given community was, for example, producing cloth for exchange, although these factors were obviously of great importance.

The domestic animals represented in early medieval faunal assemblages invariably consist primarily of differing proportions of cattle, pig, and sheep or goat.[5] The minimum number of individual animals represented by these remains is often not stated in published reports, and the proportions of different species are calculated merely on the basis of the absolute number of bones recovered. This makes it difficult to assess with any accuracy the economic importance of different species for a particular community. Cattle, for example, are often

---

[3] Hunting rights in Drenthe, for example, were given to the Bishop of Utrecht in 944 (Waterbolk 1991*a*, 101).

[4] This approach is implicit in the assumption made by Chapelot and Fossier that the Carolingian rural economy 'would not have been able to rise above the level of subsistence production', and that the early medieval peasant 'seems to have been incapable of recovering from [farm animals] anything more than a little bacon, some leather, a few tufts of wool and some thin milk' (1985, 18 and 23).

[5] It is often not possible to distinguish between the archaeological remains of sheep and goats. Here it is assumed that primarily sheep, rather than goats, are represented. Horses do not appear to have been a major source of food or of secondary products in the early Middle Ages, although a small percentage of horse bones do show signs of butchery and the consumption of horse meat is likely to have been ideologically charged.

assumed to have been the main source of meat, since they usually account for the greatest number of surviving bone fragments.[6] Yet, in most cases, cattle were slaughtered and eaten at a relatively advanced age when they could no longer be used for any other purpose, indicating that they were in fact reared primarily for traction and dairying, not for meat. Pigs, on the other hand, are probably under-represented in archaeological assemblages precisely because they were generally killed off for meat as soon as they reached full size, and the bones of very young animals do not survive well in archaeological deposits (Hagen 1995, 115–17). At Lundeborg, for example, over 90 per cent of pigs were slaughtered before the age of 2, and half before they reached one year (Hatting 1994). Similarly, sheep reared for wool production would not be slaughtered annually on reaching a certain age, and so fewer sheep bones would enter the archaeological record, leading to an underestimation of their economic importance.[7]

Comparatively little evidence exists for highly specialized animal husbandry regimes, although the emphasis on different species varied geographically and through time. Whether a high percentage of a particular species actually reflects the rearing of surplus animals for exchange is, in any case, difficult to determine. It is almost certain, however, that some exchange of animals took place. Most communities would periodically have produced surplus livestock, and not all of this would have ended up on the tables of lords. It is also possible that the exchange of produce between communities was regularized, even if this cannot be proven from archaeological remains alone. Even settlements within a few kilometres of one another could have had access to quite different natural resources and would have benefited from exchange with their neighbours. As Wickham has observed: 'All forms of even quite slight imbalance lead to exchange, to some form of local market system, embedded in the network of social relationships, doubtless, but nonetheless present' (Wickham 1985, 451). For example, the exchange of cattle from marsh settlements in return for quern-stones, timber, heather, charcoal, and iron ore from communities on the *Geest* seems likely (Schmid 1995, 238).[8] Similarly, the Frisians managed to obtain better cereals than could be grown on coastal soils, as well as timber and even wine, by exchanging these for marine products such as salt and fish with merchants along the Rhine valley (Lebecq 1983, 126–31). Such exchange need not,

---

[6] Randsborg, for example, considers that the meat diet of the whole of the first millennium 'comprised almost exclusively beef' (1985, 237).

[7] It is also likely that fish, whose bones are unlikely to be recovered without the systematic sieving of archaeological deposits, played a more significant economic role than has generally been allowed. At Feddersen Wierde, for example, bones from only twenty-nine fish were recovered, despite the settlement's coastal location (Reichstein 1991).

[8] Alternatively, the marsh settlements may have had rights over land on the *Geest*—sandy soils lay only 4 km from Feddersen Wierde, for example. Later evidence for trade in crops comes from the plant remains recovered from the eleventh/twelfth century Warft village at Hundorf on the salt marshes near the mouth of the River Eider, which suggest that at least some of the villagers' plant foods were grown on the Geest, roughly two hours' walk to the south, and so may have been traded (D. Meier, pers. comm. 1993).

however, have been governed solely by economic factors, especially where the participants in the transaction were near neighbours; even exchange of produce which perished quickly may have played a role in fostering social relations,[9] but it was the exchange of livestock, above all cattle, which seems to have had particular significance.

Cattle Of all the major domestic species, cattle require the longest time to reach maximum size and are the most demanding in terms of shelter and fodder. It is not surprising, therefore, that written and philological evidence indicates that cattle were a key measure of wealth in the late Roman Iron Age and Migration period. Tacitus (*Germania* V) claimed that 'it is the mere number of [cattle] that the Germans take pride in; for these are the only form of wealth they have, and are much prized'. The old Germanic word *fehu* (from which the modern German word for livestock, *Vieh*, derives), referred to 'money' or 'possessions' as well as to cattle (Zimmermann 1986, 82).

The economies of most regions of the North Sea zone had a strong pastoral component, at least until the eighth century, which found physical expression in the longhouse (see Chap. 2).[10] Some archaeologists have argued that land was therefore more likely to have been owned collectively and regarded as inalienable (Roymans 1996, 54). In such a society, as already noted, the exchange of cattle played an important role in maintaining social relations, quite apart from their economic importance (ibid.).[11] Indeed, the eating of meat, especially beef, may have been a means of expressing status (cf. Wickham 1985, 429). If this was the case, the shift away from cattle-rearing in favour of arable farming which took place in many regions during the eighth and ninth centuries (see below) must have had considerable repercussions for attitudes towards the land.

What do we know about the size of early medieval cattle herds? The ground-plans of longhouses are often sufficiently well preserved to enable the number of stalls to be counted, providing an indication of the minimum herd size.[12] At Flögeln, for example, some 300 cattle could have been overwintered indoors during the fourth and early fifth centuries (Zimmermann 1986). The size of the herd must have been still larger in summer, since some animals were slaughtered in the autumn, as the faunal remains from Feddersen Wierde and other settlements indicate (Reichstein 1991, 73).

Calculating the size of herds from the numbers of stalls is not a

---

[9] In some societies, for example, it would not be keeping 'good faith' to sell certain foods (such as dairy products, fruit, or vegetables), which are instead given to friends, relatives, and neighbours (Bourdieu 1990, 115).

[10] Longhouses may, of course, have accommodated animals other than cattle. A longhouse in northern Jutland which burned down contained sheep/goat, a pig, and a horse as well as cattle (Hedeager 1992, 197).

[11] See e.g. the role of cattle in early Irish mythology (Kelly 1998, 28–9).

[12] The width of cattle stalls also seems to be a fairly accurate reflection of the size of cattle; the gradual decrease in the width of stalls from the Bronze Age to the Iron Age in the Netherlands is mirrored in the reduction in the size of cattle as indicated by skeletal remains (Waterbolk 1975, 392–3).

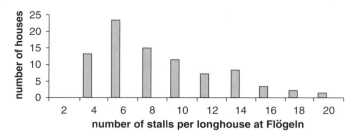

Fig. 5.1. Flögeln-Eekhöltjen: histogram showing the number of stalls per longhouse.

straightforward matter, however. First, only part of the herd, for example, dairy cows, may have been stabled indoors. Phosphate analysis carried out at Flögeln suggests, furthermore, that a few stalls in some of the fifth- and sixth-century longhouses stood empty (see Chap. 2). That said, of the eighty-three longhouses (of all periods) for which the number of stalls could be counted, 62 per cent had between four and eight stalls (Fig. 5.1). At Feddersen Wierde, where cattle played a more prominent role in the economy, all but one of the thirty-four long-houses with byres dating to the later settlement horizons (Phases 6 and 7) had room for at least twelve cattle (Haarnagel 1979*b*, 251 and Tafel 7).[13]

Assuming, despite these caveats, that the number of stalls is a reasonable indi-cator of herd size, how would the nutritional requirements of an early medieval community compare with the herd sizes indicated? According to one estimate, a household would consume approximately 140 kg of meat per head, per year (Schmid 1995, 237). Cattle in this period were relatively small and would have had a dressed weight (i.e. minus the inedible parts) of around 100 kg. A house-hold of five would thus require at least five cattle to be slaughtered per annum. The size of herd needed to provide that number would be very large, although meat would, of course, also have been supplied by sheep and pigs. This estimate of meat consumption may, however, be far too high. Prummel has noted that a household with ten head of cattle could slaughter at most only two per year without decreasing the size of the herd (1983, 249). During the nineteenth century, furthermore, in the province of Drenthe, even wealthy farmers slaugh-tered only one cow and one pig per year (Pals 1987*b*, 124). In this case, only a small proportion, around 10 per cent, of caloric intake would have been pro-vided by meat.

Such averages in any case conceal the considerable differences in the quantity of meat consumed by individuals based on rank, age, or gender, and do not take into consideration the potentially high percentage of protein and caloric intake

---

[13] The *Lex Salica* mentions two categories of herds, those containing fewer than twelve cattle and those containing more than twenty-five (Wickham 1985, 419), although the absence of longhouses in the Frankish regions makes it impossible to compare this against the archaeological evidence. It is interesting to note that even a demesne herd in fourteenth-century England averaged only around twelve cattle (M. Thompson, pers. comm. 1999).

which could have been supplied by dairy products. According to one estimate, an early medieval cow could produce up to 1,350 litres of milk per year, with an annual surplus (allowing for the milk consumed by calves) of several hundred litres per cow (Pals 1987*b*, 120).

For coastal communities such as Feddersen Wierde, provisioning would have become increasingly difficult as the population grew. The settlement is estimated to have had some 300 ha of usable land, of which only 50 ha could be cultivated (Schmid 1995, 237). In the third century, when the settlement housed some 300 villagers and 450 cattle, the surrounding farmland may not have been adequate to feed them all[14] and significant quantities of cereals may have had to be brought in, exchanged, perhaps, for dairy products and wool (Zimmermann 1995*b*, 302).[15] If the supply of winter fodder was insufficient to feed this number of cattle,[16] one would expect calves to have been killed off, and indeed, some 11 per cent of newborn calves were slaughtered. At the eighth- to eleventh-century *Wurt* settlement of Elisenhof (Eiderstedt) the percentage is even higher: over 30 per cent were killed before they reached six months. Such a kill-pattern also points to an emphasis on dairying, as does the fact that some 80 per cent of the cattle from Feddersen Wierde and Elisenhof were cows (Reichstein 1991, 73; 1994). The fact that 66 per cent of cattle at Feddersen Wierde reached the age of four is also suggestive of a regime which was not geared primarily towards meat production, but in which surplus animals, above all male calves, were slaughtered.

Pig   In contrast to cattle, pigs are meat-only animals which cannot be used for traction and do not yield usable by-products while alive. They do, however, produce two or three litters of piglets each year, are easy to rear, and cost little to keep if pannage is locally available. They can therefore be considered as 'low risk' animals, suitable for marginal areas. Alternatively, a community specializing in meat production might for the same reasons choose to rear pigs rather than cattle. Since meat-eating may furthermore have been a mark of status, a high percentage of pig bones could indicate a high-status community.[17] Indeed, the exceptionally rich community at Sorte Muld in Denmark appears to have eaten primarily pork.[18]

As already mentioned, pigs may be considerably under-represented compared to cattle in animal-bone assemblages due to differential preservation. If, furthermore, pig meat was consumed in the form of salt pork, bones would not be found

---

[14] Based on Slicher van Bath's calculations, one medieval cow would need 1.5–2 ha of grassland (Groenman van Waateringe and van Wijngaarden-Bakker 1987, 122).

[15] It has been suggested elsewhere, however, that the cattle were reared primarily for consumption by the villagers (Kossack 1984, 307 ff.; Reichstein 1991).

[16] According to one estimate, one cow would have needed some 400 kilos of hay during the winter months (Kooistra 1996).

[17] The *Lex Salica* (XXVII, 1) appears to indicate that pigs were high-value animals.

[18] See Chap. 6 and the discussion of the Anglo-Saxon settlement of Wicken Bonhunt, below.

at the point of consumption (Hagen 1995, 115). A deposit of pig mandibles in a sunken-featured building at the Carolingian village of Kootwijk reflects a 'well organized pig-breeding scheme' which allowed for twenty pigs of the same age class to be slaughtered at one time, even though, overall, cattle bones far outnumbered pig bones in the faunal assemblage (van Wijngaarden-Bakker 1987).

Sheep   The mature age at which most sheep from rural settlements were slaughtered suggests that most were reared for their wool (as well as dairying, see Fig. 5.2) and reflects the importance of textile production in these communities. Many of the coastal *Wurten*, such as Hessens and Elisenhof, appear to have specialized in wool production. At the latter, 80 per cent of sheep were kept until mature (Bender-Jørgensen 1992, 149). Not only were local conditions on the marshes well suited for sheep-rearing, but these settlements were ideally located for sea transport of cloth. Indeed, a range of Merovingian and Carolingian textiles, whose production seems to have been centred on the Frisian coast, have been tentatively equated with the *pallium fresonicum*, or Frisian cloth, which was widely traded in this period (ibid. 143). Bender-Jørgensen's work on early medieval textiles has pointed to a proliferation of cloth-producing centres in

Fig. 5.2. Milking cattle (below, left) and milking goats or sheep (below, right), as depicted in the Utrecht Psalter. MS 32, fo. 86ʳ, University Library, Utrecht.

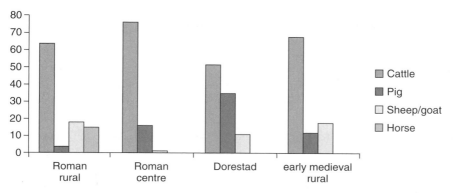

Fig. 5.3. Percentages of bones of the main domestic animals from Dutch settlements. After Randsborg 1985.

northern Europe after the collapse of the western Empire, each producing a distinctive 'brand' of cloth (ibid. 148). Thus, while trade in other commodities such as stone and metals appears to have declined with the collapse of the imperial economy, trade in textiles thrived, further emphasizing the importance of sheep-rearing to the economy.

General Trends

From such evidence, some general trends in animal husbandry can be discerned. The geographical and chronological variations in the predominance of different species is of course in large part due to environmental factors, with pigs, for example, being more prominent in forested areas, whereas sheep predominate in open sandy areas.[19] Socio-economic and demographic factors also had a role to play, however. Randsborg has compared the percentages of animal bones from Dutch settlements which lay within and just outside the western Empire, in order to assess the impact of the imperial market on rural animal husbandry (Randsborg 1985, 238–9). While his study is based on crude measures which are therefore likely to be somewhat biased in favour of cattle, the results shown in Fig. 5.3 are nevertheless revealing.

---

[19] Within the Netherlands, such a geographical trend is clearly evident, with pigs becoming increasingly important further away from the North Sea coast; in inland regions pigs could account for over 20% of domestic animals (Groenman van Waateringe and van Wijngaaden-Bakker 1987, 219). It is possible, however, to overstate the connection between pig-rearing and woodland: a study of medieval England revealed that woodland faunal assemblages could contain the same percentage of pig as arable regions (G. Astill, pers. comm. 1997).

The high proportions of cattle and pig in Roman rural settlements (the horses were used as draught animals) presumably reflect the provisioning of Roman centres with meat by rural producers. The trend towards fewer cattle and more pigs from the seventh and eighth centuries onwards, seen at the trading settlement of Dorestad in the Netherlands as well as in ordinary rural settlements, may have something to do with the expansion of settlement into forested areas, but population growth and the need to provision a growing number of consumers, particularly those in towns, with meat is likely to have played a more significant role. The most striking trend, however, and one which is clearly visible in the course of the eighth and ninth centuries, is the increasing importance of arable production, particularly of bread cereals, over cattle-rearing (ibid. table 9.3).

CROP HUSBANDRY REGIMES

Sources of Evidence

Despite Caesar's account of the early Germans' appetite for meat ('They make not much use of corn for food, but chiefly of milk and of cattle and are much engaged in hunting', *de bello Gallico* IV, 1), it is in fact unlikely that early medieval communities had a heavily meat-based diet. A vast area of pasture is needed if a community is to meet most of its caloric requirements from beef (see above), and most of the caloric intake was almost certainly obtained from cereals (Kooistra 1996, 70).

Contemporary charters and law-codes tell us relatively little about early medieval crop husbandry, although some early sources do record the value of particular cereals. A late Carolingian charter relating to the estates of Werden names wheat and rye as the main crops of the Saxon and Frisian regions; one *Modius* (*c.*9 litres) of wheat was worth 8 denarii (*c.*8 gm of silver), approximately as much as half-a-litre of honey or one cow (Wulf 1991, 337).

Archaeological evidence for the crops grown by individual communities is far more abundant and comes primarily in two forms: seeds and pollen grains. In most cases, the chief evidence for crops is cereal grains which have been preserved through becoming charred (whether accidentally or deliberately, in order to protect the remainder during drying) and discarded.[20] In general, it is difficult to date such evidence with any precision, and comparing late Roman agrarian regimes with the immediately post-Roman situation is therefore extremely difficult.[21]

---

[20] Of course, what was preserved as charred grain is not necessarily representative of what was actually grown. At the settlement of Ullandhaug in southern Norway, for example, the pollen samples taken from the settlement area indicate a predominance of oats, whereas some 75% of the cereal grains preserved from the settlement were barley (Myhre 1982, 212).

[21] See Kooistra 1996, 128 for an attempt to do just this.

The Economic Importance of Different Crops

Certain broad trends can nevertheless be discerned regarding the proportion of crops grown in different regions and in different periods. While barley remained an important cereal throughout northwest Europe (and, in Denmark at least, continued for centuries to be the most important summer-sown cereal: Näsman 1989, 165),[22] emmer, which had played such a significant role in prehistory, declined steadily in importance in the course of the early Middle Ages.

It is, however, the cultivation of rye which increased in importance most markedly in this period. Indeed, rye was to become the chief bread cereal of northern Europe during the Middle Ages, having been introduced into north-west Europe in the Roman Iron Age, initially as an arable weed (associated, for example, with barley). It was later sown in the autumn as a winter crop and occurs in significant proportions throughout our period on sites in northern Germany, Denmark, and the Netherlands (Behre 1992, table 1). By the start of the Migration period rye was already being cultivated in southern Denmark and northern Germany (Behre 1992, 148); from the eighth century onwards its cul-tivation increased markedly, a critical development which relates more generally to a period of intensified production (see below).[23] Interestingly, rye became dominant not only on the poor sandy soils where it first gained a foothold, and where it clearly out-performs other cereals, but even on richer soils in parts of central Europe, suggesting there was a cultural, as well as an environmental, reason behind the preference for rye (ibid. 150; Kooistra 1996, 128).

This rise in the importance of rye is graphically illustrated at Kosel in eastern Schleswig-Holstein, where a fourth- or fifth-century storage vessel found in a drying pit contained over 5 kg of carbonized grain, over 90 per cent of which was barley, the remainder being rye which, at Kosel at least, was not yet a separate cultigen (Dörfler and Kroll 1992, 134). A Viking period cache of grain from the same site (which had been discarded after becoming accidentally charred in the drying process) shows that by this time the winter cultivation of rye, which accounted for 96 per cent of the total quantity of grain, was well established (Kroll 1986). The weed-seed assemblage at Kosel also points to this change in cultivation regimes. In the Migration period summer annual weeds such as cockspur grass, black nightshade, and others were more numer-ous than in the Viking period, reflecting the importance of spring-sown, summer annual cultigens such as emmer, barley, oats, gold-of-pleasure, and millet (Müller-Wille *et al.* 1988, 65). This changed in the Viking age, when weeds with a long growing period, such as curled dock, sheep's sorrel, chess, and corn

---

[22] In parts of southern Germany, by contrast, oats may have been the dominant cereal (Kokabi and Rösch 1990).

[23] In poor soils, where rye copes much better than other cereals, it played a major role much earlier. At Flögeln and in the surrounding region, for example, rye was the main cereal crop as early as the second century AD (Behre 1992, 146).

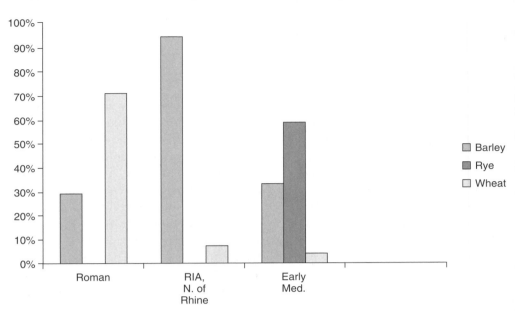

Fig. 5.4. Histogram showing the proportions of cereals present in Roman and post-Roman rural settlements in the Netherlands. After Randsborg 1985, table 9.3.

cockle, became characteristic, presumably reflecting a shift in emphasis to autumn-sown rye (ibid. 66).

Occasionally, changes in the types and proportions of crops grown can be traced at a single settlement. Kosel again provides a useful case study, as two clear phases of occupation—Migration period and Viking period—were separated by an apparent hiatus in settlement (see Chap. 6). While rye, oats, and barley occurred widely in both periods, bread wheat appears to have replaced emmer in the Viking period, and flax replaced gold-of-pleasure as an oil plant (ibid. 65).[24] Peas and beans were found exclusively in Viking period contexts, as were plants which may have been put to medicinal uses, such as common mallow and henbane (Kroll 1990).

The role of socio-economic factors in determining the kinds of crops grown is hinted at by Randsborg's comparison of the percentages of different cereals present in Roman and post-Roman rural settlements in the Netherlands (Fig. 5.4). The high percentage of wheat grown in Roman regions must reflect its exportation to imperial markets, whereas the high percentage of barley north of the Rhine may reflect the production of beer in *Germania libera* (Randsborg 1985). What comes across very clearly is the dramatic increase in the cultivation of rye in the post-Roman period, a trend which is apparent across much of

---

[24] Indeed, the appearance in the Viking age of a weed specifically associated with flax points to its increased importance in this period (Müller-Wille *et al.* 1988).

northwest Europe and which became particularly marked during the eighth to tenth centuries.

Evidence for Exchange of Agricultural Surpluses

Exchange of surplus crops between rural communities must have taken place in certain circumstances, for example, between communities on sandy, inland soils and those on the coastal marshes. The latter, as well as obtaining timber for their buildings from the sandy regions, could also have obtained heather and perhaps cereals such as emmer, rye, and bread wheat in this way (van Zeist 1988). The rye found at Feddersen Wierde, for example, could not have been grown locally (Behre 1999). At the Carolingian period settlement of Dalem, a few kilometres inland on the *Geest*, the storage capacity provided by granaries and barns appears to have exceeded the needs of the local community (see Chap. 3). This, together with the evidence that several buildings were used for cloth production and the settlement's location on a main waterway leading to the coastal marsh settlements, suggests a community engaged in trading grain and cloth with these regions and perhaps beyond (Zimmermann, 1991*a*).

In the Netherlands, however, settlements on the coastal marshes lay a considerable distance from sandy soils, from which they were separated by peat bogs. How did these communities obtain the timber and cereals essential for their survival? A study of the botanical remains from several settlements on the sandy soils yielded no direct evidence of exchange with the marsh regions (van Zeist 1988). However, weeds found in sheaves of rye dating to the eighth or ninth century from the coastal settlement of Leeuwarden indicate that these must have been imported from sandy regions to the east or southeast, although given that Leeuwarden was a port and regional market-place, this is hardly surprising (ibid.). There is also some documentary evidence for trade in cereals, notably Einhard's reference to merchants from Mainz who purchased grain, apparently regularly, from northern Germany and transported it to Mainz by river (Dutton 1998, 95–6; *Translatio et miracula sanctorum Marcellini et Petri*).

The production of significant surpluses of cereal crops by Carolingian farmers can be inferred from a study of the potential grain yields for the village of Kootwijk, which had some 150 ha available for cultivation. Pals has estimated that, if the twenty or so farms each housed on average five working members, a total of 84 ha of grain could have been harvested by the villagers (Pals 1987*b*, 126), implying that nearly half of the fields lay fallow at any one time. If, furthermore, the yield per hectare is estimated at 800 kg of grain, one farmstead would have produced some 3,360 kg of grain, of which 1,120 kg would be used as seedcorn and around 950 kg would be eaten. Even if some of the remainder were used as fodder, each farm would still have, in a good year, a surplus of around 1,000 kg of grain, or between one quarter and one third of the total yield.

Such a level of surplus production must have acted as a considerable stimulus to both market and barter economies.[25]

CONSUMERS AND PRODUCERS

Archaeological evidence for the transfer of livestock as food renders in the North Sea zone is comparatively rare (though see the discussion of animal bones from *wics*, below). It is, furthermore, unclear whether elites had preferential access to good-quality meat. The analysis of the animal bones from Feddersen Wierde, for example, does not state whether there was any material which could be specifically associated with the *Herrenhof* (Reichstein 1991). Clearly, the great majority of excavated settlements represent 'producer' communities, growing food to provision themselves, to pay tribute, and for local exchange. Yet there are exceptions. The community at Gennep in the Netherlands (see Chaps. 4 and 6) appears to have been one primarily of consumers, possibly engaged in rearing horses, but obtaining its food animals and grain from elsewhere, presumably via a system of clientship (Heidinga 1994, 206; 1998). At the trading settlement of Lundeborg on the island of Funen, roughly 70 per cent of the very large number of animal bones recovered derived from cattle, and roughly 25 per cent from pig. Seventy-seven per cent of these cattle were slaughtered as adults; the small number (6 per cent) of juvenile animals and the large quantity of butchery debris suggest that most cattle were delivered on the hoof and were not reared at the site (Hatting 1994). Preliminary investigation of the botanical remains has revealed, furthermore, that very few cereal grains were preserved by charring, again suggesting that the drying of cereals took place elsewhere, and that they arrived at the site fully processed (Robinson 1991). The animal bones and plant remains thus support the impression that the Lundeborg settlement was primarily one of consumers rather than producers of food, in this case traders (see Chap. 6).

As Lundeborg demonstrates, botanical remains can tell us something about the status of communities. Each stage of crop processing—harvesting, threshing, winnowing, and so on—produces distinctive by-products. The presence or absence of chaff and rachis fragments among cereal grains can, for example, reveal whether they arrived at a settlement in an unprocessed or semi-processed state, or whether they were delivered ready for consumption, having been fully cleaned and processed elsewhere. The seed remains from the Dutch settlements of Odoorn, Gasselte, and Pesse, for example, all contained considerable quanti-

[25] The fields associated with Dalem (see Chap. 3) have been mapped through the use of phosphate analysis, thereby identifying which areas had been manured: some ten to fifteen farms of the Carolingian/Ottonian periods appear to have made use of some 167 ha (i.e. 10–16 ha per farm), though whether this ratio remained constant throughout the life of the settlement is impossible to say (Wulf 1991, 337). This can be compared with tenth-century farms in the Veluwe, which are estimated to have had at least 8–10 ha of arable per farm (Heidinga 1987, 89).

ties of arable weed seeds, indicating that the grain was unprocessed when it was brought to the village, where the cleaning and threshing of the crop would have taken place (van Zeist *et al.* 1986, 270). The plant remains from the high-status settlement at Lejre (Zealand), however, suggest that grain arrived partly or fully cleaned. Botanical samples were taken from the postholes of the Great Hall (see Chap. 2) and from the floor layers of two contemporary sunken-featured buildings (Robinson 1991). Some 700 carbonized grains were also taken from an oven (radiocarbon-dated to between AD 660 and 780). These proved to consist almost exclusively of rye which had been fully cleaned and was presumably being dried prior to grinding. The grain samples from the Great Hall and one of the sunken-featured buildings were likewise fully processed. The samples from 'Pit House' XIV, however, contained rachis fragments, indicating a partly processed supply (ibid. 195).

INTENSIFICATION OF PRODUCTION

The intensification of agricultural production, a prerequisite of early state formation, is indirectly reflected in the appearance of new house types, new forms and greater numbers of crop-storage facilities, and changes in the layout of farmsteads and villages, particularly during the eighth and ninth centuries. It was stimulated not only by the growth of 'consumer' communities such as towns and monasteries, but also by the increased demand for food and other rents and tributes from landlords, and almost certainly—even if this is impossible to prove—population growth. The social implications for rural communities which such increased production carries with it are, however, rarely given explicit consideration.[26] More intensive farming methods would, for example, have required either an expansion in the size of households to meet their increased need for labour (which may explain the larger size of some farms in Viking-period Denmark, as at Vorbasse) or a pooling of labour and 'capital' (such as oxen or ploughs) within villages, with collective rights over and access to certain resources such as pasture and pannage. The introduction of demesne systems in particular brought with it the need to produce a substantial agricultural surplus. To meet this new demand, farmers could adopt one of two basic strategies: intensification or specialization. In other words, they could either produce more of what they were already growing in order to pay rents, or they could specialize in certain crops and/or animals, perhaps leading to diminished self-sufficiency, at least where food was concerned. A combination of these strategies is, of course, also possible. Direct archaeological evidence for such specialization is, however, hard to come by, as already seen. It is, furthermore, impossible to define with certainty the level of surplus produced on average by a

---

[26] I am particularly grateful to Ros Faith and Debbie Banham for their comments on this topic.

particular community or region, although, given enough information, potential productive capacity can be estimated, as Pals has done for Kootwijk (see above) and Kooistra has done for the Kromme Rijn region of the Netherlands (Kooistra 1996).

There is, nevertheless, evidence for a general intensification of farming practices, in the form of turf manuring and more intensive rye cultivation, the introduction of new field systems and crop rotation, and, at the level of individual settlements, increased grain-storage capacity.

Turf Manuring and 'Perpetual' Rye Cultivation

A marked increase in the cultivation of rye is apparent across northwest Europe from the eighth century onwards (see above; Behre 1992, 150). From around this time, 'perpetual' rye cultivation was introduced in regions with poor, sandy soils, from the Netherlands to Schleswig-Holstein, enabling winter rye to be grown on the same fields year after year by means of 'turf-manuring' (the German *Plaggendüngung*), a labour-intensive technique particularly associated with rye cultivation (ibid. 152; 1988). The practice of turf-manuring involved treating fields regularly (usually annually) with a mixture of manure and turves, sometimes with the addition of peat, clay, or sand, primarily in order to improve the soil's ability to retain moisture. Limited use was probably made of turf-manuring as early as the seventh century, for example in Lower Saxony, although the practice did not become widespread in northwest Germany, the Netherlands, and northern Belgium until the ninth and tenth centuries (Häßler 1991, 292).[27] In these regions at least, the ability to maintain the same fields under permanent cultivation must have contributed to the demise of shifting settlement (Müller-Wille 1979, 368).

New Field Systems

The introduction of new field systems also reflects an intensification of production. A review of the field systems of the Migration and Merovingian periods published in 1979 described them as virtually unknown (ibid. 367). Today, not only is it possible to recognize a development during this period from extensive field systems with long fallow periods, to fields under permanent cultivation with probable crop rotation, but this critically important change can also be linked to the reorganization of villages and farmsteads outlined in Chapter 3.

In northwest Germany, as in southern Scandinavia and parts of Britain, small, enclosed, irregularly shaped, so-called 'Celtic' fields were in use during the

---

[27] There is some evidence to suggest that the technique was already known in the pre-Roman Iron Age (Müller-Wille 1973, 47).

Roman Iron Age and Migration period (Häßler 1991, 293; e.g. at Flögeln: Zimmermann 1974). Strip fields, sometimes associated with individual farmsteads, appear to have emerged in the seventh century (Häßler 1991, 293; Zimmermann 1995b). At Dörverden (Lkr. Verden), for example, a Merovingian-Carolingian cemetery lay within a long, narrow parcel of land which closely matched the outlines of a field which appears on a tithe map of 1755, suggesting that strip fields were already in existence here by the seventh century (Häßler 1991, 293). In Drenthe such fields are clearly in evidence by the ninth century, as at Gasselte, where strip fields abutted directly onto the farmyard (see Chap. 3). The earliest written evidence for the use of strip fields is contained in the *Pactus Legis Salicae*, in a clause which refers to strips of land (Pact. XXVII, 32; Eckhardt 1955, 210; Boelcke 1974; Ennen and Janssen 1979, 127n.). Hints of an infield/outfield system[28] are contained in Frankish charters of the eighth and ninth centuries. In these documents, the words *campu*s and *terra* are used to refer to fields which underwent lengthy fallow periods during which they were used for pasture. *Terra aratoria*, on the other hand, referred to arable under more intensive cultivation (Theuws 1991). Such an infield/outfield system required a careful balance to be maintained between the size of the infield, which needed intensive manuring, and the number of cattle and sheep which could be supported on the land (Hedeager 1992, 219).

The replacement of Celtic fields with infield/outfield systems and strip fields is of considerable significance. It meant that each village's arable land no longer needed to be redistributed every year, as described by Tacitus in the *Germania* (XXVI). Instead, ownership of fields became established and a more direct link was forged between the individual household and the land it cultivated (Hedeager 1992, 222). The preservation of the boundaries of abandoned farmsteads in overlying fields (as at Odoorn and Gasselte: see Chap. 3) graphically illustrates this link.

The physical link between infield and farm was not always direct, however. At Kootwijk a single block of fields appears to have been divided up between individual farms which were not directly joined to their fields, as they were at Gasselte.[29] But the distinction between a relatively small, intensively cultivated infield and larger outfield, used as pasture and occasionally as ploughland, was clearly present from the eighth century onwards (Heidinga 1987).

---

[28] Following Hooke's definition, the infield was a comparatively small area of arable close to the settlement which was divided up, probably into strips, and kept under permanent cultivation through intensive manuring. The outfield lay beyond this and consisted of common pasture, part of which was periodically cultivated, 'as the need arose' (Hooke 1998, 115–16).

[29] Part of the eighth- to tenth-century fields at Kootwijk could be 'reconstructed' thanks to the survival of ancient fence-lines and plough furrows. The fences often followed the boundaries of the underlying farmyard and 'probably [marked] out different people's fields' (Heidinga 1987, 88). These small, presumably intensively manured fields were 10–20 m wide and of unknown length.

Crop Rotation

The practice of crop rotation is likely to have been associated with this reorganization of field systems. Two- and three-field crop rotation requires the sowing of both a winter and summer crop, thereby keeping fields under permanent cultivation. Fertility is maintained through intensive manuring, alternating the type of crop planted in a field, and allowing a brief fallow period for each field every third year or so, during which it may be used for grazing. Direct evidence for crop rotation prior to the tenth century is scarce, but it is hinted at by a range of indirect evidence. At Vreden in Westphalia, two strip fields (each roughly 25 m wide) shown on the cadastral map of 1827 were excavated, revealing beneath them farmsteads of the seventh to eighth centuries (Reichmann 1982, 175). These fields had earlier been part of a larger field which consisted of twelve such 'double fields'. A deep furrow in the middle of the excavated area, which was aligned with the earliest fence-line and house, indicated that these two strip fields had originally been a single parcel of land which was subdivided in the early Middle Ages. Similar bisection of early fields occurred at Telgte, also in Westphalia (ibid. 181, fig. 25). Whether this indicates two-field rotation or merely a shortage of infields must, however, remain a matter for speculation.[30]

Some attempt has also been made to find botanical evidence for the introduction of the three-field system. In Drenthe, for example, rye, barley, and oats may have been cultivated in somewhat more equal proportions after the eighth century, to judge from a detailed paleobotanical study carried out for three settlements. At Odoorn (occupied from the sixth to the ninth centuries), rye accounted for well over 90 per cent of the cereal remains. At Gasselte (ninth to twelfth centuries) and Pesse (seventh to twelfth centuries), however, rye constituted only between 65–7 per cent, with hulled barley and oats comprising the other most common cereals (van Zeist *et al.* 1986; van Zeist 1988). This has been interpreted as heralding the introduction of three-field agriculture (Waterbolk 1991*a*, 101), but the evidence as it stands is too limited to be conclusive. A more thoroughgoing change in cultivation technique—the introduction of three-field rotation together with the widespread use of the mouldboard plough, which turned the soil over, thus enhancing its fertility—could in any case be best identified not from the ratio of cereals recovered, but through an examination of arable weed-seed assemblages; the types of weed which would flourish under these conditions should be distinct from those which would thrive in small, enclosed fields ploughed without the use of a mouldboard. Such work, however, remains to be done.

The role of the mouldboard plough in the intensification of cereal production

---

[30] At Kootwijk the initial analysis of pollen and seed assemblages suggested intensive cultivation and short fallow periods, which would fit well with three-field rotation (Heidinga 1987, 87 and 90). This interpretation, however, was subsequently revised, and a simple infield/outfield system now appears more likely (Groenman van Waateringe and van Wijngaarden-Bakker 1987, 26).

remains ill-defined. It is widely assumed that its introduction enabled such intensification to take place: more intensive cultivation regimes needed more intensive manuring, and for this the mouldboard was enormously helpful in sealing in the manure and nitrogen as the soil was turned over. In fact, however, mouldboard ploughs are known to have been in use since the first century BC, to judge from surviving furrows in the Netherlands, northern Germany, and Belgium, where they enabled the heavy soils of the coastal regions to be cultivated (Glob 1951; Chapelot and Fossier 1985, 19). Several fragments of Iron Age or Migration period mouldboards were, for example, found at Feddersen Wierde (Haarnagel 1979*b*, Tafel 16). The mouldboard plough and the ard (or 'scratch plough') remained in contemporary use for centuries (Zimmermann 1995*b*, 308), as illustrated at the ninth- to eleventh-century *Wurt* of Elisenhof, where both an ard and traces of turned furrows survive (Szabó *et al.* 1985, 19 ff. and Taf. 2.17; Bantelmann 1975, 52 ff.; see also Lerche 1996).

The key question, therefore, is not when did the mouldboard come into use, but when did it come into *widespread* use? We are still some way from being able to provide a definitive answer. Iron shares and a team of oxen were needed for a mouldboard plough (the former was already in use in the Iron Age: Müller-Wille 1973), and the availability of these resources was perhaps the chief constraint on its use becoming widespread. It is again the indirect evidence provided by weed seeds which, because of their ubiquity in seed assemblages, may offer the best chance of ultimately tracing the spread of the mouldboard plough.

THE INTENSIFICATION OF ARABLE PRODUCTION: REGIONAL TRENDS

Northwest Germany

In northwest Germany, turf-manuring was practised at least from the seventh century but did not become widespread until the ninth, when it may have been linked to a reorganization of settlement (Zimmermann 1995*b*, 303; Wulf 1991).[31] This reorganization has already been touched upon in Chapter 3 and can be seen most clearly by comparing Migration period Flögeln-Eekhöltjen, with its longhouses and multiple farmsteads, with the Carolingian period settlement of Dalem, with its wider range of building types and storage structures (Figs. 3.19 and 3.6).

A number of the changes apparent in the structure and layout of farmyards and houses in the Carolingian period suggest a need for increased storage capacity and reflect a new agricultural regime which arrived with the introduction

---

[31] The practice continued into the modern period, and *Plaggen* layers up to a metre thick can be found in parts of northwest Germany (Wulf 1991, 336; Heidinga 1987, 91).

of *villae* and increased lordly control over production, resulting in a larger grain yield which could no longer be threshed in its entirety immediately after the harvest. In Westphalia changes in the form of the farmhouse in the ninth century appear to be related to this need to store larger harvests (see Chap. 2; Reichmann 1991, 284). In particular, changes in roof construction and the addition of side aisles allowed large quantities of grain to be stored in houses. This can also be seen at Dalem, where a side-aisle was added to the largest ninth-century farmhouse, presumably for similar reasons (Zimmermann 1991*a*). Reichmann has suggested that this increase in the size of the harvest was connected with the increased use of turf manuring which enabled year-round cultivation to take place (1991). The unthreshed grain which needed to be kept over the winter would have been stored in the roof-space of houses, where the smoke from the hearth would help to preserve it. A greater variety of storage structures also came into use during the seventh and eighth centuries, as can be seen from the range of barns, granaries, and helms used at Dalem and Warendorf, for example.

Southern Scandinavia

In southern Scandinavia two broad periods of agricultural intensification have been identified during the first millennium AD, the first occurring in the third century, the second around 700 (Näsman and Roesdahl 1993). From *c.*200 onwards the old, extensive 'Celtic' field systems were replaced by intensively cultivated, permanent infields situated next to villages, with pasture and meadow located some distance away. This transition can be firmly dated to the third century in Norway and Sweden, where stone field boundaries of this period survive to this day. It is generally assumed that a similar development occurred in Denmark at around the same time, and the appearance at some sites of drove-ways for leading cattle safely through the infields to pasture supports this assumption (Hedeager 1992, 205 and 221). This indicates a more intensive crop husbandry regime than was practised when the *Germania* was written: 'Ploughlands are changed yearly, and still there is enough to spare. . . . Although their land is fertile and extensive they fail to take full advantage of it because they do not work sufficiently hard' (*Germania* XXVI; Layton 1995, 707).

The second phase of intensification, occurring around AD 700, has been largely inferred from the restructuring of so many farmsteads and villages at this time (as at Vorbasse), and the appearance, at some settlements at least, of larger farmsteads (Fig. 5.5; see Chaps. 2 and 3). These changes have been linked by Danish archaeologists with the advent of two- and three-field rotation, the increased use of the mouldboard plough, and the more widespread cultivation of rye, although only the last of these is clearly attested in the archaeological record (Näsman and Roesdahl 1993, 183).

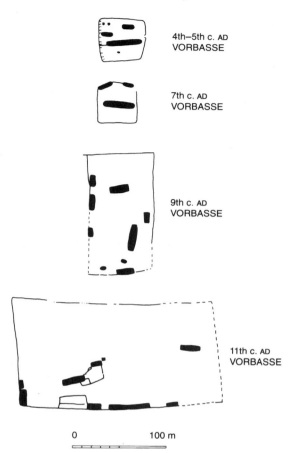

4th–5th c. AD
VORBASSE

7th c. AD
VORBASSE

Fig. 5.5. Vorbasse: the size of farmsteads from the fourth to eleventh centuries AD. After Hvass and Storgaard 1993, 190.

9th c. AD
VORBASSE

11th c. AD
VORBASSE

0   100 m

The Netherlands

Similar broad developments can be seen in the Netherlands, north of the Rhine. The transition from the regularly shifting settlements associated with Celtic fields to semi-permanent, often more structured villages began in Drenthe already in the course of the second and third centuries (Waterbolk 1982, 129 ff.). During the eighth century the appearance in parts of the Netherlands of planned villages such as Kootwijk has been associated with intensified farming methods, such as turf manuring and crop rotation.

A marked increase in the grain-storage capacity of farmsteads can also be inferred by comparing tenth-century Gasselte, with its numerous storage structures and houses with side-aisles, to the earlier settlement at Odoorn (Waterbolk 1991a; see also Chap. 3). The excavators note a marked increase over time in the percentage of each farmyard which was built on. At Odoorn the buildings occupied a total floor area of (on average) around 100 m^2 per farmyard, while at

Gasselte the floor area was up to five times greater: 'in view of the greater height of the buildings in Gasselte, the increase in volume of all the buildings would have been [at least ten times] greater' (Waterbolk and Harsema 1979, 264). As in northwest Germany, a greater variety of storage structures—barns and helms—is also apparent in the Netherlands, although this phenomenon does not become particularly marked until the ninth century.

Northwest Gaul

The Romanization of northern Gaul involved, among other things, the reorientation of farming practices towards production for markets which provisioned the military and urban centres of the Rhine *limes*, and towards meeting the demands of taxation (Roymans 1996, 58 ff.). Roymans has argued that the introduction of cash markets turned agricultural produce into a true commodity, whose social value was consequently reduced. Control over land became increasingly important and private landed property replaced the 'traditional collective claims to land' of the late Iron Age (ibid. 60). The arable regions of the loess soils became dominated by villas, while pastoral, sandy areas have yielded less evidence for intensified production. This geographical difference is also apparent in the Merovingian period, when pastoral farming was predominant on the clay, peat, and sandy soils in the far northwest of Gaul (i.e. the southern part of the Netherlands), whereas pig-rearing and arable farming were more important on the loess soils of northern France, central Belgium, and the German Rhineland (ibid. 56).

The debate regarding the degree of continuity between the late Roman and Merovingian landscapes of northern Gaul has become polarized, with some scholars envisaging economic catastrophe leaving ruined fields in its wake, while others argue for broad continuity without any major upheavals in the rural economy during the whole of the first millennium AD (Ouzoulias 1997). While no general model can be proposed for the whole of the region, studies of animal bones do reflect how the decline of large urban centres, and hence the main markets for meat, prompted a return to less specialized, more self-sufficient animal-husbandry regimes.

A comparative study of the animal bones from settlements in the Île-de-France, the Pas-de-Calais, and Picardy is particularly revealing in this regard (Leblay *et al.* 1997). Even within the Île-de-France, considerable local variation is apparent during the late Roman period with regard to the relative percentages of pig, cattle, and sheep, although sheep usually represent between 30 per cent and 50 per cent of animal-bone assemblages (ibid., fig. 4). In the sixth century, however, this picture changed: the proportion of cattle increased markedly, from around 27 per cent to around 55 per cent, at the expense of sheep (which dropped to *c*.15 per cent), while the proportion of pig changed little, remaining at around 30 per cent (ibid., fig. 6). In the Pas-de-Calais and Picardy the picture is somewhat different. Here the percentage of both cattle and sheep dropped slightly in the sixth century, to around 50 per cent and 15 per cent respectively, while the percentage of pig increased from *c.*20 per cent to *c.*35 per cent. Across all three regions, however, there is markedly less local variability in the proportions of species in the Merovingian period compared to the late Roman period, perhaps indicating less specialization (ibid. 53).

As for the animals themselves, a decrease in the withers-height of cattle from the sixth century onwards is presumably due either to a decline in animal-husbandry skills, or to a deliberate decision on the part of farmers to breed smaller cattle which could be more easily maintained.[32] The fact that almost all domestic species were affected by a reduction in size in the Merovingian period, however, suggests that this was not deliberate choice but rather a gradual development, perhaps imperceptible to the farmers themselves (ibid. 54). Such a reduction in the size of livestock is also apparent in southwest Germany during the same period, where it has been attributed to the demise of the Roman practice of systematic cross-breeding (Damminger 1998, 65).

In all of the regions under study, more labour-intensive forms of farming are apparent by the eighth century and, from the ninth century at the latest, a marked intensification of bread-cereal production and a decline in the economic importance of cattle-rearing is apparent. How does Anglo-Saxon England compare with this picture?

FARMING IN ANGLO-SAXON ENGLAND

Comparisons between the farming practices prevalent in northwest continental Europe and England are complicated by the paucity in England of large-scale settlement excavations and hence of large assemblages of animal bones and plant remains. As a result, Anglo-Saxon archaeologists and historians have tended to focus on issues of local land use and 'resource areas', rather than on the economy of individual communities (cf. Hooke 1998). Remarkably little has been published on Anglo-Saxon arable farming practices *per se* (although see Clutton-Brock 1976; Fowler 1997; Rackham 1994*a*), and most of the relevant data remains appended to excavation reports, with little attempt at synthesis.[33] These differences in emphasis notwithstanding, enough detailed studies do exist to allow Anglo-Saxon farming to be set alongside and compared, if only in very general terms, with developments in the North Sea zone generally.

---

[32] This reduction in the size of cattle is apparent, for example, at Villiers-le-Sec, a villa of the abbey of St-Denis (Ruas 1988, 228).

[33] In a review by a palaeobotanist of the evidence for arable farming in Hampshire published in 1991, the available sample is described as 'hopelessly inadequate' (Green 1991, 367).

Iusbandry

nt emphasis in studies of Anglo-Saxon animal husbandry has been
___ ___ nimal bones from *wics* and what these tell us, indirectly, about the
rural settlements that provisioned these trading centres (e.g. Bourdillon 1994;
O'Connor 1994; Crabtree 1996). This is unsurprising, as there are still few
sizeable faunal assemblages from rural settlements. At the time of writing, only
one published study of an animal-bone assemblage from an early Anglo-Saxon
settlement attempts the kind of detailed reconstruction of animal-husbandry
practices undertaken, for example, for Feddersen Wierde or Kootwijk, namely,
Crabtree's detailed investigation of the large assemblage of animal bones
(*c*.175,000 bones and fragments) from the settlement at West Stow, Suffolk
(Crabtree 1990).

Despite the lack of detailed studies, it is clear that the animal-husbandry
regimes of the fifth and sixth centuries had, in several important ways, more in
common with those of the Iron Age than of Roman Britain, although some
underlying continuities from the Roman period are, unsurprisingly, also indicated. This is largely accounted for by the fact that early Anglo-Saxon farming
was not market-oriented. Crabtree's study suggests that the community at West
Stow practised a diverse, relatively balanced animal economy, a pattern which
seems to be repeated at most early Anglo-Saxon settlements. Compared to
northwest Germany and southern Scandinavia, most regions of Anglo-Saxon
England placed a greater emphasis on sheep over cattle, a trend which becomes
particularly marked by the late Saxon period.[34] The West Stow animal bones
illustrate this gradual trend towards more sheep and pig at the expense of cattle
(Crabtree 1994, 41). The predominance of sheep, many of which were kept until
maturity, furthermore reflects the importance of wool production and, presumably, dairying. As on the continent, the percentage of game in early Anglo-Saxon
animal-bone assemblages is usually tiny (cf. Crabtree 1996, 70), although the
fact that hunting played only a minor role in Anglo-Saxon subsistence strategies
should not lead us to underestimate the social importance of wild animals such
as deer, boar, beaver, and bear, as attested by their appearance in the literature,
iconography, and amulets of the period (Crabtree 1995). Indeed, recent research
suggests that already in the mid-Saxon period (*c*.650–850), high-status settlements produced a considerably higher percentage of game, around 2.5 per cent,
compared to around 0.5 per cent on ordinary rural settlements and towns (Sykes
2001).

Crabtree has argued, based primarily on evidence from East Anglia, that early
Anglo-Saxon husbandry practices were quite unlike those across the North Sea,
not only in terms of the greater emphasis on sheep, but also with regard to kill

---

[34] Regional diversity is, however, clearly apparent, and largely related to the quality of the available
pasture: along the middle and the upper Thames valley, in contrast to East Anglia, cattle appear to have
been economically more important (e.g. at Yarnton, Oxon.: Hey, forthcoming).

patterns. Thus, for example, at Feddersen Wierde 66 per cent of cattle reached the age of 4 and 20 per cent of sheep were killed during their first year; at fifth-century West Stow only 39 per cent of cattle survived beyond the age of 4, and over 40 per cent of sheep were killed in their first year. Crabtree notes, further-more, certain similarities at West Stow with the Iron Age and Roman periods in terms of animal sizes, butchery practices, and kill patterns, leading her to argue for long-term continuities in animal-husbandry strategies. In contrast to northern Gaul, for example, there was no general decline in the size of livestock in early Anglo-Saxon England (Crabtree 1990, 68; Hagen 1995, 59). While such continuity is entirely plausible, indeed likely, her comparisons with the continent are based heavily on the evidence from Feddersen Wierde and thus remain too limited to enable clear distinctions to be drawn with the situation in England. The farming strategies of a *Wurt* community living on the marshes of northwest Germany are, in any case, unlikely to be closely similar to those of settlements in the sandy regions of East Anglia. Above all, her conclusions do not take into account the considerable regional variation in kill patterns and species ratios even within 'Saxon' and 'Anglian' regions. Clearly, more comparative work needs to be done by palaeozoologists before early Anglo-Saxon animal-husbandry practices can be properly considered within a wider northwest European context.

It is noticeable by the mid-Saxon period that, although sheep were predomi-nant on rural sites, cattle were the main meat animal at *wics* such as Ipswich, London, Hamwic, and York (Crabtree 1994, 43; Bourdillon 1994; O'Connor 1994), as they were at the continental *wics* of Ribe, Dorestad, and Hedeby (Hatting 1991; Prummel 1983; Reichstein and Tiessen, 1974). This is particu-larly surprising in the case of Ipswich, which is situated in a region of sandy soils which are better suited for grazing sheep. Indeed, the heavy reliance on cattle as the main meat source, the fact that many of these were well beyond prime market age, and the limited range of other food species (domestic or wild) present in the *wics*, suggest that these settlements were, at least partly, provisioned by a system of food renders which were redistributed in such a way that meat producers and meat consumers were not in direct contact (Crabtree 1996, 64; O'Connor 1994).[35] Furthermore, Anglo-Saxon law-codes suggest that, as on the continent, cattle were the most valuable farm animal, even though they may not have been the most important animal in economic terms.[36]

The emergence of this system of food renders had an observeable impact on animal-husbandry practices in the mid-Saxon period, in that some farmers moved away from a diverse regime geared essentially towards self-sufficiency, to

[35] Lundenwic may have been an exception, however; the evidence from a number of sites in London that most cattle were slaughtered as sub-adults has led Rackham to argue for 'a market economy rather than a controlled supply through food rents', in contrast to O'Connor's interpretation of the animal bones from York (Rackham 1994*b*, 131; O'Connor 1994).

[36] A clause in the late seventh-century laws of King Ine of Wessex may indicate that two fully grown cows were equivalent in value to ten wethers (LXX, 1; Whitelock 1955, 371).

a more specialized strategy which was oriented towards emerging markets for meat and wool, not only in order to provision trading towns, but also monasteries and royal and aristocratic centres. A number of settlements have produced evidence for specialized livestock rearing, including several fen-edge settlements in Norfolk which have produced faunal evidence suggesting that these communities specialized in cattle-rearing and salt production (Andrew 1992). They lie, furthermore, only a few kilometres from high-status sites, probably monasteries or estate centres, identified at Bawsey and Wormegay. Surplus production of beef and hides may also be indicated at the primarily mid-Saxon settlement at Pennyland (Bucks.). The age profile of the cattle bones suggests that these were primarily raised for meat; unlike the cattle bones from most of the *wics*, some 70 per cent were killed by the age of 3, that is, on reaching their full weight (Williams 1993).

Excavation of a high-status mid- to late Saxon settlement at Flixborough (Lincs.), which was probably originally monastic, later perhaps becoming a secular estate centre, has yielded an exceptionally large and well-preserved assemblage of animal bones, suggesting an abundant meat supply (Loveluck 1998). During the late seventh and eighth centuries, when the site was clearly of high status and probably monastic, the animal bones are suggestive of a 'consumer community'. Cattle were the main meat animal and were exceptionally large,[37] matched in size only by cattle from London and the Low Countries. A peak in the percentage of cattle was reached in the late eighth and early ninth centuries, and as it appears that nearly all were mature animals, these must have been reared elsewhere. During the same period there was a decline in the consumption of pig and sheep and a rise in the consumption of wildfowl and fish. During the mid- to late ninth century the percentage of cattle dropped dramatically, and sheep became the predominant species. A large quantity of textile-production equipment also dates to this period, when the character of the settlement changed markedly, perhaps to that of a secular 'producer' community (C. Loveluck 2001 and pers. comm.).

Brandon in northwest Suffolk was, like Flixborough, a high-status settlement of the seventh to ninth centuries, likely to have been monastic, and it too has yielded a large assemblage of over 150,000 animal bones (Crabtree 1996). Here the species ratios and age profiles are suggestive of specialized wool production, and evidence for intensive craft activity, including cloth production and dyeing, lends further support to this theory. Interim reports also state that the plant remains reflect a community which was not primarily engaged in food production, although the detailed evidence for this must await full publication (Carr *et al.* 1988, 375).

At Wicken Bonhunt in Essex, on the other hand, analysis of over 100,000 animal bones dating to the mid-Saxon period revealed an exceptionally high

---

[37] Crabtree (1990, 107) notes a general increase in the size of cattle during the mid-Saxon period.

proportion of pig: around 70 per cent of the identifiable large domestic animals (Crabtree 1996, 63).[38] The evidence is difficult to interpret, but appears to indicate pork/bacon production and export on a considerable scale (ibid. 70; 1994, 50; Wade 1980). Generally, pig makes up a relatively small percentage of the animal bones recovered from Anglo-Saxon settlements, as in many parts of northwest Europe. However, as Clutton-Brock (1976) has noted, the written sources suggest much larger numbers of pigs than are indicated by the archaeological evidence[39] and, as has already been observed, pigs are probably under-represented in assemblages of animal bones.

The only royal settlement from this period to be excavated, the Northumbrian vill at Yeavering, regrettably produced a rather limited animal-bone assemblage, although it does point to an overwhelming preponderance of cattle among the domestic species. Very few juvenile animals were present, the great majority having been slaughtered between 18–35 months (Higgs and Jarman 1977, 331).

The appearance of specialized animal-husbandry practices during the mid-Saxon period has often been attributed to the need to provision the *wics*, although in fact their populations were probably too small to have had a significant impact on farming strategies which extended beyond their immediate hinterlands. Yet the evidence from Yeavering, Flixborough, and Wicken Bonhunt suggests that religious and high-status secular communities would also have drawn upon a system of tribute which involved the movement of livestock around the countryside. Unlike the *wics*, however, these communities would have been in direct contact with meat producers and have had access to a greater variety of foods and more palatable meat.[40] As yet, the archaeological evidence remains inconclusive on this point.

The impact of such communities on the organization of animal husbandry must have been considerable. The creation of hay-meadows, for example, and the increasing importance of oats in the mid- to late Saxon period are suggestive of more intensive animal-rearing (Hooke 1998, 133).[41] The cattle herds associated with monastic estates must, furthermore, have been larger than anything seen previously. The Lindisfarne Gospels, produced in seventh-century Northumbria, famously required 127 calf-skins, while the Codex Amiatinus, one of three complete Bibles produced around the same time at the twinned

---

[38] Wicken Bonhunt is generally considered to have been a settlement of relatively high status, based on its layout and the large quantity of imported pottery found there (Wade 1980). Very little metalwork was recovered, however, although this may merely reflect the fact that, unlike many sites of this period excavated more recently, no metal-detector was used.

[39] She cites the example of the ninth-century ealdorman Alfred of Surrey, who bequeathed 2,000 pigs to his wife (Clutton-Brock 1976, 378).

[40] A large deposit of animal bones from an eighth-century pit on the site of the late Saxon abbey at Eynsham, Oxon., indicates wasteful butchery practices in which large chunks of bone were thrown away without any attempt to extract the marrow. This is suggestive of an abundant meat supply, although whether the community at Eynsham was already monastic at this date is uncertain (Keevil, forthcoming).

[41] For evidence of Anglo-Saxon hay-meadows from Yarnton, Oxon., see Hey, forthcoming.

monasteries of Monkwearmouth/Jarrow, required 515 (Brown 1991, 47; Bruce-Mitford 1969).[42] On one recent estimate, some 1,500 acres of pasture would have been necessary to sustain a herd large enough to produce one gospel book of the size of the Lindisfarne Gospels per year (Härke 1999).

Crop Husbandry and Field Systems

Pollen studies have demonstrated that in many, perhaps most, regions of England Roman fields were maintained as open, cleared land through the early and mid-Anglo-Saxon periods, although there is evidence from East Anglia to suggest an increase in pastoral over arable farming during the fifth and sixth centuries (Murphy 1994). Farming systems, however, were clearly less intensive during this period than they had been previously: with no urban populations or armies to provision, there was neither the need for intensive production of cereals, nor the labour forces previously associated with villas to sustain it. Roman drainage systems fell into disuse, and light soils which were easy to cultivate, such as river gravels, were generally favoured over heavier soils (Hamerow 1992). This indicates not a major discontinuity as such, but essentially a partial reversion or retreat to a pre-Roman pattern of land use which was to continue until the eighth century, when the heavier soils of the claylands began again to be widely exploited. This change in settlement patterns at the end of the Roman period can be seen in regions as diverse as the Upper Thames Valley, North Yorkshire, northwest Essex, and southeast Suffolk (ibid.).

The maintenance of old field systems is unsurprising. The inhabitants of post-Roman Britain are unlikely to have been 'pioneers' where farming was concerned and the evidence suggests that for the most part they took over farmland which was still in reasonable working order. The legal basis of landholding and the payment of food rents had, by the time of the earliest written sources in the seventh century, become reorganized along 'Germanic' lines, as evidenced, for example, in the law-codes of King Ine of Wessex (Fowler 1997, 248); until the eighth or ninth century, however, the range of crops grown (apart from spelt and emmer—see below—and 'cash crops' such as dill, lentils, grapes, etc.) and even farming practices probably differed little from those of the small farms of Roman Britain or even the late Pre-Roman Iron Age (Millett 1990, 97 ff.; Jones 1982, 103).

Such underlying continuities notwithstanding, by the mid-Saxon period crop-husbandry regimes differed from those of the late Roman period in some important respects. One of the most notable differences is the decline of spelt, which had been the chief crop of Roman Britain, yet is found in only small quantities in Anglo-Saxon settlements (Murphy 1994).[43] In eastern England spelt was rapidly

---

[42] Although Gameson (1992) warns us against overestimating the cost of producing such books.

[43] At West Stow, spelt occurred in contexts dating up to the mid-fifth century, but not later. Where spelt does appear in early Anglo-Saxon settlements, it provides strong evidence of the continuous cultivation of the same fields since the Roman period (Murphy 1994, 37).

replaced by bread wheat, which had been comparatively rare in Roman Britain. This is in contrast to northern Germany and the Netherlands, where emmer wheat, which was of great importance in prehistory, continued to be grown in the early Middle Ages, only gradually being replaced by bread wheat. Emmer declined in importance, however, in post-Roman lowland Britain and is scarce in Anglo-Saxon settlements.[44]

In England, as on the continent, bread cereals had replaced barley as the dominant cereal by the ninth century, although the emphasis in England was on bread wheat rather than rye (Hagen 1995, 21). Bread wheat required, in comparison to barley, a greater investment of labour in terms of cultivation and manuring in order to obtain the potentially high yields; the increase in its cultivation thus implies higher levels of agrarian organization. Late Saxon written sources also indicate that wheat was considered preferable to barley: barley bread, for example, was the preferred food of saints as a mark of their self-denial and asceticisim (Hagan 1995, 19). It is, in any case, likely that by the mid-Saxon period barley was primarily used for brewing, or as fodder, rather than baking.[45] This can be inferred from the fact that 'naked' varieties of wheat, which were clean-threshing and so did not need to be parched, became more popular, while naked varieties of barley did not, with hulled barley remaining prevalent. This suggests that the latter was used for malting and therefore did not need to be threshed (Hagen 1995, 28).

Rye appears to have been grown as a separate crop in England from the seventh century onwards. There seem to have been regional differences in its popularity: rye occurs only rarely in late Saxon towns in Wessex, but may have been more common in the Danelaw, to judge from the situation in ninth-century Stafford (Fowler 1997, 255). The fact that rye was generally much less prevalent in most parts of England compared to northwest Europe must be due primarily to the richer soils and damper conditions here, the latter making the fungal disease ergot a greater problem. The possibility that cultural choice also played a role, however, should not be entirely discounted (see above, p. 135).

At Yarnton in Oxfordshire, where large-scale excavation of an Anglo-Saxon settlement in the 1990s produced an exceptional range of environmental data, this evidence points to an intensification of farming in the later eighth and ninth centuries. A somewhat wider range of crops was grown, including rye and legumes, compared to the early Saxon period, and there is indirect evidence of improved soil fertility and weeding techniques (Hey, forthcoming). At Pennyland too the excavator has seen the predominance of bread wheat and the weed types present as demonstrating 'that deep cultivation was practised' (Williams 1993, 96). The evidence, furthermore, for flax processing and brewing on a large scale

---

[44] Some significant quantities of emmer have, however, recently been identified along the Thames valley (R. Pelling, pers. comm. 1999).

[45] Work in Hampshire suggests, however, that barley may have been more prevalent on later Saxon rural settlements than was once thought, while bread wheat may have been consumed largely in urban centres (Green 1991, 375).

by the late Saxon period, as well as for two- or three-field rotation (Campbell 1994, 81; Hey, forthcoming), also point to an intensification of production.[46] Where surplus was stored, however, is unclear. Unlike their continental counterparts, Anglo-Saxon settlements for the most part lack structures which are clearly identifiable as barns or granaries (see Chap. 2). There is evidence, as yet unpublished, from West Heslerton that sunken huts were used for grain storage (as, for example, at Kootwijk: see Chap. 2), and possible granaries have been identified at Orton Hall Farm near Peterborough, Catholme, Staffs., Pennyland and Yarnton (at least those at Pennyland and Yarnton probably date to the mid-Saxon period: Powlesland 1997; MacKreth 1996, 89–90; Kinsley, forthcoming; Williams 1993, 82; Hey, forthcoming). There are no discernible architectural changes to buildings, however, which could indicate increased storage capacity, as seen on the continent at around this time.

As for field systems, early attempts to devise general models for the way in which these developed (e.g. Orwin and Orwin 1938) have given way in recent years to a recognition that different types of both 'evolved' and 'created' field systems existed in Anglo-Saxon England, sometimes side by side (Fowler 1997, 252; Dodgshon 1980). It is likely that, as on the continent, infield/outfield systems were common by the mid-Saxon period along with some form of common fields, although these would be very difficult to detect archaeologically. There are indications of a reorganization of fields in the eighth century, presumably to meet the growing demands from elites for surplus to support their estates and projects such as the building of churches, as well as to feed the growing populations in towns (Fowler 1997, 252). The widespread appearance of enclosures associated with individual settlements, not only around groups of buildings but also defining paddocks, kitchen gardens, and perhaps even infields (see e.g. the settlements at Riby Crossroads and Pennyland, Chap. 3) may reflect a more general reorganization of farming practices.[47]

The evidence for Anglo-Saxon crop-husbandry regimes thus remains patchy, and despite the evidence for intensification and the increase in the cultivation of bread wheat, the view that there was little improvement in farming techniques during the Anglo-Saxon period persists (e.g. Fowler 1997, 256). Written sources, above all Domesday Book, should leave us in no doubt, however, that late Saxon farmers were able to produce enough agrarian surplus to supply large cash rents and support a large population, some 10 per cent of which lived in towns. The nature of land use by the later Anglo-Saxon period has been neatly

---

[46] Two large stone and clay ovens dating to the late seventh to eighth centuries found at Gillingham in Dorset may represent a centralized grain-processing facility; they could, however, have been used to roast ore (Heaton 1993, 114, 125).

[47] An extensive literature dealing with the origins of open fields exists (e.g. Dodgshon 1980; Hall 1995; Rowley 1981; Orwin and Orwin 1938). The creation of open fields associated with planned villages appears to have been essentially a late Saxon phenomenon (Hooke 1998, 115; though in some parts of the country, notably Northamptonshire, open field systems may have been introduced as early as the ninth century: Hall, 1995), and their development will not be entered into here.

summarized by Della Hooke: 'The system was efficient enough to remain the basis of development well into late medieval times, adapting, but not necessarily altering, as populations waxed and waned and as economic pressures changed. It was capable of maintaining a network of small towns and markets, rather more successfully, some would argue, than during Roman times' (Hooke 1988, 151).

6

Rural Centres, Trade, and Non-Agrarian Production

INTRODUCTION

In contrast to the relative scarcity of publications dealing with the buildings and layouts of rural settlements, many volumes have been devoted to the development of early medieval trade and craft production (e.g. Jankuhn *et al.* 1981; 1983; K. Düwel *et al.* 1987, vols. 1–4; Hodges and Whitehouse 1983). Archaeological research into these topics has been made more fruitful—as well as more complex—by the contributions of neighbouring disciplines such as history, geography, and numismatics. It has, however, tended to focus almost exclusively on towns, monasteries, and royal centres, yet craft production, trade, and exchange also played a significant role in farming communities before and after the emergence of such specialized centres. Indeed, the rural settlements of northwest Europe were already significantly differentiated in their economies in the Migration period, suggesting a high level of socio-economic complexity several centuries earlier than has generally been supposed. The evidence now available for trade and non-agrarian production, which derives almost wholly from archaeology, calls for a thoroughgoing reassessment of when and how centralized authorities emerged in northern Europe after the collapse of the western Empire. This is particularly true for northern Germany and southern Scandinavia, where early state formation has conventionally been dated to the late Viking period. Research into state formation has in the past focused on the origins of towns and market centres, the latter usually seen as arising from participation in long-distance trade which was controlled by kings or magnates. Yet, several centuries before there were kings or towns in northern Europe, rural settlements emerged which point to a degree of political centralization. This chapter considers the evidence for these rural centres and the role of non-agrarian production and exchange in rural settlements generally: what was the scale and context of the production, distribution, and consumption of non-agrarian goods? Who controlled these activities, and how, if at all, did the long-distance trade networks which fuelled the nascent towns of Merovingian and

Viking Age Europe affect the economies of the communities which lay in their hinterlands?

RURAL CENTRES

The discovery of high-status rural centres in southern Scandinavia has provided some unexpected answers to the first of these questions.[1] An astonishing number of hoards of precious metals dating from the fourth to seventh centuries has come to light with the increasing use of metal-detectors, particularly in Denmark. The spectacular nature of this 'treasure' has spurred archaeological exploration of its wider context. The resulting excavations have uncovered a previously unrecognized type of settlement which emerged during the Migration period, in which trade and manufacture constituted primary economic activities, a scenario previously unimagined. These communities also farmed; they built buildings and laid out their settlements in ways which are largely indistinguishable from those of ordinary villages. We are not, therefore, dealing with so-called 'proto-towns' such as Hedeby (Denmark), Ipswich (Suffolk), or Dorestad (Netherlands), which first emerged in the seventh century and display some distinctively urban characteristics (Jankuhn 1986; Wade 1988; van Es and Verwers 1980). It is also important to note that none of the rural centres discussed below developed into a town. Instead, they seem to represent a distinct type of community which appeared some three centuries before one can speak of 'kingdoms' and 'towns', and followed a distinct economic trajectory. Their appearance raises important questions, above all, to what extent did these settlements function as centres with administrative, market, and religious functions, and what does their appearance signal in terms of changing political and economic organization?

The discovery of such a settlement at Gudme on the Danish island of Funen dazzled the archaeological world, for Gudme has yielded the largest body of 'treasure'—fifteen hoards so far—known from the whole of Migration period Scandinavia (Kromann *et al.* 1991). Excavation has demonstrated that these hoards were buried within one or more settlements and that occupation at Gudme, which was uninterrupted from the third to eleventh centuries AD and spread across at least 500 ha, experienced an economic flowering between *c.*AD 400 and 600. Archaeologists have thus far opened up only relatively small windows onto this very large complex (Fig. 6.1), but the finds demonstrate conclusively that the Gudme community had access to exceptional wealth. A single hoard from Gudme III, for example, contained 285 late fourth-century *siliquae*, all but one of which was struck in the eastern Empire, the first hoard of this type to be found in northern Europe (Fig. 6.2). The other hoards can be divided

---

[1] These settlements are often referred to as 'central places' even though true 'central place theory', devised to explain the location of centres in societies with a competitive market economy, is not strictly appropriate for this period.

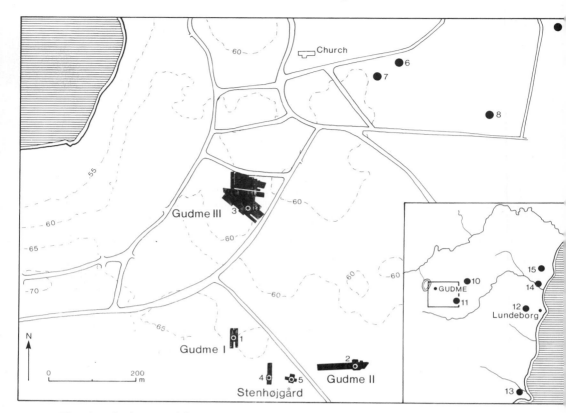

Fig. 6.1. Gudme-Lundeborg: Location map. 1. Gudme I. Solidi; 2. Gudme II. Bracteates, finger ring, gold and garnet jewellery; 3. Gudme III. Siliquae; 4. Stenhøjgård I. Molten silver; 5. Stenhøjgård II. Molten silver and gold; 6. Laurits' Mark I. Gold neck- and finger-rings; 7. Laurits' Mark II. Silver sheet; 8. Jordbaermarken. Gold ingot and sheet metal; 9. Egsmosegård. Gold ring; 10. 'Oure'. Sheet metal; 11. Lillesø. Arm-ring, finger-rings, sheet metal; 12. Broholm hoard. Finger-, arm-, and neck-rings, bracteates, brooches, solidus, gold ingots, etc.; 13. Elsehoved. Solidi, brooch, finger-ring, gold ingot; 14. Hesselager Fredskov I. Neck-ring, gold bracteates; 15. Hesselager Fredskov II. Gold chain with gold and garnet ornaments, silver sheet. After Vang Petersen 1994, fig. 1.

broadly into four types (Vang Peterson 1994, 38): most consisted of scrap metal to be melted down for reuse, and included Roman coins and even massive silver fragments from a Roman monument or building; the second type contained jewellery, for example, a hoard of bracteates (pendants which appeared in southern Scandinavia in the fifth century, originally modelled after Roman coins and medallions, but later depicting mostly supernatural scenes) from Gudme II; the third type of hoard can be described as prestigious objects to be given by magnates to their followers, such as gold scabbard mounts (Fig. 6.3) and a collection of gold rings weighing nearly half a kilo; the fourth type is represented by the Broholm hoard found near Gudme in the nineteenth century, which contained

Fig. 6.2. Siliqua hoard from Gudme III: 285 Roman silver coins from AD 337–78. Photo: Courtesy of the National Museum of Denmark.

Fig. 6.3. Gold scabbard-mount from Gudme. After Thrane 1994, fig. 7.

over 4 kilos of gold and may represent a 'treasure chest' from which such gifts would have been selected (ibid.). In addition to these hoards, the number of Roman imports is such that we can safely assume at least some members of this community dined from Roman dishes and drank from Roman glass beakers (ibid.).

Despite the enormous wealth reflected in these hoards, excavations at Gudme have, with one important exception (see below), so far revealed farmsteads of the type seen at Vorbasse and elsewhere—large, but not extraordinarily so, on average about 3,000–4,000 m², with a main house and adjacent smaller buildings, although the normally ubiquitous sunken huts appear to have been absent (Jørgensen 1993, 60). Even so, Gudme is distinct from contemporary settlements such as Vorbasse, Flögeln, and Wijster, not only in terms of the sheer quantity, variety, and richness of its material culture, but also in its spatial development and size. Rather than the periodic shifting characteristic of this period and seen so clearly at Vorbasse and Nørre Snede (see Chaps. 2 and 4), the buildings at Gudme were rebuilt repeatedly on the same spot up to eight times, and occupation appears to have been dense. Such stability (also seen at Sorte Muld; see below) contrasts with most rural settlements of this period in the region, and 'must represent a different organization from an ordinary agrarian village community' (Jørgensen 1993, 60). If, furthermore, the site contained as many as fifty homesteads each with six to ten occupants, as has been suggested (ibid. 60)— and this is a modest estimate—a community of 300–500 people is represented, a far larger population than the average settlement.

The question of who presided over this remarkable community is an intriguing one. Particularly splendid pieces of ornamental metalwork indicative of very high status, such as gold sword-fittings and neck-rings, have been found to the north and east of the excavations, and it may be that a magnate's residence has yet to be uncovered there. A possible candidate has already been found, however, in excavations at Gudme II. A massive timber building once stood here, nearly 50 m in length and over 9 m wide (Figs. 2.3 and 2.4). Fragments of gold and glass were found in its postholes (probably associated with a foundation ritual), and phosphate analysis indicates that it did not contain a cattle byre. The smaller building adjacent to it was also exceptionally wide, and contained a small gold hoard (P. Ø. Sørensen, pers. comm. and 1993). On the basis of these and other finds, it appears that the craftworkers, traders, and farmers of Gudme were under the protection and control of a leading family (Jørgensen 1993).

Gudme lay only *c.*4 km from the contemporary coastal manufacturing centre and seasonal trading station at Lundeborg, the earliest such site known in southern Scandinavia (Fig. 6.1). Here, craftspeople working in amber, bone, and metal manufactured and marketed their goods in exchange for Roman imports such as glass vessels and beads (Thomsen 1994). Both Gudme and Lundeborg have yielded abundant evidence for the working of precious and other metals in the form of molten bronze, silver, and gold, as well as unfinished objects (Thrane 1987).

Gudme, for all its wealth, is not unique. Indeed, the fourth to seventh centuries saw the emergence of a whole class of rich, sometimes spectacularly rich, rural communities in southern Scandinavia whose wealth appears to have derived primarily from control over trade and craft production. Other Migration period settlements in Denmark which have produced finds of comparable richness include Sorte Muld on the island of Bornholm, as well as Lejre, Neble, and Lake Tissø on Zealand (Axboe 1992; Jørgensen 1998 and 2000). Comparable rural centres have also been identified in southern Sweden, for example, at Gamla Uppsala and Uppåkra (Brink 1996; Hårdh 2000). Although work on these sites is still under way, all have yielded rich, high-status objects—symbols of lordship—as well as abundant evidence of specialized craft production, long-distance contacts, and in at least some cases, a religious function.

At Sorte Muld, just 2 km from the coast in southeast Bornholm, metaldetector finds and limited excavation suggest several foci of occupation dating from the Pre-Roman Iron Age to at least the seventh century (Axboe 1992). The site has yielded over 2,300 *guldgubber*, gold sheet plaques dating to the sixth and seventh centuries, showing male and female figures, often in pairs, which are believed to have served a religious function, perhaps as 'temple money' (Watt 1999; Fig. 6.4); in addition, gold bracteates, weapons, ingots, coins, and metalworking debris were recovered. At Neble, small-scale excavations have yielded casting debris, weights, a matrix for manufacturing *guldgubber*, arabic coins, and jewellery (Axboe 1992).

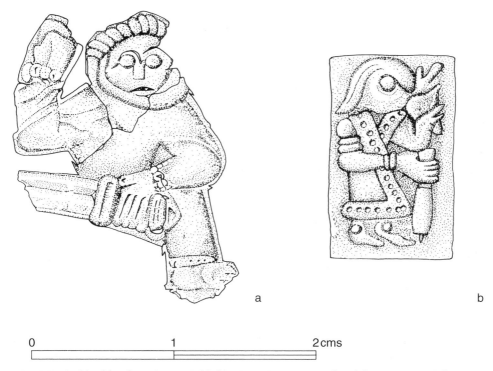

a   b

0   1   2cms

Fig. 6.4. *Guldgubber* from Sorte Muld showing (a) a ring sword and (b) arm-rings. After Watt 1999, figs. 3 and 4.

The settlement complex along the western shore of Lake Tissø in western Zealand spanned the seventh to eleventh centuries and covered some 50 hectares (Jørgensen 2000). Two main zones have been defined, one identified as a 'manor', the other as a market. A sequence of monumental timber halls as well as other buildings was built within the enclosed yard of the manor. This area yielded no evidence of agrarian production but did produce large quantities of jewellery, weaponry, and Frankish imports dating to the late eighth and ninth centuries, as well as the first sceatta (a small, silver coin) to be found on Zealand. By the end of the ninth century the number of buildings within the manor had increased markedly. The market area, which appears to have been in intermittent use, contained primarily or exclusively sunken-featured buildings and produced evidence of ferrous and non-ferrous metalworking (including the manufacture of jewellery), weights, and a ninth-century Byzantine seal.

Gammel Lejre was, according to legend, the capital of the first Danish royal dynasty in the eleventh century. The existence here of Migration period burials, including some exceptionally rich graves and a stone ship-setting, has been known about since the 1940s. Excavations in the late 1980s revealed in addition two zones of settlement covering in total some 200,000 m², less than 5 per cent of which has so far been excavated (Fig. 6.5; Christensen 1991). The vast timber hall

Fig. 6.5. Lejre: plan of settlement. After Christensen 1991, fig. 6.

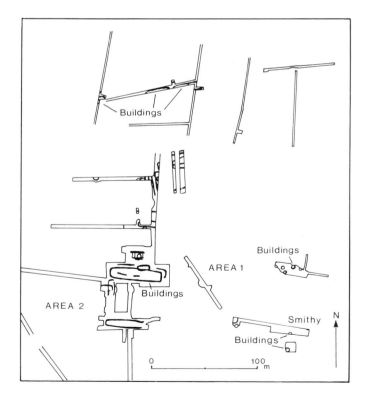

at Lejre has already been described in Chapter 2 (Fig. 2.2). A smaller building, perhaps a kitchen or sleeping quarters, lay immediately to the north of the hall, and around a dozen other buildings lay in its immediate vicinity. A smithy, which yielded a massive layer of iron slag as well as smiths' tools, was excavated some 100 m southeast of the hall complex, in an area which also produced evidence of non-ferrous metalworking. Finds include some fifty copper-alloy ornaments, including high-quality pieces and imports. The settlement at Lejre can thus be divided into two functionally distinct zones: Area 1, the focus of craft activity, and Area 2, the domestic area. The exceptional capacity of the hall, the evidence of specialist craft activities, and the fact that Lejre was later chosen as the burial place of Viking kings leaves little doubt that already in the Migration and early Viking periods Lejre was the central settlement of an aristocratic estate (Christensen 1991: 183).

Unlike the sites just mentioned, occupation at Dankirke in southwest Jutland appears to have been more limited in extent, to judge from metal-detector prospection undertaken in the area of a small-scale excavation carried out in the 1960s (Jarl Hansen 1989*a* and *b*). The excavations did, however, yield a variety of rich finds and imported goods. Associated with one house were gold bullion, numerous sherds of Frankish glass, and lead weights. The latest datable finds from the excavation are thirteen coins—three from Dorestad, two from England, and eight from Frisia—dating to the early eighth century and coinciding roughly with the founding of the trading town of Ribe, just 7 km distant, after which Dankirke declined.

All of these settlements vary in both date and detail, and it would be rash to assume that all represent the same phenomenon, yet they do share certain key characteristics. First and most obviously, they are exceptionally rich in metal finds, particularly gold and silver, in comparison to other rural settlements. To take Vorbasse as an example, occupation from the fifth century to the early Viking period covered an area of $c.60,000\,\text{m}^2$ but yielded only some six bronze objects, in comparison to the thousands of metal finds found at Gudme (Axboe 1992). These metalwork assemblages invariably include precious metals, weapons, and continental imports such as coins and jewellery. Second, all of these settlements were located within 5 km of the sea. Dankirke, near the west coast of Jutland, was ideally sited for trade with both the Frankish and Anglo-Saxon worlds. Neble, on the southwest coast of Zealand, lies just opposite Gudme, and Lejre is sited near the Roskilde fjord. These first two characteristics—rich and exotic finds, and a coastal location—suggest that these were strategic places for exchange, redistribution, and long-distance contacts, and that control over them would have bolstered the power of those who lived in these settlements. The third shared feature is that most of these settlements were large (Fig. 6.6). Gudme, as already observed, may have contained as many as fifty contemporary farms and Sorte Muld must have had at least thirty (ibid.). These sites thus represent exceptionally large population clusters for this period.

Fig. 6.6. Sizes of Danish 'rural centres' compared to the village of Vorbasse. After Hvass and Storgaard 1993, 193.

Yet they were distinct from the *emporia* which emerged in the seventh century, and, as already observed, none of these early centres developed into towns. A possible analogy for the separate but associated clusters of settlement seen at Gudme, and probably at Sorte Muld and Neble, are the *oppida* of Iron Age Britain such as Verulamium and Camulodunum, where groups of buildings were spread across a wide area, within which lay zones with religious, trading, craft, and perhaps military functions (J. Gunby, pers. comm. 1999; Cunliffe 1974, 90–1). While it is possible to stretch the comparison too far, the model of separate clusters of buildings operating as a single unit is a useful one.

A fourth, religious and administrative, character is indicated for some of these settlements by the presence of gold bracteates and the enigmatic *guldgubber*, of which Sorte Muld, as already noted, has produced well over 2,000 and Gudme-Lundeborg ninety-five (Axboe 1992). Some of the most striking images on the bracteates, including some from Gudme, depict a potent mixture of political and religious symbolism, and the production of such bracteates appears to have been closely connected with centres of cult and power (Hauck 1987, 156 ff.; Näsman 1989, 170). The central image on some bracteates appears to be that of a 'god-king' and deploys a synthesis of symbols of Roman imperial authority, such as a head in profile wearing a diadem, with those of Germanic power, such as Woden imagery (Fig. 6.7). A group of bracteates from Funen depicts the head in profile with long braided hair, a symbol of lordship amongst Frankish rulers—the *reges criniti* depicted most famously on the signet ring buried with the Merovingian king Childeric at the end of the fifth century (Hauck 1987). Some versions show the head 'on horseback'. Some *guldgubber* (which appeared in the sixth and seventh centuries, somewhat later than the bracteates) also depict symbols of power such as swords as well as neck-, arm-, and ankle-rings (Fig. 6.4). The figures on these gold plaques are often shown embracing, but are occasionally depicted making gestures similar to those of prayer and blessing seen on contemporary early Christian art (Watt 1999). A religious function for Gudme is also indicated by the place-name: the medieval form, *Gudhem*, means 'home of the gods', and neighbouring place-names refer to 'gods' hill' and 'hill of sacrifices' (cf. Lake Tissø, 'The lake of the god Tiw'; Hauck 1987, 148; Jørgensen 2000). This association of secular and supernatural power must surely represent an attempt at legitimation by rulers who were not merely tribal 'big men', but the heads of leading dynasties; it may not be an exaggeration to suggest that the roots of sacral kingship can be seen in these images.

If some gold bracteates and *guldgubber* do indeed depict 'god-kings', then the settlements where these objects were produced and/or used in significant numbers provide signposts to the geography of power in southern Scandinavia during the Migration period (Fabech 1994). Interestingly, the earliest written sources to mention Danish 'kings' date to the sixth century (Axboe 1995, 217; see below, n. 3). Hauck adduces two further sources of indirect evidence for the existence of such early rulers: the genealogies of early Anglo-Saxon kings who

Fig. 6.7. Gold bracteate depicting long-haired god-king. After Hauck 1994, fig. 8*a*.

traced their ancestry back to still earlier Scandinavian god-kings, and the presence at Gudme of lordly insignia such as gold sword-rings and arm-rings directly comparable to those buried with the Merovingian king Childeric I (Hauck 1987; Werner 1980). The interpretation of these settlements as early magnate centres finds further support in the fact that Gudme, Sorte Muld, and Lejre all held the status of administrative and, in the case of Lejre, royal centres in the later medieval period.

In trying to set these rural centres into a wider socio-political context, there is always the risk of oversimplification. Nevertheless, a plausible model sees a transition in Denmark which began at around the beginning of the third century AD from a society in which wealth and power were relatively widely spread, to one in which they were concentrated in the hands of a small number of magnates and their military retinues and clients. This development was stimulated by increasing economic contact with the Roman Empire, which actively cultivated links with Germanic chieftains, although internal changes in agricultural systems and productive capacity must have provided the underlying foundation (Randsborg 1994, 209; Kromann *et al.* 1991; Hedeager 1992, 285; 1993). The increasing quantities of Roman provincial imports found beyond the frontier reflect these external contacts; thus Lundeborg experienced a boom in imports in the third and fourth centuries at roughly the same time as Gudme acquired the trappings of exceptional wealth and international trade connections. The number of imports began to decline after AD 400, and by the sixth century Lundeborg had largely lost its role as a trading centre although, interestingly, craft production appears to have been unaffected by this decline (Thomsen 1994, 28).

When the 'prestige goods economy' of *Germania libera*, fed by Roman luxury imports (and reflected in the potlatch-style votive offerings of the late Roman Iron Age), collapsed, it left an opening for new forms of authority. The development of a heritable system of power would have enabled leading families to accumulate wealth and ever larger numbers of followers by maintaining long-term control over trade and over access to precious metals and cult centres. They could thereby establish control over ever wider territories, with land, rather than mobile wealth, becoming increasingly important as a source of power. The appearance of rural centres is thus best explained as the result of a growth in the size of territories under the control of a single magnate. In Näsman's words, 'they were places where agrarian surplus was mobilised for use in the construction of a more complex social system' (2000, 53). By centralizing such resources, and by forging strong links with Frankish elites, these centres set the scene for early state formation.

Agrarian production must have played an important role in the emergence of central places in southern Scandinavia, as suggested by a study of the island of Bornholm in the western Baltic (Jørgensen 1991). At the end of the Roman Iron Age the settlement structure of Bornholm underwent major changes: large villages were replaced by small, scattered hamlets, while the number of burials decreased and some cemeteries were abandoned altogether. Exceptions to this pattern, however, are found on the fertile soils of northeast Bornholm, particularly in the parishes of Ibsker and Østerlars, where exceptionally large settlements were formed at this time. Ibsker, furthermore, contains a remarkable concentration of settlements with precious-metal finds dating from c.175–950 AD, including Sorte Muld (ibid. 167). The settlement pattern on Bornholm thus appears to have consisted of a few large, rich settlements, and a much larger number of small settlements consisting of perhaps one to three farms (ibid. 171).

The number of gold finds on Bornholm peaked between c. AD 480 and 600. This can be broken down into a brief phase of hoarding (c.480–520/30), followed by a period (c.550–600) of richly furnished weapon graves which emulated the Merovingian burial rite. Jørgensen (ibid.) has suggested that this later phase reflects a period of rivalry between several leading families on the island who had connections with Merovingian elites. In the course of the seventh century the richly furnished burials came to an end and were replaced by a more standardized burial rite. Jørgensen sees this as an indication of a more stable social structure with clearly defined positions, where status no longer needed to be expressed through burial rite (ibid. 178–9).

For only one of the high-status settlements on Bornholm, Rytterbakken, have associated burials been found, at the cemeteries of Baekkegård and Glasergård. Although Baekkegård yielded no burials of exceptionally high status, Glasergård contained two of the richest graves found to date on Bornholm, both dating to the second half of the sixth century and containing rich weaponry and horse gear similar to that found in Merovingian burials. Indeed, the close similarities between the weapon graves of Bornholm and Francia, as well as the large number of Frankish imports in Bornholm dating to *c*.550–650, indicate close links between the leading families of the two regions (ibid. 179–80). In the seventh century the central places of Bornholm lost many of their special functions. Only Sorte Muld maintained its status into the eighth century, suggesting that authority was becoming increasingly centralized, a hypothesis which appears to be supported by ninth-century sources referring to a 'king' of Bornholm (ibid. 180).

On Bornholm agricultural productivity seems to lie behind the establishment of these centres, enabling them to gain a virtual monopoly on precious metals and imports.[2] The parish of Ibsker is situated on fertile loam soils in an area of rich pasture, which in the early part of the twentieth century had a crop yield which was 30 per cent higher per hectare than comparable parishes. Even in the early Middle Ages Ibsker must have possessed the resources to feed a larger population than other parts of the island. It was not only densely populated but also rich: Ibsker has produced 30 to 80 per cent more gold finds than any other parish on Bornholm (ibid. 176). The theory that communities in this region were able to maintain exceptionally large cattle herds is supported by archaeological excavation as well as by medieval and later sources. At Sorte Muld, for example, the ratio of cattle : sheep : pig bones is 6 : 3 : 1; at Lundeborg the faunal remains consist primarily of cattle bones (ibid. 181; see Chap. 5) and in southeast Funen as a whole, in the Middle Ages, taxes were paid in cattle.

The appearance in the Migration period of objects such as gold bracteates and *guldgubber* corresponds with wider changes in the structure of power and ritual in southern Scandinavia. The transferral of sacral rites from traditional 'communal' places such as lakes, where votive offerings had been made for centuries, to the settlements and homesteads of elite families, suggests a profound transformation (Fabech 1994). Fabech has argued that this mirrors the actions

---

[2] A comparable situation may be seen in the district of Jaeren, a strip of fertile lowland in southwestern Norway for which detailed demographic and archaeological surveys have been carried out (Myhre 1982). Of the 260 farms present today, most show evidence of Iron Age/Migration period occupation. A further 200 farms have been identified which are now deserted but most of which were occupied during the Iron Age/Migration period. While not all of these farms were necessarily contemporary, they do indicate a substantial population during the Migration period. This becomes more striking if one considers the population of one parish which in the seventeenth and eighteenth centuries contained 38 farms, each housing 17–23 people. During the Migration period the same area contained approximately 60 farms; even allowing for a modest average of around 10 people per farm, the population would have been comparable to that of the seventeenth century, and each farm may have housed considerably more than 10. Certainly the largest farms at Ullandhaug (see Chap. 2) could have accommodated households of more than 25. Jaeren seems to have been home to a number of chiefly centres, and this may have resulted in an exceptional concentration of surplus and consequently of population during the Migration period (ibid. 213 ff.).

of the Frankish aristocracy who, beginning in the sixth century, ceased to bury their dead in community cemeteries, establishing instead separate burial grounds and ultimately churches for this purpose. She suggests that the adoption of new sacral sites in southern Scandinavia could reflect a similar process, whereby authority was no longer based on a prestige-goods economy fuelled by luxury imports, external raids, and tribute, as the votive offerings of the late Roman Iron Age suggest, but increasingly on exploitation of the land, as the supply of imports dwindled (ibid. 175–6). Long-distance contacts did not, however, cease. Indeed, links between southern Scandinavian and Frankish elites in this period are clearly demonstrated by their shared use of symbols of authority such as ring-swords and helmets.[3] Fabech argues that by the end of the sixth century, 'petty kings and lords with royal estates and manorial dwellings' had emerged in southern Scandinavia, who sought to emulate Frankish elites (ibid. 176).

These links with the Merovingian world raise the issue of economic relations between southern Scandinavia, Francia, and the Anglo-Saxon kingdoms in the pre- and early Viking period. The emergence in the late seventh and early eighth centuries of nascent market centres such as Ribe, Hedeby, and Åhus demonstrates the existence of long-distance trade on a substantial scale. The origins of the goods traded through these centres and how that trade was controlled are issues around which debate has revolved for decades (cf. Hodges and Whitehouse 1983), yet the impact of these trade networks on rural communities has only recently begun to be considered.

NETWORKS OF TRADE AND EXCHANGE

Southern Scandinavia

The long-distance exchange networks which reached northern Europe during the late Roman Iron Age and Migration period served the purpose of transporting relatively small quantities of luxury goods such as jewellery, glass vessels, and other costly items from the Empire to high-ranking individuals beyond the *limes*, as diplomatic gifts to cultivate allegiances, or in exchange for commodities such as corn and slaves or even as dowries. A marked change in this pattern occurred in the eighth century when, in addition to objects whose value lay in their rarity, more mundane goods such as whetstones, querns, and pottery began to be imported from distant places via trading centres and put to everyday use in ordinary farming settlements.[4] These imports came from both within Scandinavia—

---

[3] Such links are also documented in Gregory of Tours's account of the ill-fated seaborne invasion of Gaul led by a sixth-century Danish 'king', Chlochilaich (possibly the Hygelac referred to in *Beowulf*) in the *History of the Franks*, III, 3.

[4] The survival in large quantities of such durable goods suggests a parallel, but archaeologically invisible, large-scale trade in more perishable commodities.

for example, whetstones and soapstone vessels from Norway—and from further afield—for example, quernstones and pottery from the Rhineland and pottery from the Slavonic-Baltic region. Such goods had a relatively low intrinsic value and must, therefore, have been produced and exported in bulk for economies of scale to apply (Näsman 1987, 465; Näsman and Roesdahl 1993, 184). The flourishing in the late seventh and eighth centuries of emporia in southern Scandinavia (but also outside Scandinavia: for example, at London and Dorestad), as well as improvements in shipping technology and the construction of canals and harbours, suggest that these 'trading towns' served as redistribution centres or entrepôts for precisely such goods. The burgeoning agricultural production which fed this 'boom' in long-distance trade, manifest, for example, in the increased size of individual farmsteads at Vorbasse, has already been examined (see Chap. 5).

Schleswig-Holstein: Hedeby and its Hinterland

One of the most thoroughly studied of the trading towns of southern Scandinavia is Hedeby, established in the eighth century in eastern Schleswig-Holstein, at the politically volatile interface between the Danes, Frisians, Saxons, and Obodrites (Jankuhn 1986). Research into this remarkable settlement, with its harbour, street plan, and rich material culture, spanned much of the twentieth century, yet systematic investigation of contemporary rural settlements in the surrounding region has only begun relatively recently. Indeed, the economic dynamic between the earliest north European trading centres and their hinterlands has yet to be characterized. Did farms and villages export agricultural surplus to Hedeby to support its craftspeople and traders? Did, in turn, imported goods and manufactured items from Hedeby 'trickle down' to its hinterland? The excavations of two settlements, Schuby and Kosel, suggest some unexpected answers.

The Viking period settlement of Schuby lay a mere 6 km from Hedeby, and its successor, Schleswig, 3 km from the Danevirke, and only a few hundred metres from a major north–south road known as the *Heerweg* (Kühn 1993, Abb. 4). Excavation of part of the settlement revealed thirty-three houses as well as hearths, ovens, and, to the north of the settlement, numerous iron-smelting pits and smithies dating from the the early ninth to fourteenth centuries. The settlement yielded large quantities of grain as well as evidence for textile production, amber-, and metalworking. It is, however, not possible to ascertain from this evidence how much, if any, agricultural surplus (and perhaps iron) from Schuby found its way to Hedeby. The high percentage of meat animals, namely, cattle and pig, from southern Scandinavian towns in general (including Hedeby) in comparison to rural settlements does suggest that they were provisioned by surrounding villages (Randsborg 1980, 57 and fig. 13). It is easier to recognize goods travelling in the other direction. Indeed, virtually all categories of long-distance trade goods found at Hedeby are also represented at Schuby, apart from some made of organic materials which were not preserved at the latter. Indeed, whetstones and soapstone vessels from Norway and lava querns from the Rhineland were so common at Schuby that they must have been used by virtually every household (Kühn 1993, 47). The presence of more exclusive imports, such as jewellery, glass, and carnelian beads, provides further evidence that this village in the hinterland of Hedeby had access to the same range of long-distance trade goods as the emporium itself.

A similar picture emerges from the excavations at Kosel, 3 km north of the Danevirke on a river leading into the Schlei, the main waterway of the region (Meier 1990b). Occupation at Kosel commenced in the Migration period, when it consisted of a small, rather dispersed settlement. Both archaeological and pollen evidence indicate that the site was unoccupied from the sixth to eighth centuries, and re-established in the ninth. The later Viking-period phase consisted of ground-level houses as well as numerous sunken-featured buildings, with abundant evidence of textile manufacture and iron-smithing. Imports from northern and western Europe were found in impressive quantities. These included a bronze comb of a type manufactured at Hedeby and exported as far afield as the Netherlands, as well as whetstones and soapstone vessels from Norway and numerous fragments of Rhenish lava querns. In addition to these relatively cheap trade goods there were pieces of high-quality metalwork, including Frankish jewellery and an Irish or Scottish ring-headed pin (which may, of course, have been looted rather than traded), as well as fragments of costly pottery containers from the Rhineland, such as Tating and Badorf wares (ibid. 23; 1994; Dörfler *et al.* 1992, 126 ff.). Although most of the metalwork found at Kosel was imported, the vast majority of the pottery was of local manufacture, suggesting that the community was indigenous and not an international population of traders, as has been suggested for Hedeby.

For neither Kosel nor Schuby can it be proven that a significant agricultural surplus was produced, although such evidence would inevitably be elusive. The excavator of Kosel has argued that trade drove the village's economy and that agriculture was a secondary activity (Meier 1990b, 26). Indeed, Kosel's position along the most important trade route of the region is unlikely to have been fortuitous, and the discovery of a scale pan from a pair of folding scales of the type widely used by traders in this period, as well as a weight and an Arabic silver coin cut in half, underscore this point. It seems that inhabitants of Kosel and other communities in this region actively participated in and benefited from the same exchange networks as Hedeby itself. In fact, as yet not a single primarily agrarian settlement has been identified in the immediate hinterland of Hedeby. The exact relationship between settlements such as Kosel and Schuby and the trading town remains unclear, however. What is certain is that trade goods from regions to the north, south, east, and west of Schleswig-Holstein found their way not only to Hedeby and other emporia, but also to rural settlements all around the North Sea zone. Clearly, these settlements, even those in the immediate hinterland of Hedeby, did not act merely as victuallers of their 'proto-urban' neighbour, nor should we assume that all long-distance trade was necessarily channelled through Hedeby.

Not all villages, however, had ready access to the *Importstrom* which flowed across northern Europe in the Carolingian/Viking period. The eighth- to tenth-century settlement of Elisenhof lay at the mouth of the Eider, yet excavation here revealed a community which was economically rather isolated and possessed few luxury goods or imports, despite its advantageous topographic position (Steuer 1979).[5] Plough-marks and seed remains demonstrate that some cereals were cultivated, although the emphasis was probably on cattle-rearing and wool production. A coarse shelly ware, so-called *Muschelgrus* pottery, which was widely traded along the North Sea coast in the ninth century makes up some 25 per cent of the assemblage. The finer, more costly Rhenish pottery which was traded along these same routes is, however, scarcely represented (ibid.).

NON-AGRARIAN PRODUCTION

The preserved textiles and leather and wooden objects which come from water-logged settlements such as Feddersen Wierde serve as a reminder of the wide range and sophistication of even the more mundane crafts of this period, only a hint of which survives on most sites where organic preservation is poor or non-existent (Hayen *et al.* 1981). Several major studies are devoted to the technology of early medieval crafts such as iron-, wood-, and leatherworking as well as cloth production (e.g. Jankuhn *et al.* 1983; Haarnagel *et al.* 1984; Bender-Jørgensen 1992). Craft technology as such is not, therefore, considered here. Instead, the focus is on the economic role that these activities played in rural settlements, especially those crafts for which we have reasonably abundant archaeological evidence, namely, metalworking, pottery production, stone-working, and cloth production. Throughout the fifth to ninth centuries rural communities existed which appear to have been engaged in craft production beyond the needs of the local community. How was this surplus distributed? To what degree was it detached from agrarian production and controlled from above? How did the mechanisms of distribution differ from those of later market centres, or was there in fact little significant difference between Migration period ports such as Lundeborg in Denmark (see above) and emporia such as Ribe which emerged some three centuries later? (Näsman 1989, 170).

---

[5] Part of a folding scale and a few Carolingian imports were, however, found at Elisenhof (Müller-Wille 1994/5, 51; 1989).

Ironworking

Tracing the development of ironworking is particularly important, as control over its production would have conferred considerable political power. The landscapes of Schleswig-Holstein and Jutland are rich in bog iron, and there is scarcely a late Iron Age or Migration period settlement in the region that has not yielded evidence of ironworking (Müller-Wille 1983, Abb. 1 and 2). The great increase in iron-smelting sites, the greater frequency and size of iron tools, and the hundreds of hoards of iron ingots deposited in southern Scandinavia and Schleswig-Holstein during the Migration period all suggest that intensification of ironworking helped to fuel the economy of this period (C. Zimmermann 1998). A period of intensified iron production in the fifth century has been associated with the penetration of the Danes into Jutland, the ensuing conflict, and a resulting increase in the demand for weapons.[6] In support of this thesis is the complementary distribution of bog iron and evidence for ironworking in western Jutland, and the great votive deposits of war booty to the east, for example, at Illerup and Nydam. The marked decrease in evidence for iron production from the sixth century onwards furthermore corresponds to the period when, according to the Byzantine historian Procopius, the Danes had become established in Jutland (ibid. 88).

A number of Migration period communities in Schleswig-Holstein and Jutland practised iron-smelting on a scale which suggests surplus production. An archaeological survey at Joldelund (Nord Friesland) has identified several concentrations of ironworking debris, the largest of which covers an area of *c.*8 ha (Backer *et al.* 1992; Jöns 1993; 1999). Excavations here have revealed part of a village, occupied between *c.*350 and 450, which was engaged in both farming and iron production. Some 500 slag-pit furnaces (the chief type of iron-smelting furnace in use up to the seventh century) have been identified, as well as substantial dumps of ironworking debris. Joldelund is providing archaeologists with unparalleled insights into iron production during the Migration period, for all stages of iron-smelting and smithing are represented, including evidence for charcoal production, several large slag-heaps covering up to 100 m², hammer scale, and four or five buildings used as smithies. It is notable, however, that the buildings and layout of the settlement are not obviously different from those of ordinary farming settlements (Fig. 6.8).

While all of this suggests some iron production beyond the needs of the local community, it is unlikely that the settlement was economically dependent on iron production, for the furnaces represent ironworking over a period of 100–150 years and each furnace represents only one smelting. The excavator estimates a yield of around 50–70 kg of iron per year, sufficient to supply Joldelund and some neighbouring settlements, but not enough to suggest an

---

[6] Although it could be argued that this increase in production was merely to compensate for the loss of iron imported from the Empire (Jöns 1993, 50).

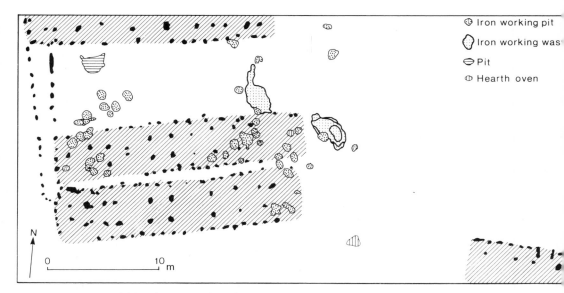

Fig. 6.8. Joldelund: partial plan of settlement. After Backer *et al.* 1992, Abb. 20.

entire community specializing in iron production. Plough-marks, botanical evidence, and the presence of enclosed farmsteads with longhouses all indicate, furthermore, permanent, year-round occupation at Joldelund and an unexceptional agricultural regime (Backer *et al.* 1992; Jöns 1999, 258; C. Zimmermann 1998, 88).

The ability of a community of farmers to produce iron, particularly a surplus of iron, was of course dependent on ready access to the essential raw materials: bog iron, timber, and clay. Charcoal samples from Joldelund, and a comparable fourth- to sixth-century iron-producing site at Snorup in western Jutland, suggest that coppiced oak was the favoured timber for charcoal production, although alder was also used. Voss has estimated that one cluster of 170 furnaces at Snorup would have consumed 43 tonnes of charcoal, which in turn would have required a coppice of some 20 ha (Voss 1993, 208). As many as 5,000 furnaces have been identified at Snorup, some of which were aligned in 'strings' associated with individual farmsteads (Nørbach 1999). It is estimated that the village would, nevertheless, have had fewer than twenty furnaces in use per season, although here too some surplus iron was presumably traded to settlements such as Nørre Snede, which produced little evidence of iron production, or to centres such as Dankirke and Lundeborg, where iron ingots of a type similar to those produced at Snorup were found (Müller-Wille 1999, 208–9).

Joldelund, Snorup, and other iron-producing settlements in the region provide an important corrective to the notion that centres such as Gudme and Sorte Muld had a monopoly on concentrated industrial activity in the Migration period. Indeed, it seems likely that throughout the early Middle Ages surplus production and exchange of basic commodities such as iron were undertaken by individuals or communities where the essential raw materials were readily to hand, while daily life remained dominated by the rhythms of the agricultural cycle. The social mechanisms which governed the extraction, exchange, redistribution, or external trade of iron in southern Scandinavia and northern Germany during the Migration period remain ill-defined, although there is nothing to indicate that the surplus production of iron was under the direct control of a centralized authority,[7] as the evidence from Gudme and other centres suggests was the case for non-ferrous metalworking (see below).

The south Scandinavian 'boom' in iron production during the Migration period thus appears to have taken place within the context of numerous, primarily agrarian, settlements. By the Viking Age, however, iron-smelting seems to have been restricted to relatively few communities, such as Schuby (see below), where a separate craftworking quarter lay at the northern edge of the settlement, a further sign, perhaps, of increasing specialization.[8] Certainly, the 3.4 tonnes of smithing slag recovered from Hedeby point to the importation of substantial quantities of iron, probably from smelting centres in southern Norway and, especially, southern Sweden (Jöns 1993; Voss 1993, 206).

In the northern Netherlands evidence has also come to light which suggests an intensification and reorganization of iron production in the fourth century (Groenewoudt and van Nie 1995). At Heeten, a small-scale excavation in 1991 uncovered part of a settlement dating from the late second to fifth centuries. In the fourth century a large fenced farmyard containing timber buildings, sunken-featured buildings, and wells was constructed. The large amount of smelting-slag present in some of the features (bog iron from nearby marshes was in plentiful supply) led to further prospection outside of the excavated area, revealing at least seventeen slag-pit furnaces and massive quantities of slag, indicating that this was no ordinary farm. Dendrochronological dating indicates a limited period of iron production lasting only around thirty to thirty-five years, and ending by *c*.345. It is estimated that around half a ton of iron could have

---

[7] Ironworking at Feddersen Wierde, which had to import iron from the *Geest* regions, was originally thought to be largely confined to the area around the *Herrenhof*, the occupants of which were assumed to have overseen the importation of the iron as well as the production of agricultural and other iron implements (Haarnagel *et al.* 1984, 300–1). A recent re-evaluation of the metalworking evidence from Feddersen Wierde, however, has noted two further concentrations of ironworking debris which lay well to the north and west of the *Herrenhof*, casting doubt on the original interpretation. Even the main concentration of ironworking debris just to the east of the *Herrenhof* could have been dumped there as a means of building up the edge of the *Wurt* (Schuster and de Rijk 2001).

[8] Alternatively, the lack of evidence for iron-smelting in this period could be the result of a switch to a less easily identifiable type of furnace (C. Zimmermann 1998, 95).

been produced each year, far beyond the needs of a single settlement. Very little smithing slag was found at Heeten, however, indicating that the bloom was worked into objects elsewhere. This was confirmed by excavations some 4 km to the west, at Wesepe, which produced significant quantities of smithing-slag, and it has been suggested that Heeten and Wesepe were 'elements of one regional or even supra-regional system in which iron production and the working of bloom was [*sic*] spatially separated' (ibid. 208). Whatever gave rise to the increased need for iron (the suggestion that it was the demand for military equipment by the Salian Franks seems insufficient to explain it: ibid.), Heeten was clearly home to specialist iron-smelters, particularly in light of botanical evidence which indicates that no processing of crops took place at the settlement. Heeten could have supplied 'a large population' with iron, although whether its distribution was overseen directly by a local elite, as the separation of smelting and smithing activities suggests, or was 'run by some kind of entrepreneur' (ibid. 209), is a matter for speculation. The lack of Roman imports at least suggests that this production was not driven by trade with the Empire.

The Veluwe district in the central Netherlands has also produced evidence for intensive iron production, though at a somewhat later date (Heidinga 1987, 194–6). Despite the fact that this was an agriculturally marginal area, settlements such as Kootwijk were able to obtain strikingly high proportions (80–90 per cent) of imported pottery, largely from the Rhineland. This is most plausibly explained by the fact that the Veluwe is rich in limonite, a type of iron ore, and appears to have been the main iron-producing region in the Netherlands in the early Middle Ages. One surviving slag-heap, for example, broadly dated to the Carolingian period, represents the production of 165 metric tons of iron. Small-scale excavation of a Merovingian settlement south of Hoog Buurlo revealed evidence for specialist iron production as early as the seventh century in the form of some 30 kg of iron bloom. The metalworking debris found suggests that smelting took place elsewhere, while the bloom was brought to the settlement, either to be worked into iron or simply sorted and traded. Heidinga interprets Hoog Buurlo as a settlement of professional iron-smelters, and suggests that the iron industry of the area met the needs of an extensive region (ibid.). He argues that, even though a proportion of the iron flowed ultimately to the king, monasteries, and great landowners, it is unlikely that its production and distribution were essentially controlled from above, and argues instead that this lay largely 'in the hands of the communities of iron smelters themselves' (ibid. 198). The iron appears to have been traded via a long-distance network reaching other parts of the Netherlands, and perhaps beyond, along which Rhenish pottery also circulated. Deforestation by the tenth century in the region around Kootwijk has been attributed to a demand for charcoal to support this iron production, an industry which appears to have declined dramatically by the twelfth century (ibid. 136).

Non-ferrous Metalworking

Non-ferrous metalworking, unlike ironworking, appears to have been closely associated with the settlements of elites during the fifth to seventh centuries, including communities with Roman affiliations such as Gennep, the defended *Höhensiedlungen* of the Frankish and Alamannic elites (discussed below), and rural centres such as Gudme. These groups appear to have achieved a near-monopoly over the manufacture and distribution of fine metalwork in these regions, which in turn enabled them to strengthen their positions still further (Steuer 1994, 133). Whether this situation had changed by the Viking/Carolingian period is unclear, for although several metalworking sites of this period have been identified, their wider settlement context is unknown (Capelle 1974; Winkelmann 1977, 105). Despite the lack of excavated workshop sites, it appears from the finished products that some larger-scale, centralized production of cast copper-alloy jewellery had begun by the sixth century, for example, of S-shaped and bird brooches (in apparent contrast to gold and garnet cloisonné jewellery, which appears to have been made primarily to commission: Arrhenius 1985, 194). This trend towards standardized production became still more marked in the jewellery of the eighth century, a development perhaps linked in part to the new bulk trade in everyday objects which emerged at roughly the same time. Eventually new workshops appeared under the aegis of the Church and under the protection of ecclesiastical lords, and these, at least in part, replaced the workshops of the earlier *Herrenhöfe* (Steuer 1982, 486).

Case Study: Gennep—Metalworking at a Northern 'Bridgehead' of the Empire
The late Roman/Migration period settlement of Gennep (N. Limburg) lay near a large *castellum* at the confluence of the rivers Meuse and Niers (Fig. 6.9; see also Chap. 5) (Heidinga 1994; Heidinga and Offenburg 1992). It has added considerably to our understanding of craft production, especially metalworking, at the chronological and geographical interface between the western Empire and the Frankish world, from which numerous cemeteries but few settlements are known. Some 34,000 m² were excavated, revealing approximately 120 sunken-featured buildings, eight ground-level timber buildings (including several long-houses), a few granaries, nineteen inhumation graves, and over 100 oven pits, some of which served industrial functions (Fig. 6.10). Due to erosion, the original extent of the settlement is unknown. Despite the presence of longhouses, the botanical and faunal evidence suggests that the community at Gennep was not primarily engaged in food production,[9] and the excavator has suggested that the longhouses did not contain cattle byres but were instead large assembly halls

---

[9] Horses may, however, have been reared, and 20% of the faunal remains are of red deer, indicating hunting on a considerable scale.

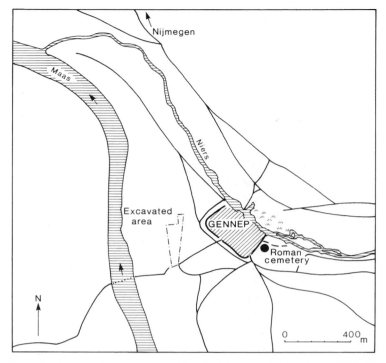

Fig. 6.9. Gennep: location map. After Heidinga and Offenberg 1992, 53.

(Heidinga 1994: 205). Metalworking, however, appears to have played a central economic role.

Every stage of copper-alloy working was represented at Gennep, from scrap metal in the form of cut-up brooches and ingots to crucibles, moulds, and both unfinished and finished objects. Substantial evidence was also recovered for the working of gold and silver. The evidence for ironworking is more limited and consists only of smithing slag. Ample evidence was also recovered for contacts with the Roman world, including, significantly, a mould for making bronze fittings for the *cingulum*, the belt worn by Roman officials and the military (Figs. 6.11 and 6.12; Heidinga 1994). In addition, some 350 Roman coins from the late fourth and early fifth centuries were recovered, as were substantial quantities of imported Gallo-Roman pottery as well as thousands of fragments of Roman glass vessels and military gear. It appears that this privileged community of Germanic settlers and craftworkers was closely associated with the Gallo-Roman military in the early fifth century; indeed, this may have been, at least for a time, a 'federate' settlement of considerable status (ibid. 206–7). The settlement shrank in size in the second half of the fifth century and by AD 500 appears

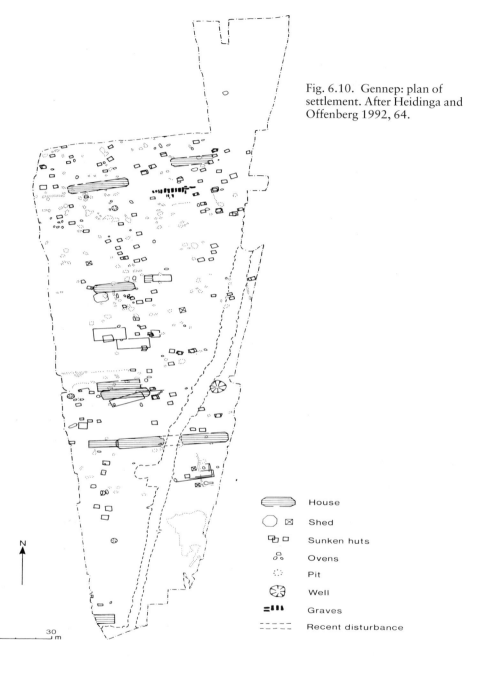

Fig. 6.10. Gennep: plan of settlement. After Heidinga and Offenberg 1992, 64.

		House
○	⊠	Shed
		Sunken huts
		Ovens
		Pit
⊕		Well
		Graves
- - - - -		Recent disturbance

N

0   30
m

Fig. 6.11. Gennep: mould for making a bronze, tubular-sided attachment plate for a Roman *cingulum*. Photo: Courtesy of H. A. Heidinga.

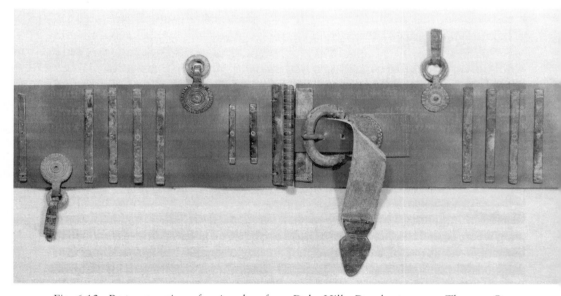

Fig. 6.12. Reconstruction of a *cingulum* from Dyke Hills, Dorchester-upon-Thames, Oxon. The Gennep mould is for making a tubular-sided plate attached to the end of the belt, similar to the fifth-century example seen here. Photo: Courtesy of the Ashmolean Museum, Oxford.

either to have been abandoned or to have shifted to a new location. This discontinuity could be linked to Clovis's annexation of the region *c.* AD 507, after which the military role of the Rhineland-Frankish elites who lived at Gennep would have come to an end (ibid. 206).

Case Study: The Höhensiedlungen—Craft Centres in Northern Francia
In contrast to the abundance of archaeological data available for southern
Scandinavia, northwest Gemany and the Netherlands, our knowledge of rural
settlements in the northern Frankish regions remains based on a relatively
small number of sites (see Chap. 3). Amongst those which stand out most clearly
are a few defended hilltop settlements which were established near the Rhine
and Danube frontiers, and which served as both craft centres and the homes
of elite families and their followers. These are the so-called *Höhenburgen* (or
Höhensiedlungen), the most striking of which emerged in the Alamannic regions
during the late Roman and post-Roman periods. The original *Höhenburge* were
vici and *villae rusticae* in the frontier zones of the Empire which moved to higher,
more easily defensible locations after the Germanic incursions of the early third
century (Steuer 1994). The Frankish, Alamannic, and Burgundian elites who
later settled in this region adopted this Roman fashion for hilltop settlements.

The most thoroughly investigated of these settlements is Runde Berg near
Urach, at the edge of the Black Forest (Christlein 1978, 42–9; Steuer 1994). The
settlement was founded in the mid-third century shortly after the takeover of the
region by the Alamanni, and consisted of timber buildings and a craft area pro-
tected by a 250 m steep drop and, by the fifth century, a palisaded enclosure. The
romanized lifestyle of at least some of its occupants—generally believed to have
been an Alamannic leader, his war band, and dependants—and their close links
with the Roman world are reflected in their use of Roman glass vessels, fine
pottery wares, coins, and games (Steuer 1994; Christlein 1978, 44). In the fifth
century bronze- and silver-working were carried out close to the palisaded enclosure, while ironworking was sited further away. Although few traces survive
of the buildings of this period, the chiefly household is believed to have been sited
within the palisaded enclosure, based upon the concentration there of weapons,
horse gear, and imported glass (Steuer 1994, 138).

Manufacture of fine metalwork and other prestigious items such as glass
vessels was a characteristic feature of the *Höhenburgen* of the fourth to sixth
centuries. Roman scrap metal, glass cullet, brooch moulds, and belt fittings,
touchstones for testing the purity of gold, tools, and glass slag are typically found
at such settlements. The presence of traders is attested by finds of scales and
weights of both local and Byzantine origins (Christlein 1978, 100).

In the fifth and sixth centuries these workshops produced unique pieces such
as finely worked gold and garnet brooches—symbols of power and privilege for
leading families. The production of such jewellery as well as weaponry must
have been controlled by the residents of the *Höhenburgen*, who distributed them
as gifts to their followers in the surrounding region (Steuer 1994, 139). These
impressive defended sites with their resident craftspeople provide a striking
image of the power wielded by these families.

Runde Berg was abandoned in the early sixth century. Resettlement of several
hill-top sites, including Runde Berg, took place in the later seventh century, when

they became home to new 'Frankish' elites who were ostentatiously buried at places like Niederstotzingen, near Ulm (Christlein 1978, 48; Paulsen 1967). Thereafter, the *Höhensiedlungen* were largely abandoned, and specialized craft production presumably shifted to royal, monastic, and aristocratic centres (Steuer 1994).

Pottery Production

During the Migration period pottery across much of northwest Europe was hand-built, tempered with local materials, and included both plain, relatively coarse wares used as storage vessels, cooking pots, and so on, and finer, thin-walled, decorated vessels found in settlements but above all used as cremation urns in cemeteries, the latter reaching a peak in quality and complexity in the fifth and sixth centuries. Such pottery was presumably fired in simple clamp kilns, and its highly individual character is not suggestive of centralized production.[10] Although plain, hand-built wares continued to be made throughout the Merovingian/early Viking periods, long after the decorated pottery of the Migration period ceased to be produced, they too were largely replaced by harder fired, mass-produced, wheel-turned pottery. These later wares tend to be bag-shaped or ovoid in form, sometimes with rouletted or stamped decoration. One of the most thoroughly studied of these is the *Kugeltopf*, the dominant pottery type found in much of northwest Germany and along the Frisian coast from the ninth to twelfth centuries, made using a wooden mould and a turntable (Wulf 1991, 346).

The majority of early Frankish pottery kilns appear to have been sited in rural locations,[11] with the major production centres lying along the middle and lower Rhine, the earliest in the region of Mayen (Janssen 1983, 349). In the south German village of Wülfingen (Nordwürttemberg) a pottery kiln was producing plain, coarse, wheel-thrown vessels in the seventh century (Schulze 1982). A similar situation can be seen further to the north in the village of Geseke (Westphalia), where excavation revealed a well-preserved pottery kiln which was in operation in the late sixth or seventh century (Winkelmann 1977, 115–19). The region supplied by the Geseke pots has not yet been defined, but the fact that Geseke was a Saxon royal estate in the ninth and tenth centuries, and that Wülfingen was a probable *Herrenhof* in the eleventh and twelfth centuries (Janssen 1983, 349 ff.), suggest that this production was, at least to some degree, controlled from above. It appears that most 'late Saxon' pottery in north-

---

[10] Although there may be exceptions such as Charnwood Forest Ware (see below) and Illington–Lackford pottery, which could have been produced in special workshops (Williams and Vince 1998; Myres 1977, 60–2; Russel 1984, 525 ff., 528).

[11] The assumption that pottery industries were not based in towns until the twelfth century (Janssen 1983, 351 ff.; Müller-Wille 1983, Abb. 6) cannot, however, be accepted uncritically since the discovery in the 1980s in Ipswich, Suffolk, of a pottery kiln used to fire a mass-produced pottery which was marketed primarily throughout East Anglia during the eighth and ninth centuries (Wade 1988). Urban pottery industries such as Stamford Ware were also a feature of the Danelaw in England (Kilmurry 1980).

west Germany was manufactured in small workshops such as these, serving the local region, so that the degree of contact between producer and customer would have been considerable (Häßler 1991, 295). In southern Scandinavia, too, pottery does not generally appear to have been traded over long distances; thus, in eighth-century Hedeby and Ribe only some 5–7 per cent of the pottery was imported (Näsman 2000).

Stone-working

Quernstones were traded both locally and inter-regionally. The clearest example of the latter is the basalt lava querns produced in the region of Mayen which, like the pottery from the same region, were exported via the Rhine harbour of Andernach to southern Scandinavia and England (Janssen 1983, 352; Steuer 1987). Local trade in querns can also be seen to have taken place between settlements on the marsh and those on the Geest in the Elbe–Weser triangle. Although Rhenish lava querns were imported into this region, locally available granite was also used. A number of these granite querns were found in various stages of manufacture at the settlement of Flögeln, whereas only finished examples were found at the nearby marsh settlement of Feddersen Wierde, suggesting a priori a local trade in these objects (Haarnagel *et al.* 1984, 288–9).

Cloth Production

Early written sources, most famously the letter from Charlemagne to the Mercian king Offa, with its mention of English cloaks being sent to Francia (Whitelock 1955, no. 197), highlight the key importance of textile production in the economies of England and Frisia in the early Middle Ages. Frisian cloth was being traded at least as early as the seventh and eighth centuries, and high-quality textiles have been recovered from a number of settlements excavated in this region. At the east Frisian *Wurt* of Hessens, situated between two watercourses southwest of Wilhelmshaven, a group of longhouses was excavated which were occupied during the seventh to tenth centuries. In the seventh century one of these buildings was partly demolished and converted into a dock for a small boat, after rising water levels had rendered it uninhabitable. The dock, fragments of boats, and numerous pieces of high-quality cloth all suggest that the community was involved in the trading of textiles (Wulf 1991).

Clauses in early law-codes dealing with cloth production, and the ubiquity of loomweights and spindlewhorls on rural settlements throughout the early Middle Ages, confirm that textile production played a major role in the economies of these communities.[12] At Warendorf, for example, loomweights,

---

[12] Title II in the *Lex Frisionum*, 'Iudicia Wulemari', states that crimes committed against women who know how to make 'frese' (*foeminae fresum facienti*) are fined four times more heavily than those committed against other women. 'Frese' may refer to a woollen cloth (Dölling 1958, 35).

spindlewhorls, and a flax comb, as well as the emplacements for warp-weighted looms,[13] suggest that most if not all farmsteads had a building in which weaving took place, indicating cloth production at household level (Winkelmann 1977, 105). Workshops for specialized cloth production, however, do not become evident in the archaeological record until the Viking and Ottonian periods. At the Ottonian palace at Tilleda (Harz), for example, several large, elongated, sunken-floored buildings situated in the craftworkers' quarter appear to have served as weaving sheds (Grimm 1968). Textile production also assumed a new prominence in the villages of this period. At Dalem, for example, which was well situated for trade with coastal settlements, several large sunken-featured buildings have been identified as weaving sheds (Zimmermann 1991*a*; see Chap. 3), while at Næs on Zealand, 'large scale production' of linen took place from the second half of the eighth century to the tenth century (Møller Hansen and Høier, 2000).

The Social Position of the Rural Craftworker: The Smith

It is difficult to counter the assertion that by the reign of Charlemagne the economic activities of the great majority of people living in northwest Europe were, to a greater or lesser extent, 'controlled from above' (Duby 1968, 34). Archaeology suggests, however, that a degree of economic independence was exercised with regard to non-agrarian production in the countryside. Although the social position occupied by the rural craftworker in general remains poorly understood, a good deal of consideration has been given to the status of the early medieval smith, primarily because the ability to produce metal objects was closely linked to political and military power and the smith, therefore, appears in a variety of written sources. Discussions have tended to centre on whether the smith was itinerant and 'free' or bound to a lord: the situation, in fact, is unlikely to have been so clear-cut.

The number of graves containing smith's tools which have been excavated in Merovingian and Viking cemeteries remains relatively small. Furthermore, these usually contain only one or two tools, not a complete 'kit', the most common combinations being a hammer and tongs, or hammer and file (Müller-Wille 1983, 251). In most cases the tools are those of a smith, but several burials also contained carpentry tools, suggesting competence in a range of crafts (ibid., Abb. 16). The fact that only a tiny percentage of the thousands of the Frankish burials excavated to date contained tools suggests that only a small proportion of craftspeople—perhaps only those who were particularly skilful or who

---

[13] The upright, warp-weighted loom of the type known since the Neolithic was used in northwest Europe throughout the early Middle Ages (Zimmermann 1982). The more efficient horizontal loom came into use from about the tenth century, but the warp-weighted loom, which did not restrict the width of the cloth being woven, maintained an important role; one of the looms from Dalem, for example, allowed cloth with a width of *c*.3.5 m to be woven (Zimmermann 1995*a*, 282).

belonged to a high social stratum (see below)—were buried with symbols of their crafts (Winkelmann 1977, 97 ff.; 103).

There is evidence to suggest that, while goldsmiths may have been followers of lords, some at least were free to move periodically to take up commissions (James 1988, 207). The freeborn goldsmith Eligius who became bishop of Noyon is the most striking example of this (Wicker 1994, 147; Steuer 1982, 479). Seventh-century Anglo-Saxon law-codes, however, indicate that some smiths were not 'free agents' (Hinton 1998, 10); the laws of King Ine of Wessex, for example, state that 'if a *gesith*-born man moves elsewhere, he may then have with him his reeve and his smith and his children's nurse' (Whitelock 1955, no. 32. 63)

Steuer has argued that a craftworker's station depended upon his or her social status at birth (1982). In other words, an unfree potter was not unfree *because* he or she was a potter, but was already unfree. The fact that the craftworkers mentioned in law-codes are generally unfree may be because so many of the laws are to do with establishing the value of property, including slaves; it does not ne-cessarily follow that all specialist craftworkers were unfree.[14] Craftworkers could be part of a lord's household but could also have independent status. The status of the smith may also have been related to the kind of objects he or she produced, for example, jewellery and swords as opposed to, say, nails and knives. The *wergelds* assigned by the law-codes of the Burgundians also indicate that there were social distinctions made between a goldsmith, a silversmith, and a blacksmith (Wicker 1994, 146). Certain crafts clearly possessed a greater cachet than others, and smiths are assigned a particularly high value in the laws of the period (James 1988, 207).

During the Migration and Merovingian periods it appears that everyday goods were produced at the level of both the individual household and of the community as a whole. Thus, smithies could be associated with individual farm-steads, as at Joldelund or Vorbasse, where three of the fourth-century farmyards contained smithies, and where, in the Viking period, several smithies were actu-ally incorporated into longhouses, while others lay in separate buildings (C. Zimmermann 1998, 86; Müller-Wille 1983, 235). More specialized production, for example, of certain types of ornamental metalwork and weaponry, seems, however, to have been based at the settlements of elites whose occupants also controlled their distribution.

PRODUCTION, EXCHANGE, AND RURAL CENTRES IN ANGLO-SAXON ENGLAND

What evidence do we have for rural, secular centres of production and trade in Anglo-Saxon England during the early and mid-Saxon periods? For the fifth and

---

[14] Nehlsen (1981) concludes, however, that most craftworkers were in fact unfree.

sixth centuries, direct evidence for workshops and craft production is negligible, apart from artefacts related to bone/antler-working and textile production. The rare exception, such as the brooch mould from Mucking in Essex (Webster 1993), only serves to highlight the extreme paucity of such evidence. For the mid-Saxon period, trade networks—both international and regional—come more clearly into focus, though production sites remain scarce. Ipswich Ware, a type of pottery produced primarily from the early eighth to mid-ninth centuries, provides a rare example of a commodity for which both the production site and distribution have been studied in considerable detail. A pottery kiln and large quantities of potting debris associated with the production of Ipswich Ware have been found in Ipswich itself, while Ipswich Ware is found widely on settlements within East Anglia, and must have been distributed by an efficient marketing system (Scull 1997, 277–8; Wade 1988, 95–6; Blinkhorn 1999).

It has often been assumed that participation in long-distance trade networks and intensive craft production was primarily the preserve of towns, royal estates, and monasteries, yet the widespread distribution and rapid circulation of coinage by the early eighth century suggests a comparatively high level of economic integration in the Anglo-Saxon countryside.[15] The settlement context of this activity remains elusive, as most of these coins are metal-detector finds and do not derive from excavations: did it take place in ordinary farming settlements, in special markets, estate centres, or all three? In terms of trade and craft production, we have as yet to find settlements equivalent to Kosel, Schuby, Snorup, or Joldelund in England.

In contrast to northern Germany and southern Scandinavia, there is as yet little evidence from England that continental trade goods, which presumably entered principally via the emporia, reached their hinterlands in any quantity. As yet, however, little systematic work to quantify and plot such material has been undertaken (an exception being Coutts 1992), and this impression may yet prove misleading.[16] A study of the distribution of Rhenish lava querns in Anglo-Saxon settlements, for example, suggests that these were widely distributed, indeed much more so than imported pottery (Parkhouse 1997). The late seventh- to tenth-century settlement at Yarnton, Oxon., despite its inland location, produced fragments of between eight and fourteen such querns (Gill Hey and Paul Blinkhorn, pers. comm. 1997; Roe 1997). This material was presumably transported up the Thames from London, where a dump of over 200 fragments of

---

[15] The situation on the continent is markedly different. Whereas in England there are some 600 to 700 find-spots of the silver coins known as sceattas, in southern Scandinavia 'there are hardly six or seven' and monetary exchanges there appear to have been almost entirely restricted to emporia (Metcalf 1996). Thus in England, coinage was clearly integrated into local economic activity, while in Scandinavia and Frisia, coins were almost exclusively associated with long-distance trade. The picture is somewhat different in the region of the Rhine estuary which was heavily coin-using, and the number of single sceatta finds in the Netherlands is gradually increasing, although the settlement context of these finds remains unclear (M. Metcalf, pers. comm.).

[16] Moreland (2000, 69), for example, has argued that the level of production in eighth-century England 'has been massively underestimated'. See also Palmer, 2002.

lava querns exported to England as rough-outs have been recovered from the late Saxon waterfront embankments (Freshwater 1996). The quernstones could have been obtained in exchange for agricultural produce or perhaps for the shelly pottery wares which appear to have been exported from the Upper Thames Valley to London (Roe 1997; Vince 1985, 30–1). Alternatively, Yarnton may have obtained these imports via the nearby monastery at Eynsham, where a similar number of lava quern fragments was found. The possibility, however, that ordinary villages had independent access to a trading network based on the Thames should not be discounted.

An exceptional opportunity to investigate the economies of communities in the hinterlands of English *wics* is offered by two sites within some 10 km of Ipswich which have produced large numbers of coins and other metal finds. These sites have not been subjected to large-scale excavation, however, and it therefore remains impossible to characterize the nature of these settlements in any detail. The first is at Barham, on a ridge overlooking the Gipping valley some 7 km northwest of Ipswich. Excavation of approximately 1 per cent of the site (estimated to cover 6–7 ha) has failed to uncover structures, leading to the suggestion that it may not have been a settlement at all, but rather a market or open-air meeting place, although given that 99 per cent of the site remains unexcavated, this must remain little more than speculation (Newman 1999 and forthcoming). The imports date primarily from the seventh to mid-ninth centuries (although some earlier material was recovered) and come primarily from the western Frankish and Frisian regions. These include a gold *tremissis* minted at Quentovic *c.*640, a number of Frisian *sceattas*, two equal-armed brooches dating to between the mid-eighth and mid-ninth centuries, and an enamelled saint's brooch of the mid-ninth to early tenth century (Wamers 1994, 595). Other finds include a garnet-and-gold cloisonné stud, a silver disc-headed pin, and several hanging-bowl escutcheons. Certainly, in comparison to contemporary settlements which have been identified in the Deben valley to the east, Barham is exceptionally rich in metalwork and coins. Its inclusion in an eleventh-century charter confirming estates held by Ely Abbey, where it is listed along with important places such as Brandon and Barking, further suggests an earlier significance as a regional centre (Sawyer 1968, no. 1051).

At Coddenham, a former Roman small town at a major river crossing only 2.5 km northwest of Barham and likewise known primarily from metal-detector finds, a large number of coins, mostly of mid-seventh to early eighth-century date have been recovered. These include four Merovingian *tremisses*, twelve gold 'thrymsas', and some fifty primary *sceattas*, along with other metal objects including three gold fragments, two with repoussé decoration and one originally with a cloisonné inset. Among the imported finds were a sixth-century Frankish bird brooch and part of a radiate-headed brooch (Fig. 6.13, 1, 4) (Newman, forthcoming *a* and *b*). The majority of the finds, however, date to the seventh and eighth centuries. Of particular interest are a number of pieces of metalwork

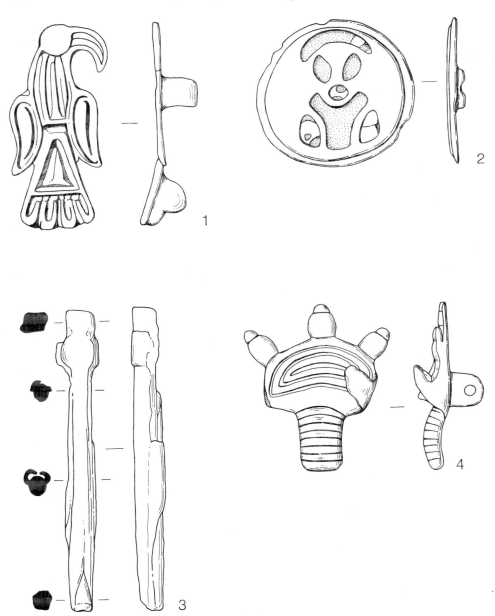

Fig. 6.13. Coddenham: metal finds. 1. Frankish bird brooch; 2. Saint's brooch; 3. Unfinished pin; 4. Radiate-headed brooch. Scale: 1 : 1. With kind permission of Suffolk County Council.

which appear to have been broken up for reuse and which, along with at least one unfinished copper-alloy pin (Fig. 6.13, 3), two unfinished buckles, and offcuts of sheet metal and other metalworking debris, indicate intensive metalworking. This range of imports, together with the evidence for metalworking and the fact that the lower Gipping valley was a major communications and trade route in the later prehistoric and Roman periods, hints at the existence of a metalworking and redistribution centre which in origin pre-dated Ipswich. It is interesting to note that neither Coddenham nor Barham became towns (Newman, forthcoming).

While the evidence that some rural settlements of the seventh to ninth centuries had access to long-distance as well as regional trade networks is thus growing, no early or mid-Anglo-Saxon settlement has yet been found which engaged in non-agrarian production on a scale comparable to, say, Gennep or Joldelund. The limited evidence for non-ferrous metalworking uncovered so far from settlements (listed by Hinton 1998, 3–4) indicates almost exclusively small-scale, dispersed production to serve the needs of local communities. As for iron-working, even regions which were centres of iron-smelting in the Roman and medieval periods, such as the Weald of Sussex and the Forest of Dean, have produced virtually no evidence for smelting during the Anglo-Saxon period; the evidence for smithing in rural settlements, while widespread, is not substantial (McDonnell 1989; Bayley 1991). There are a few exceptions, however, notably at Ramsbury in Wiltshire, where an iron-smelting and smithing site dating to the late eighth and early ninth centuries has been excavated, although on too limited a scale to establish its wider context (Haslam 1980, 56). Iron ore was transported to Ramsbury from between 5 km to 30 km away. Ramsbury, however, was the seat of the West Saxon bishopric from 909 to 1058, and it seems likely that the earlier iron-producing site was part of an important royal estate. Indeed, Hinton has plausibly argued that the advent of kingship and the emergence of ecclesiastical centres may in part account for the increased archaeological evidence for metalworking (especially ironworking) associated with rural settlements from the eighth century onwards, as estates were more intensively exploited (Hinton 1998, 17–18).[17] An earlier iron-smelting site, described as 'extensive', was uncovered at Little Totham, near the estuary of the River Blackwater in Essex, with a number of slag-pit furnaces and smithing hearths, possibly associated with sunken-featured buildings, dated by thermoluminscence and radiocarbon to the seventh century (Selkirk 1989). Regrettably, only limited information regarding this important site is available (O. Bedwin, pers. comm. 1997; Wallis 1998). What evidence we do have, however, suggests that iron production in England during the fifth to the seventh centuries at least was largely

[17] A small excavation c.30 m southwest of Romsey Abbey in Hampshire, also uncovered evidence of intensive iron-smelting (Scott 1993). A mid-Saxon date, perhaps related to a secular/royal estate pre-dating the foundation of the abbey, is postulated for some of this material based on the evidence for the use of slag-block technology (I. Scott, pers. comm.).

integrated into the agrarian economy and was primarily carried out by farmers, rather than specialist smelters (G. McDonnell, pers. comm.).

The possibility that surplus pottery production took place in rural settlements cannot be ruled out, although the lack of known kiln sites makes this a matter of pure speculation. There is as yet little evidence for the regularized exchange of pottery prior to the widespread appearance of Ipswich Ware in the eighth and ninth centuries, despite the recent recognition of a type of pottery made in the Charnwood Forest region of Leicestershire which travelled some distance from its area of production (Williams and Vince 1998). It is likewise probable that surplus cloth for trade or exchange was manufactured in rural settlements,[18] as was certainly the case along the Frisian coast by the seventh century (see above), but it is impossible to quantify this production purely on the basis of the spinning and weaving equipment which survives in rural settlements.

The current interpretative paradigm for mid- and late Saxon England sees participation in long-distance trade and intensive craft production as having been the prerogative of *wics*, minsters, and royal estates. Evidence from southern Scandinavia as well as sites such as Yarnton, Barham, and Coddenham should warn us against this assumption, however. We now know that a wide range of rural communities in mid-Saxon England had access to a range of trade goods broadly similar to those in southern Scandinavia and northern Germany. The lack of comparable evidence for intensive production such as major concentrations of smelting and smithing debris, crucibles, and moulds, remains puzzling, however. A possible solution may be that archaeologists have been looking in the wrong places and that the main metalworking sites lie outside of settlements: the discovery by geophysical prospection of massive slag deposits outside what otherwise appeared to be an 'ordinary' settlement at Heeten (see above) could provide a salutory lesson. It is interesting to note in this connection that recent radiocarbon dates from massive slag-heaps in the Rockingham Forest region of Northamptonshire indicate that the same heaps remained in use from the fifth to the thirteenth centuries (Foard, 2001). The legend of Weland the Smith (Hinton 1998, 11 ff.), as well as some evidence for rituals associated with iron-smelting, such as the quantities of animal bones found in smelting pits at Joldelund (Jöns 1997), indicate, furthermore, that the smith's ability to transform ore into metal was seen as a mysterious, indeed magical process, which needed to be kept at a safe distance; this, combined with the need to keep noxious or dangerous craft activities well away from the farmyard, may explain why evidence for metal-working within settlements themselves is comparatively rare.

---

[18] One of Ine's laws (XLIV.1) seems to show the king defining the quality of woollen cloth with a view to its collection as a form of render from each household, or perhaps each hide (Whitelock 1955, no. 32). I am grateful to John Maddicott for drawing this to my attention.

7

Epilogue: Trajectories and Turning-Points

A survey such as this one can only present a fraction of the archaeological evidence available for early medieval settlements, yet even a relatively brief review of this evidence makes plain the remarkable diversity of these settlements in terms of form and economy; the communities they represent were far from being simple, isolated, and economically primitive as so often portrayed in traditional historical scholarship. In particular, the recognition on the one hand of high-status complexes dating to the Migration period and, on the other, farming communities of 'ordinary' status which were extensively engaged in trade and non-agrarian production, points to a higher degree of economic complexity, integration, and resilience than was previously imagined.

Furthermore, the archaeology, when viewed *in toto*, points to what has aptly been dubbed 'the long eighth century', namely the period from *c.*680 to 830,[1] as a turning-point, not only in terms of settlement structure and architecture, but also in the organization of landed production and regional exchange. By 800, as we have seen, rural settlements in the North Sea zone were configured in ways that were markedly different from their Migration period predecessors. The longhouse had, in most regions, undergone a radical transformation or been given up altogether; settlements were increasingly planned and bounded; farming and craft activities, as well as the circulation of goods, showed signs of a wide-ranging reorganization; and elite families had stamped an increasingly separate group identity onto the landscape as they established distinctive settlements and buried their dead in new burial grounds away from the communal cemeteries of their ancestors. While the very nature of archaeological evidence does not permit us to point with certainty to the specific causes which lay behind these changes, the emergence of kingdoms in northwest Europe provides the backdrop against which they can best be understood.

The development of early states—specifically in Denmark and England—and the northward expansion of Frankish colonial activities required both increased production and the mobilization of agrarian resources into an increasingly

---

[1] In his introduction to a volume devoted to 'the long eighth century', Wickham defines this period as the first fully post-Roman century in the West and one which displayed 'a general homogeneity', at least in terms of production, distribution, and demand (Wickham 2000*a*).

centralized political system. Indeed, an increased emphasis on surplus extraction must lie behind many of the changes observable in the plant and animal remains of this period and in the remnants of craft production, as well as in the greater size and storage capacities of at least some farmsteads in central Jutland, Lower Saxony, Westphalia, and Drenthe. These changes suggest a shift away from essentially (though never entirely) self-sufficient communities, whose economies involved reciprocal exchange and the circulation of prestigious goods, towards an economy based on the redistribution of surplus production and trade of commodities via regional networks.

The impact which the intensification of production would have had upon rural communities is also manifested in the increased access which farmers had to imported goods through a redistributive network which ultimately connected them to the emporia. The latter, of course, played a key role in the economic florescence of the 'long' eighth century. Even if the precise economic mechanisms which linked farms to emporia remain unclear, these trading centres must have affected the character of life in their hinterlands, as testified by the widespread presence in rural settlements of imported quernstones, pottery, glass, and other items which must have come into daily use around this time.[2] It can hardly be a coincidence, for example, that the eighth century saw the doubling in size of Ipswich and the marketing of Ipswich Ware in large quantities to rural settlements throughout East Anglia.

The intensification and reorganization of production must of course be seen as responses to increased demand (Wickham 2000*b*, 349). In England and Francia this demand was partly created by monasteries who oversaw a large-scale reorganization of landed production—production which, in effect, paid for these communities. Intensification was not, however, restricted to the monastery- and town-dotted landscapes of northwest Gaul and England, but is also apparent in southern Scandinavia and northern Germany.[3] This increase in demand must therefore have sprung not only from the requirements of so-called 'consumer communities', but also from a general growth in population.

Intensification of production, particularly of cultivation, would have brought with it important social changes, stemming in part from the need for the labour force to be in closer contact. These would have contributed to, and in turn been shaped by, changes in the structure of settlements and of houses. Indeed, given the important role of the house in the reproduction of social relationships, the widespread appearance of the Warendorf-type house takes on a new significance, as does the change from farmsteads in which several functions were combined under the single roof of the longhouse, to those containing a variety of

---

[2] Moreland has argued that, in England, the intensification of production actually preceded the founding of the emporia, but the archaeological dating remains too inexact to establish this with certainty (Moreland 2000).

[3] Randsborg notes that the expansion of pasture and cereal production from *c*.700 onwards was 'a general pattern throughout the north-western parts of the Continent' (1998, 83. See also Chap. 5).

buildings, each serving a different function. While the more bounded, measured, and defined use of space within settlements may in part reflect the increasingly firm grip exerted by local aristocrats on the land and the people who worked it, it is also likely to reflect more closely defined social roles and relationships, such as an increased concern with marriage patterns and rights of inheritance (Bourdieu 1973; Brück 2000; Barrett 1994, 151). Thus the more uniform layouts of farmsteads apparent in the eighth century may have developed as much in response to changes in power structures within households and communities as to wider economic or political developments. Similarly, the greater standardization of burial practices in the later seventh and eighth centuries, seen not only in England and at the northern fringes of the Frankish world, but also in southern Scandinavia, may signal more closely defined social roles and ranks (Jørgensen 1991).

It will be apparent from the preceding chapters that, while early medieval cemeteries are often discussed in terms of ritual and symbolism, settlements still tend to be analysed in largely functional terms. Yet the early medieval house in particular would have been closely bound up with the life-cycle of the household and ritual activities would almost certainly have accompanied the building, modification, dismantling, and abandonment of houses (Bloch 1995; Gerretsen 1999). It is difficult to 'write the biography' of a timber structure from postholes alone, yet traces of ritual associated with buildings can be found. At the Frisian terp of Wijnaldum, for example, five newborn infants were buried within the settlement, and one was positioned in direct association with a building, apparently as a so-called 'foundation offering'[4] (Gerrets 1999, 337); a pit containing a cow next to an entrance to Building C13 at Cowdery's Down is a particularly clear example of such an offering (Millett 1984, 221). The bracteates deposited in the posthole of a house at Gudme must also have served a ritual, perhaps protective, purpose (Vang-Petersen 1994, 35, fig. 12). Human inhumations were positioned at the entrances to two of the enclosed farmsteads at Catholme, Staffordshire (Kinsley, 2002) and immediately outside the east entrance to Building A4 at Yeavering (Burial AX; Hope-Taylor 1977, 67, fig. 25).

It is an inescapable fact that the quantity of detailed, published data concerning early medieval settlements is for the moment comparatively small, certainly in relation to that available for burials—too small, for the most part, to undertake meaningful statistical analyses or, in some cases, even basic comparisons. It is unsurprising, therefore, that the great potential of settlement archaeology to reflect the changing relationships between individuals, households, and communities remains to be fully realized. Yet the evidence already available does much more than merely provide a guide to the scale of the unknown. Excavation has revealed the degree to which developments in rural life transcended political

---

[4] It is probable, however, that such offerings could also mark other significant events in the 'life-cycle' of a building and household.

boundaries and events. Architecture, settlement structure, and agrarian practices underwent strikingly similar transformations all around the North Sea zone, as communities in these regions reacted against, but also adapted themselves to, Mediterranean culture and as individuals saw themselves increasingly as members of several communities—not only of a household, farm, and village, but also of a district or territory.

As the number of excavations and archaeological surveys grows, it is becoming increasingly possible not only to chart large-scale developments in settlement form and land use, but to relate these to the changing ideologies of power during the second half of the first millennium AD. This must surely rank among archaeology's most significant contributions to the study of the early Middle Ages.

References

ADDYMAN, P. 1972, 'The Anglo-Saxon house: a new review', *Anglo-Saxon England*, 1: 273–308.

——and D. LEIGH 1973, 'The Anglo-Saxon village at Chalton, Hampshire: second interim report', *Medieval Archaeology*, 17: 1–25.

ANDERSEN, S. W. and F. RIEK 1984, 'Mølleparken: a settlement of the 4th–5th centuries A.D. at Løgumkloster, S. Jutland', *Journal of Danish Archaeology*, 3: 170–6.

ANDREW, P. 1992, 'Middle Saxon Norfolk: evidence for settlement 650–850', *The Annual 1992: Norfolk Archaeological and Historical Research Group*: 13–28.

ARNOLD, C. and P. WARDLE 1981, 'Early medieval settlement patterns in England', *Medieval Archaeology*, 25: 145–9.

ARRHENIUS, B. 1985, *Merovingian Garnet Jewellery: Emergence and Social Implications*, Stockholm: Almqvist & Wiksell International.

ASTILL, G. and W. DAVIES 1997, *A Breton Landscape*, London: UCL Press.

ASTON, M. and C. GERRARD 1999, ' "Unique, traditional and charming": the Shapwick Project, Somerset', *Antiquaries Journal*, 79: 1–58.

AUSENDA, G. 1995 (ed.), *After Empire: Towards an Ethnology of Europe's Barbarians*, San Marino: Boydell Press.

AXBOE, M. 1992, 'Metal og magt? Detektorfund fra jernalderbopladser', *Arkaeologiske udgravninger i Danmark 1991*, Copenhagen: 18–32.

——1995, 'Danish kings and dendrochronology: archaeological insights into the early history of the Danish state', in Ausenda (ed.): 217–38.

BACKER, S., W. DÖRFLER, M. GANZELEWSKI, A. HAFFNER, A. HAUPTMANN, H. JÖNS, H. KROLL, and R. DRUSE 1992, 'Frühgeschichtliche Eisengewinnung und Verarbeitung am Kammberg bei Joldelund', in Müller-Wille and Hoffmann (eds.): 83–110.

BALKWILL, C. 1993, 'Old English *wic* and the origin of the hundred', *Landscape History*, 15: 5–12.

BALZARETTI, R. 1995, 'Cities and markets in the early Middle Ages', in Ausenda (ed.): 113–33.

BANTELMANN, A. 1975, *Die Frühgeschichtliche Marschensiedlung beim Elisenhof in Eiderstedt*, Bd. 1, Frankfurt: P. Lang.

BARDET, A., P. KOOI, H. T. WATERBOLK, and J. WIERINGA 1983, *Peelo, Historisch-Geografisch en Archeologisch Onderzoek naar de Ouderdom van een Drents Dorp* (*Mededelingen der Koninklijke Nederlandse Akademie van Wetenschappen, afd Letterkunde, Nieuwe Reeks*, Deel 46.1), Amsterdam.

BÄRENFÄNGER, R. 1998, 'Von der Steinzeit bis zum Mittelalter: Ergebnisse archä-ologischer Forschung in Hesel', in P. Weßel (ed.), *Hesel: 'Wüste Fläche, Dürre Wildnis und Magere Heidepflanzen': der Weg eines Bauerndorfes in die Moderne*, Gemeinde Hesel: 19–72.

BARNWELL, P. 1996, '*Hlafæta, ceorl, hid* and *scir*: Celtic, Roman or Germanic?', in D. Griffiths (ed.), *Anglo-Saxon Studies in Archaeology and History*, 9, Oxford: Oxford University Committee for Archaeology: 53–62.

BARRETT, J. 1994, *Fragments From Antiquity: An Archaeology of Social Life in Britain, 2900–1200 BC*, Oxford: Blackwell.

BARTON, K. 1962, 'Settlements of the Iron Age and Pagan Saxon periods at Linford, Essex', *Trans. Essex Archaeol Soc*, 3rd ser., 1: 57–102.

BAYARD, D. 1989, 'Le Village mérovingien du "Gué de Mauchamp" à Juvincourt-et-Damary: Un des premiers habitats des Moyen Age fouillés dans le Nord de la France', *Archéologie Autoroute A26, Revue Archéologie de Picardie 1989*: 101–10.

BAYLEY, J. 1991, 'Anglo-Saxon non-ferrous metalworking: a survey', *World Archaeology*, 23 (1): 115–30.

BECKER, C. J. 1971, 'Früheisenzeitliche Dörfer bei Grøntoft, Westjütland', *Acta Archaeologica*, 42: 79–110.

BEDE, *Bede's Ecclesiastical History of the English People*, 1969, ed. and trans. B. Colgrave and R. A. B. Mynors, Oxford: Clarendon Press.

BEHRE, K.-E. 1976, *Elisenhof 2: Die Pflanzenreste*, Frankfurt: P. Lang.

—— 1988, 'The role of man in European vegetation history', in B. Huntley and T. Webb (eds.), *Vegetation History*, Dordrecht/London: Kluwer Academic: 633–72.

—— 1991, 'The ecological interpretation of archaeobotanical data', in W. van Zeist, K. Wasylikowa, and K.-E. Behre (eds.), *Progress in Old World Palaeoethnobotany*, Rotterdam: A. A. Balkema: 81–108.

—— 1992, 'The history of rye cultivation in Europe', *Vegetation History and Archaeobotany* (1992), 1: 141–56.

—— 1999, Paper presented to the Arbeitsgemeinschaft für Sachsenforschung, Bederkesa.

—— and D. KUČAN 1986, 'Die Reflektion archäologisch bekannter Siedlungen in Pollendiagrammen verschiedener Entfernung—Beispiele aus der Siedlungskammer Flögeln, Nordwestdeutschland', in K.-E. Behre (ed.), *Anthropogenic Indicators in Pollen Diagrams*, Rotterdam/Boston: A. A. Balkema: 95–114.

—— and P. SCHMID 1998, *Das Niedersächsische Institut für historische Küstenforschung: 60 Jahre Forschungstätigkeit im Küstengebiet*, Wilhelmshaven: Brune Druck- und Verlagsgesellschaft.

BELL, M. 1978, 'Excavations at Bishopstone, Sussex', *Sussex Arch. Coll.* 15: 192–241.

BENDER-JØRGENSEN, L. 1992, *North European Textiles until A.D. 1000*, Århus: Århus University Press.

BERESFORD, G. 1987, *Goltho: The Development of an Early Medieval Manor, c.850–1150*, London: English Heritage.

BERESFORD, M. and J. HURST 1990, *Wharram Percy: Deserted Medieval Village*, London: English Heritage/Batsford.

BERNHARD, H. 1981, 'Ausgrabungen in der frühmittelalterlichen Siedlung Speyer "Vogelgesang", Rheinland-Pfalz', in A. van Doorselaer (ed.), *De merovingische Beschaving in de Scheldevallei*: 223–38.

—— 1982, 'Die frühmittelalterliche Siedlung Speyer, "Vogelgesang"', *Offa*, 39: 217–33.

BESTEMAN, J. C., J. M. Bos, and H. A. HEIDINGA 1990 (eds.) *Medieval Archaeology in the Netherlands*, Assen/Maastricht: Van Gorcum.

BINTLIFF, J. 1994, 'Territorial behaviour and the natural history of the Greek *Polis*', in E. Olshausen and H. Sonnabend (eds.), *Stuttgarter Kolloquium zur historischen Geographie des Altertums (Geographica Historica 7)*, Amsterdam: A. M. Hakkert: 207–47.

——and H. HAMEROW 1995 (eds.), *Europe Between Late Antiquity and the Middle Ages: Recent Archaeological and Historical Research in Western and Southern Europe*, BAR International Series, 617, Oxford: British Archaeological Reports.

BLAIR, J. 1994, *Anglo-Saxon Oxfordshire*, Stroud: Alan Sutton.

BLINKHORN, P. 1999, 'Of cabbages and kings: production, trade and consumption in middle Saxon England', in M. Anderton (ed.), *Anglo-Saxon Trading Centres: Beyond the Emporia*, Glasgow: Cruithne Press: 4–23.

BLOCH, M. L. B. 1961, *Feudal Society* (trans. L. Manyon), London: Routledge & Kegan Paul.

——1966, *French Rural History: An Essay on its Basic Characteristics* (trans. J. Sondheimer), London: Routledge & Kegan Paul. Originally published in 1931 as *Les Caractères originaux de l'histoire rurale Française*, Oslo, Cambridge, Mass: H. Aschenhoug, Harvard University Press.

——1995, 'The resurrection of the house amongst the Zafimaniry of Madagascar', in J. Carsten and S. Hugh-Jones (eds.), *About the House: Lévi-Strauss and Beyond*, Cambridge: Cambridge University Press: 69–83.

BLOK, D. 1960, *Een diplomatisch onderzeok van de oudste particuliere oorkonden van Werden*, Assen.

BLOEMERS, J. and J. THIJSSEN 1990, 'Facts and reflections on the continuity of settlement at Nijmegen between A.D. 400 and 750', in Besteman *et al.* (eds.): 133–47.

BODDINGTON, A. 1990, 'Models of settlement, burial and worship: the Final Phase reviewed', in E. Southworth (ed.), *Anglo-Saxon Cemeteries: A Reappraisal*, Stroud: Alan Sutton: 177–99.

BOELCKE, W. 1974, 'Die Frühmittelalterliche Wurzeln der südwestdeutschen Gewann-flur', in H.-J. Nitz (ed.), *Historisch-Genetische Siedlungsforschung*, Darmstadt: Wissenschaftliche Buchgesellschaft: 136–83.

BÖHM, K. 1993. ' "Elirespach" wiederentdeckt: ein neuer bajuwarischer Haustyp aus Irlbach', *Das archäologische Jahr in Bayern 1992*: 138–40.

BÖHME, H. W. 1991 (ed.), *Siedlungen und Landesausbau zur Salierzeit Teil 1: in den nördlichen Landschaften des Reiches*, Sigmaringen: Thorbecke Verlag.

BOURDIEU, P. 1973, 'The Berber house', in M. Douglas (ed.), *Rules and Meanings: An Anthropology of Everyday Knowledge*, Harmondsworth: Penguin Education: 98–110.

——1990, *The Logic of Practice* (trans. R. Nice), Cambridge: Polity Press.

BOURDILLON, J. 1994, 'The animal provisioning of Saxon Southampton', in Rackham (ed.): 120–5.

BRANDT, K. H. 1965, 'Stand der Untersuchung der Völkerwanderungszeitlicher Siedlung Bremen-Grambke I', *Germania*, 43: 395–401.

BRINK, S. 1996, 'Political and social structures in early Scandinavia', *TOR* 28: 235–81.

BRØGGER, A. and H. SCHETELIG 1928 (eds.), *Osebergfundet*, Bd. 2, Oslo: Universitets Oldsaksamling.

BROWN, M. 1991, *Anglo-Saxon Manuscripts*, London: British Library.

BRUCE-MITFORD, R. 1969, 'The art of the Codex Amiatinus', *Journal of the British Archaeol. Assoc.* 3rd ser. 32: 1–25.

BRÜCK, J. 2000. 'Settlement, landscape and social identity: the early-middle Bronze Age transition in Wessex, Sussex and the Thames valley', *Oxford Journal of Archaeology*, 19 (3): 273–300.

BULT, E. J. and D. P. HALLEWAS 1990, 'Archaeological evidence for early medieval settlement around the Meuse and Rhine deltas up to *c*. A.D. 1000', in Besteman *et al.* (eds.): 71–90.

CAESAR, *de bello Gallico IV* 1970, H. J. Edwards (ed. and trans.), revised edn., Loeb Classical Library, Cambridge, Mass: Harvard University Press.

CALLMER, J. 1987, 'Iron Age and early medieval settlement development in southern Scandinavia: some contemporary and future research perspectives', in G. Burenhult (ed.)., *Theoretical Approaches to Artefacts, Settlements and Society: Studies in Honour of Mats Malmer*, British Archaeological Reports 366 (International Series): 429–43, Oxford: BAR.

CAMPBELL, G. 1994, 'The preliminary archaeobotanical results from Anglo-Saxon West Cotton and Raunds' in Rackham (ed.): 65–82.

CAPELLE, T. 1974, 'Die karolingisch-ottonische Bronzegießersiedlung bei Kückshausen', *Frühmittelalterliche Studien*, 8: 294–302.

CARR, R., A. TESTER, and P. Murphy 1988, 'The Middle-Saxon settlement at Staunch Meadow, Brandon,' *Antiquity*, 62 (235): 371–6.

CHAPELOT, J. 1980, 'Le Fond de cabane dans l'habitat rural Ouest-Européen', *Archéologie Médiévale*, 10: 5–57.

—— and R. FOSSIER 1985, *The Village and House in the Middle Ages* (trans. H. Cleere), London: Batsford.

CHAPMAN, J. 1989, 'The early Balkan village', *Varia Archaeologica Hungarica*, 2: 33–55.

CHRISTENSEN, T. 1991, 'Lejre beyond Legend: the archaeological evidence', *Journal of Danish Archaeology*, 10: 163–85.

CHRISTIE, N. 1995, 'Italy and the Roman to Medieval transition', in Bintliff and Hamerow (eds.): 99–110.

CHRISTLEIN, R. 1978, *Die Alamannen; Archäologie eines lebendigen Volkes*, Stuttgart: K. Theiss.

——1981*a*, 'Kirchheim bei München, Oberbayern: Das Dorf des frühen Mittelalters', *Das Archäologische Jahr in Bayern 1980*: 162–3.

——1981*b*, 'Ausgrabungen 1980 und Schwerpunkte archäologischer Forschung in Bayern', *Das Archäologische Jahr in Bayern 1980*: 15–37.

CLAESSON, H. and P. SKALNIK 1978, *The Early State*, The Hague: Mouton.

CLUTTON-BROCK, J. 1976, 'The animal resources', in D. Wilson (ed.), *The Archaeology of Anglo-Saxon England*, Cambridge: Cambridge University Press: 373–92.

COLGRAVE, B. 1956 (ed. and trans.), *Felix's Life of Saint Guthlac*, Cambridge: Cambridge University Press.

COUTTS, C. 1992, 'Pottery and the Emporia: imported pottery in Middle Saxon England with particular reference to Ipswich', unpublished Ph.D. thesis, University of Sheffield.

CRABTREE, P. 1990, *West Stow, Suffolk: Early Anglo-Saxon Animal Husbandry*, East Anglian Archaeology, 47, Ipswich: Suffolk County Planning Department.

—— 1994, 'Animal exploitation in East Anglian villages', in Rackham (ed.): 40–54.

—— 1995, 'The symbolic role of animals in Anglo-Saxon England: evidence from burials and cremations', in K. Ryan and P. Crabtree (eds.), *The Symbolic Role of Animals in Archaeology*, Philadelphia: University of Pennsylvania: 21–6.

—— 1996, 'Production and consumption in an early complex society: animal use in Middle Saxon East Anglia', *World Archaeology*, 28: 58–75.

CRAWFORD, S. 1997, 'Britons, Anglo-Saxons and the Germanic burial ritual', in J. Chapman and H. Hamerow (eds.), *Migrations and Invasions in Archaeological Explanation*, Oxford: British Archaeological Reports: 45–72.

CUNLIFFE, B. 1972, 'Saxon and medieval settlement pattern in the region of Chalton, Hampshire', *Medieval Archaeology*, 16: 1–12.

—— 1973, 'Chalton, Hampshire: the evolution of a landscape', *Antiquaries Journal*, 53: 173–90.

—— 1974, *Iron Age Communities* (rev. edn.), London: Routledge & Kegan Paul.

DAMMINGER, F. 1998, 'Dwellings, settlements and settlement patterns in Merovingian southwest Germany and adjacent areas', in I. Wood (ed.), *Franks and Alamanni in the Merovingian Period: An Ethnographic Perspective*, San Marino: Boydell: 33–88.

DANNENBERG, H.-E. and H.-J. SCHULZE (eds.), *Geschichte des Landes zwischen Elbe und Weser*, Bd. 1, Stade: Ditzen Druck.

DANNHEIMER, H. 1987, *Auf den Spuren der Baiuwaren*, Pfaffenhofen: W. Ludwig.

DEMOLON, P. 1972, *Le village mérovingien de Brebières, VIᵉ–VIIᵉ siècles*, Arras: Commission départemental des monuments historiques du Pas-de-Calais.

DIX, B. 1986/7, 'The Raunds Area Project: second interim report', *Northamptonshire Archaeology*, 21: 3–29.

DIXON, P. 1982, 'How Saxon is the Saxon house?', in P. Drury (ed.), *Structural Reconstruction: Approaches to the Interpretation of the Excavated Remains of Buildings*, BAR British Series, Oxford: British Archaeological Reports, 110: 275–86.

DODGSHON, R. 1980, *The Origin of British Field Systems: An Interpretation*, London: Academic Press.

DÖLLING, H. 1958, *Haus und Hof in Westgermanischen Volksrechten*, Münster: Aschendorffsche Verlagsbuchhandlung.

DOMS, A. 1990, 'Siedlung und Friedhof der römischen Kaiserzeit und der Frühen Völkerwanderungszeit in Bielefeld-Sieker: Geschichte im Herzen Europas', in H. Hellenkamper, H. G. Horn, and B. Trier (eds.), *Archäologie in Nordrhein-Westfalen*, Köln: Römisch-Germanisches Museum der Stadt Köln: 264–70.

DONAT, P. and H. ULLRICH 1971, 'Einwohnerzahlen und Siedlungsgröße der Merowingerzeit', *Zeitschrift für Archäologie*, 5: 234–65.

DÖRFLER, K. 1990, 'Neue Untersuchungen zur Frage der Siedlungskontinuität im 6., 7. und 8. Jh. in Angeln und Schwansen', in Meier (ed.): 39–42.

—— and H. Kroll 1992, 'Von der Eisenzeit zum Mittelalter: Siedlungsforschung in Angeln und Schwansen', in M. Müller-Wille and D. Hoffmann (eds.), *Der Vergangenheit auf der Spur*, Neumünster: Karl Wachholtz Verlag: 111–40.

DOUGLAS, M. 1972, 'Symbolic orders in the use of domestic space', in Ucko *et al.* (eds.): 513–21.

DUBY, G. 1968, *Rural Economy and Country Life in the Medieval West* (trans. C. Postan), London: E. Arnold.

DUBY, G. 1974, *The Early Growth of the European Economy: Warriors and Peasants From the Seventh to the Twelfth Century* (trans. H. Clarke), Ithaca: Cornell University Press.

DUTTON, P. 1998 (ed. and trans.), *Charlemagne's Courtier: The Complete Einhard*, Ontario: Broadview Press.

DÜWEL, K., H. JANKUHN, H. SIEMS, and D. TEMPEL 1987 (eds.), *Untersuchungen zu Handel und Verkehr der vor- und frühgeschichtlichen Zeit in Mittel- und Nordeuropa: Bericht über die Kolloquien der Kommission für die Altertumskunde Mittel- und Nordeuropas in den Jahren 1980 bis 1985 Teil IV: Der Handel der Karolinger- und Wikingerzeit*, Abhandlungen der Akademie der Wissenschaften in Göttingen, Göttingen: Vandenhoeck and Ruprecht.

ECKHARDT, K. 1955 (ed.), *Pactus Legis Salicae II.i: 65 Titel-Text*, Göttingen: Musterschmidt-Verlag.

—— 1958, *Leges Alamannorum*, Bd. I, Göttingen: Musterschmidt-Verlag.

—— 1962, *Leges Alamannorum*, Bd. II, Witzenhansen: Deutschrechthicher Instituts-Verlag.

ENNEN, E. and W. Janssen 1979, *Deutsche Agrargeschichte von Neolithikum bis zur Schwelle des Industriezeitalters*, Wiesbaden: F. Steiner.

Es, W. A. VAN 1967, *Wijster: A Native Village Beyond the Imperial Frontier*, *Palaeohistoria*, 11.

—— 1973, 'Roman-period settlement on the "Free-Germanic" sandy soil of Drenthe, Overijssel and Gelderland', *Berichten der Rijksdienst voor Oudheidkundig Bodemonderzoek*, 23: 273–80.

—— and W. VERWERS 1980, *Excavations at Dorestad I: The Harbour, Hoogstraat 1*, Amersfoort: ROB.

FABECH, C. 1994, 'Reading society from the cultural landscape: South Scandinavia between sacral and political power', in Nielsen, Randsborg, and Thrane (eds.): 169–83.

—— and RINGTVED, J. 1999, *Settlement and Landscape. Proceedings of a Conference in Århus, Denmark, May 4–7 1998*, Moesgård: Jutland Archaeological Society.

FARNOUX, C. 1987, 'Les Fonds de cabane Mérovingiens Cisrhenans et leur contexte', *Amphora*, 47: 1–48.

FEHRING, G. 1991, *The Archaeology of Medieval Germany: An Introduction* (trans. R. Samson), London: Routledge.

FLANNERY, K. 1972, 'The origins of the village as a settlement type in Mesoamerica and the near East', in Ucko, Dimbleby, and Tringham (eds.): 23–53.

FOARD, G. 2001, 'Medieval woodland, agriculture and industry in Rockingham Forest', *Medieval Archaeology*, 45: 41–96.

FOWLER, P. 1981, 'Farming in the Anglo-Saxon landscape: an archaeologist's review', *Anglo-Saxon England*, 9: 263–80.

—— 1997, 'Farming in early medieval England: Some fields for thought', in J. Hines (ed.), *The Anglo-Saxons from the Migration Period to the Eighth Century*, Woodbridge: Boydell & Brewer: 245–60.

FRASER, D. 1968, *Village Planning in the Primitive World*, London: Studio Vista.

FRESHWATER, T. 1996, 'A lava quern workshop in Late Saxon London', *The London Archaeologist*, 8 (2): 39–45.

GAMESON, R. 1992, 'The cost of the Codex Amiatinus', *Notes & Queries*, Mar. 1992: 2–9.

GEBÜHR, M. 1998, 'Angulus desertus?', in H.-J. Häßler (ed.), *Studien zur Sachsenforschung*, 11, Oldenburg: Isensee Verlag: 43–86.

GERRETS, D. 1995, 'The Anglo-Frisian relationship seen from an archaeological point of view', in V. Faltings, A. Walker, and O. Wilts (eds.), *Friesische Studien III: Beiträge des Föhrer Symposiums zur Friesischen Philologie*, Odense University Press: 119–28.

——1999, 'Conclusions', in J. M. Besteman, J. C. Bos, D. Gerrets, H. A. Heidinga, and J. de Koning (eds.), *The Excavations at Wijnaldum vol. 1: Reports on Frisia in Roman and Medieval Times*, Rotterdam: A. A. Balkema: 331–42.

——and H. A. HEIDINGA 1996, 'The Frisian achievement', paper presented to the Arbeitsgemeinschaft für Sachsenforschung, York.

GERRETSEN, F. 1999, 'To build and to abandon. The cultural biography of late prehistoric houses and farmsteads in the southern Netherlands', *Archaeological Dialogues*, 6(2): 76–97.

GIDDENS, A. 1979, *Central Problems in Social Theory*, London: Macmillan Press.

GIFFEN, A. E. VAN 1936, 'Der Warf in Ezinge, Provinz Groningen, Holland, und seine westgermanischen Häuser', *Germania*, 20: 40–7.

GLOB, P. V. 1951, *Ard og Plov I Nordens Oldtid*, Århus: Univrsitetsforlaget Århus.

GOJDA, M. 1991, *The Ancient Slavs: Settlement and Society*, Edinburgh University Press.

GOODY, J. 1972, 'The evolution of the family', in P. Laslett (ed.), *Household and Family in Past Times*, Cambridge: Cambridge University Press: 103–24.

GREEN, F. 1981, 'Iron Age, Roman and Saxon crops: the archaeological evidence from Wessex', in M. Jones and G. Dimbleby (eds.), *The Environment of Man: The Iron Age to the Anglo-Saxon period*, BAR British Series, Oxford: British Archaeological Reports, 87: 129–53.

——1991, 'Landscape archaeology in Hampshire: the Saxon plant remains', in J. Renfrew (ed.), *New Light On Early Farming: Recent Developments in Palaeoethnobotany*, Edinburgh: Edinburgh University Press: 363–77.

GREGORY OF TOURS, *The History of the Franks*, 1927, O. M. Dalton (ed. and trans.), Oxford: Clarendon Press.

GRIMM, P. 1968, 'The royal palace at Tilleda: excavations from 1935–66, *Medieval Archaeology*, 12: 83–100.

GRISEBACH, H. 1917, *Das Polnische Bauernhaus. Beiträge zur polnische Landeskunde*, Berlin.

GROENEWOUDT, B. and M. VAN NIE 1995, 'Assessing the scale and organisation of Germanic iron production in Heeten, the Netherland', *Journal of European Archaeology*, 3 (2): 87–215.

GROENMAN VAN WAATERINGE, W. and L. VAN WIJNGAARDEN-BAKKER 1987 (eds.), *Farm Life in a Carolingian Village*, Assen: van Gorcum.

HAARNAGEL, W. 1979a, 'Das Eisenzeitliche Dorf «Feddersen Wierde»', in Jankuhn and Wenskus (eds.): 45–100.

——1979b, *Die Grabung Feddersen Wierde Bd. II: Methode, Hausbau, Siedlungs- und Wirtschaftsformen Sowie Sozialstruktur*, Wiesbaden: F. Steiner.

——and P. SCHMID 1984, 'Siedlungen', in Kossack *et al.* (eds.): 172–244.

HAARNAGEL, W., O. HARCK, and H.-J. HUNDT 1984, 'Güterproduktion', in Kossack *et al.* (eds.): 288–304.

HAGEN, A. 1995, *Anglo-Saxon Food and Drink: Production and Distribution*, Hockwold cum Wilton: Anglo-Saxon Books.

HALL, D. 1988, 'The Late Saxon countryside: villages and their fields', in D. Hooke (ed.), *Anglo-Saxon Settlements*, Oxford: Blackwell: 99–122.

——1995, *The Open Fields of Northamptonshire*, Northants Record Soc., 38, Northampton: Northants Record Society.

HALSALL, G. 1995a, *Settlement and Social Organization: The Merovingian Region of Metz*, Cambridge: Cambridge University Press.

——1995b, 'The Merovingian period in northeastern Gaul: Transition or change?', in Bintliff and Hamerow (eds.): 38–57.

HAMEROW, H. 1991, 'Settlement mobility and the "Middle Saxon Shift": rural settlements and settlement patterns in Anglo-Saxon England', *Anglo-Saxon England*, 20: 1–17.

——1992, 'Settlement on the gravels in the Anglo-Saxon period', in M. Fulford and L. Nichols (eds.), *Developing Landscapes of Lowland Britain: The Archaeology of the British Gravels*, London: Society of Antiquaries: 39–46.

——1993, *Mucking, Volume 2: The Anglo-Saxon Settlement*, London: English Heritage.

——1997, 'Migration theory and the Anglo-Saxon "identity crisis" ', in J. Chapman and H. Hamerow (eds.), *Migrations and Invasions in Archaeological Explanation*, Oxford: British Archaeological Reports IS 664: 33–44.

——1999a, 'Anglo-Saxon timber buildings: The continental connection', in H. Sarfatij, W. Verwers, and P. Woltering (eds.), *In Discussion with the Past: Archaeological Studies Presented to W. A. van Es*, Zwolle: SPA: 119–28.

——1999b, 'Angles, Saxons and Anglo-Saxons: rural centres, trade and production', *Studien zur Sachsenforschung*, 13: 189–207.

——2002, 'The development of the settlement', in G. Kinsley (ed.), *Catholme: An Anglo-Saxon Settlement on the Trent Gravels in Staffordshire*, Nottingham: University of Nottingham: 123–29.

HANSEN, T. E. 1987, 'Die Eisenzeitliche Siedlung bei Nørre Snede, Mitteljütland', *Acta Archaeologica*, 58: 171–200.

——D. MIKKELSEN, and S. HVASS 1991, 'Rural settlements in the seventh century', in P. Mortensen and B. Rasmussen (eds.), *Fra Stamme til Stat i Danmark, 2, Høvdingesamfund og Kongemagt*, Højbjerg/Århus: Jysk arkaeologisk Selskab: 17–27.

HÅRDH, B. 2000, 'Uppåkra—a centre in south Sweden in the 1st millennium AD', *Antiquity*, 74 (185): 640–8.

HÄRKE, H. 1992, *Angelsächsische Waffengräber des 5. bis 7. Jahrhundert*, Cologne: Rhineland Verlag.

——1997, 'Early Anglo-Saxon social structure', in J. Hines (ed.), *The Anglo-Saxons From the Migration Period to the Eighth Century: An Ethnographic Perspective*, Woodbridge: Boydell Press: 125–70.

——1999, 'Saxon warriors and Viking kings', Linacre Lecture, Oxford.

HASELGROVE, C. and C. SCULL 1995, 'The changing structure of rural settlement in southern Picardy during the first millennium A.D.', in Bintliff and Hamerow (eds.): 58–70.

HÄßLER, H.-J. 1991, 'Völkerwanderungszeit und Merowingerzeit', in H.-J. Häßler (ed.), *Ur- und Frühgeschichte in Niedersachsen*, Stuttgart: Theiss: 285–320.

HATTING, T. 1991, 'The Archaeozoology', in M. Bencard, L. Bender Jørgensen, and H. Brinch Madsen (eds.), *Ribe Excavations vol. 3*, Esbjerg: Sydjysk Universitetsforlag: 43–58.

——1994, 'The animal bones from the refuse layer at Lundeborg', in Nielsen *et al.* (eds.): 94–7.

HAUCK, K. 1987, 'Gudme in der Sicht der Brakteatenforschung', *Frühmittelalterliche Studien*, 21: 147–81.

——1994, 'Gudme als Kultort und seine Rolle beim Austausch von Bildformularen der Goldbrakteaten', in Nielsen *et al.* (eds.): 78–88.

HAWKES, S. C. and C. MATTHEWS 1985, 'Early Saxon settlements and burials on Puddlehill, near Dunstable, Bedfordshire', in S. C. Hawkes, J. Campbell, and P. D. C. Brown (eds.), *Anglo-Saxon Studies in Archaeology and History*, 4, Oxford: Oxford University Committee for Archaeology: 59–116.

HAYEN, H. 1979, *Der Bohlenweg VI (PR): im grossen Moor am Dümmer, Stand der Bearbeitung, Materialheft zur Ur- und Frühgeschichte Niedersachsens*, 15, Hildesheim: Lax.

——R. ULLEMEYER, and K. TIDOW 1981, *Einzeluntersuchungen zur Feddersen Wierde, Bd. III: Wagen, Textil- und Lederfunde, Bienenkorb, Schlackenanalysen*, Wiesbaden: F. Steiner.

HEATON, M. 1993, 'Two Mid-Saxon grain driers and later medieval features at Chantry Fields, Gillingham, Dorset', *Proc. of the Dorset Nat. Hist. and Archaeol. Soc.*, 114: 97–126.

HEDEAGER, L. 1992, *Iron Age Societies: From Tribe to State in Northern Europe 500 BC to AD 700*, Oxford: Blackwell.

——1993, 'The origin of the state in Scandinavia', in C. Prescott and B. Solberg (eds.), *Nordic TAG: Report from the Third Nordic TAG Conference 1990*, Bergen: University of Bergen: 22–30.

HEIDINGA, H. A. 1987, *Medieval Settlement and Economy North of the Lower Rhine*, Assen/Maastricht: Van Gorcum.

——1990, 'From Kootwijk to Rhenen: in search of the elite in the Central Netherlands in the early Middle Ages', in Bestemann, Bos, and Heidinga (eds.): 9–37.

——1994, 'Frankish settlement at Gennep: a Migration Period centre in the Dutch Meuse area', in Nielson, Randsborg, and Thrane (eds.): 202–9.

——1998, 'Gennep', in J. Hoops, *Reallexicon der Germanischen Altertumskunde*, Bd. 11, Berlin: W. de Gruyter: 202–9.

——and A. OFFENBERG 1992, *Op Zoek naar de vijfde eeuw: de Franken tussen Rijn en Maas*, Amsterdam: De Bataafsche Leeuw.

HERLIHY, D. 1985, *Medieval Households*, Cambridge, Mass: Harvard University Press.

HERSCHEND, F. 1989, 'Changing houses: early medieval house types in Sweden, 500–1100 A.D.', *TOR* 22: 79–103.

——1998, *The Idea of the Good*, Uppsala: University of Uppsala.

HEY, G., forthcoming, *Yarnton: Saxon and Medieval Settlement and Landscape*, Oxford: Oxford Archaeological Unit.

HIGGS, E. and M. JARMAN 1977, 'Yeavering's faunal remains', in B. Hope-Taylor, *Yeavering: An Anglo-British Centre of Early Northumbria*, London: HMSO: 325–32.

HIGHAM, N. 1992, *Rome, Britain and the Anglo-Saxons*, London: Seaby.

HILL, D. 1985, 'The construction of Offa's Dyke', *Antiquaries Journal*, 65: 140–2.

HINES, J. 1995, 'Cultural change and social organisation in early Anglo-Saxon England', in Ausenda (ed.): 75–88.

HINTON, D. 1998, 'Anglo-Saxon smiths and myths,' *Bull. John Rylands Univ. Library, Manchester*, 80: 3–21.

HODGES, R. 1989, *The Anglo-Saxon Achievement*, London: Duckworth.

——and D. WHITEHOUSE 1983, *Mohammed, Charlemagne and the Origins of Europe*, London: Duckworth.

——and B. HOBLEY 1988 (eds.), *The Rebirth of Towns in the West* A.D. *700–1050*, London: Council for British Archaeology.

HOLST, M. 1997, 'The dynamic of the iron age village: a technique for the relative-chronological analysis of area-excavated iron age settlements', *Journal of Danish Archaeology*, 13: 95–119.

HOOKE, D. 1988, 'Regional variation in southern and central England in the Anglo-Saxon period and its relationship to land units and settlement', in D. Hooke (ed.), *Anglo-Saxon Settlements*, Oxford: Blackwell: 123–51.

——1998, *The Landscape of Anglo-Saxon England*, Leicester: Leicester University Press.

HOPE-TAYLOR, B. 1977, *Yeavering: An Anglo-British Centre of Early Northumbria*, London: HMSO.

HUGHES, M. 1988, 'The Meon Valley Landscape Project', *Soc. Landscape Stud. Newsletter 1988*: 7–10.

HUIJTS, C. 1992, *De voor-historische boerderijbouw in Drenthe: Reconstructiemodellen van 1300 voor tot 1300 na Chr.*, Arnhem: Stichting Historisch Boerderij-onderzoek.

HULST, R. S. 1984, 'Ede-Op-den-Berg', *Jaarverslag ROB 1984*: 27–8.

——1985, 'Ede-Op-den-Berg', *Jaarverslag ROB 1985*: 35–6.

HVASS, S. 1979, 'Die völkerwanderungszeitliche Siedlung Vorbasse, Mitteljütland', *Acta Archaeologica*, 49, 61–111.

——1980, 'The Viking age settlement at Vorbasse, Central Jutland, *Acta Archaeologica*, 50: 137–72.

——1983, 'Vorbasse: The development of a settlement through the first millennium A.D.', *Journal of Danish Archaeology*, 2: 127–36.

——1985, *Hodde et vestjysk landsbysamfund fra aeldre jernalder*, Copenhagen: Akademisk Forlag.

——1986, 'Vorbasse: eine Dorfsiedlung während des 1. Jahrtausends n. Chr. in Mitteljütland, Dänemark', *Bericht der römisch-germanischen Kommission*, 67: 529–42.

——1988*a*, 'The status of the Iron Age settlement in Denmark', in M. Bierma, O. Harsema, and W. van Zeist (eds.), *Archeologie en Landschaap*, Rijksuniversiteit Groningen: 97–132.

——1988*b*, 'Iron Age settlements', in P. Mortensen and B. Rasmussen (eds.), *Fra Stamme til Staat i Danmark 1*, Århus Universitets Forlag: 91–2.

——1989, 'Rural settlements in Denmark in the first millennium A.D.', in Randsborg (ed.): 91–9.

——and B. STORGAARD 1993 (eds.), *Digging Into the Past: 25 Years of Archaeology in Denmark*, Copenhagen: Royal Society of Northern Antiquaries.

JAMES, E. 1979, 'Cemeteries and the problems of Frankish settlement in Gaul', in P. Sawyer (ed.), *Names, Words and Graves: Early Medieval Settlement*, Leeds: School of History, University of Leeds: 55–89.

——1988, *The Franks*, Oxford: Blackwell.

JAMES, S., A. MARSHALL, and M. MILLETT 1985, 'An early medieval building tradition', *Archaeological Journal*, 141: 182–215.

JANKUHN, H. 1979, 'Siedlungsarchäologie als Forschungsmethode', in Jankuhn and Wenskus (eds.): 19–43.

——1986, *Haithabu: ein Handelsplatz der Wikingerzeit*, Neumünster: Wachholtz Verlag.

——and R. WENSKUS (eds.) 1979, *Geschichtswissenschaft und Archäologie: Untersuchungen zur Siedlungs-, Wirtschafts- und Kirchengeschichte*, Sigmaringen: Thorbecke.

——W. JANSSEN, R. SCHMIDT-WIEGARD, and H. TIEFENBACH 1981, *Das Handwerk in vor- und frühgeschichtlicher Zeit, Teil I: Historische und rechtshistorische Beiträge und Untersuchungen zur Frühgeschichte der Gilde*, Göttingen: Vandenhoeck and Ruprecht.

——————————1983. *Das Handwerk in vor- und frühgeschichtlicher Zeit, Teil II: Archäologische und philologische Beiträge*, Göttingen: Vandenhoeck and Ruprecht.

JANSEN, H. 1999, 'Marketplaces and towns in Denmark 700–1100: a royal initiative', in C. Karkov, K. Wickham-Crowley, and B. Young (eds.), *Spaces of the Living and the Dead: An Archaeological Dialogue* (American Early Medieval Studies), Oxford: Oxbow Books: 119–32.

JANSSEN, W. 1976, 'Some major aspects of Frankish and medieval settlement in the Rhineland', in P. Sawyer (ed.), *Medieval Settlement: Continuity and Change*, London: Edward Arnold: 41–60.

——1983, 'Gewerbliche Produktion des Mittelalters als Wirtschaftsfaktor im ländlichen Raum', in Jankuhn *et al.* (eds.): 317–96.

JARL HANSEN, H. 1989*a*, 'Dankirke: Affluence in late Iron Age Denmark', in Randsborg (ed.): 123–8.

——1989*b*, 'Dankirke: Eisenzeitliche Siedlung und Handelszentrum: Übersicht über die Ausgrabungen von 1965–70', *KUML 1988/89*: 201–47.

JONES, M. 1982, 'Crop production in Roman Britain', in D. Miles (ed.), *The Romano-British Countryside*, BAR 103, Oxford: British Archaeological Reports: 97–198.

JONES, M. U. 1973, 'An ancient landscape palimpsest at Mucking, Essex', *Essex Archaeology and History*, 5: 6–12.

——1979, 'Saxon sunken huts: problems of interpretation', *Archaeological Journal*, 136: 53–9

——and W. T. JONES 1975, 'The crop-mark sites at Mucking, Essex, England', in R. Bruce-Mitford (ed.), *Recent Archaeological Excavations in Europe*, London: Routledge & Kegan Paul: 133–87.

JÖNS, H. 1993, 'Zur Eisenverhüttung in Schleswig-Holstein in vor- und frühgeschichtlicher Zeit', *Offa*, 49/50: 41–55.

——1997, *Frühe Eisengewinnung in Joldelund, Kreis Nordfriesland: ein Beitrag zur Siedlungs- und Technikgeschichte Schleswig-Holsteins*, Universitätsforschungen zur prähistorischen Archäologie, Bd. 40, Bonn: R. Habelt.

JÖNS, H. 1999, 'Iron production in northern Germany during the Iron Age', in C. Fabech and J. Ringtved (eds.), *Settlement and Landscape: Proceedings of a Conference in Århus, May 4–7, 1998*, Moesgård: Jutland Archaeological Society: 29–60.

JØRGENSEN, L. 1991, 'Schatzfunde und Agrarproduktion: Zentrumsbildung auf Bornholm in 5.–6. Jh. n. Chr.', *Studien zur Sachsenforschung*, 7, Hildesheim: Verlag August Lax: 153–86.

——1993, 'The find material from Gudme II: composition and interpretation', in Nielson, Randsborg, and Thrane (eds.): 53–63.

——1998, 'En storgård fra vikingetid ved Tissø, Sjaelland—en foreløbig praesentation', in L. Larsson and B. Hårdh (eds.), *Acta Archaeologica Lundensia*, ser. 8, no. 28: 233–48.

——2000, 'Manor and market at Lake Tissø', paper delivered to a Conference, 'The Archaeology of Inland Markets, Fairs and "Productive Sites" *c.*650–850', Oxford, 15–17 December 2000.

KEEVIL, G., forthcoming, *Excavations at Eynsham Abbey*.

KELLY, F. 1998, *Early Irish Farming: A Study Based Mainly on the Law-Texts of the Seventh and Eighth Centuries* A.D., Dublin: Institute for Advanced Studies.

KILMURRY, K. 1980, *The Pottery Industry of Stamford, Lincolnshire, c.* AD *850–1250*, BAR Brit. Ser., 84, Oxford: British Archaeological Reports.

KINSLEY, G., 2002, *Catholine. An Anglo-Saxon Settlement on the Trent Gravels in Staffordshire*, Nottingham: University of Nottingham.

KOKABI, M. and M. RÖSCH 1990, 'Knochen und Pflanzenreste des frühen Mittelalter von Lauchheim, Ostalbkreis', *Archäologische Ausgrabungen in Baden-Wurttemberg 1990*: 215–19.

KOOI, P. 1995, 'Het project Peelo: het onderzoek in de Jaren 1981, 1982, 1986, 1987 EN 1988', *Palaeohistoria*, 35/6: 169–306.

——G. DELGER, and K. KLAASSENS 1989, 'Een verkennend onderzoek op de Westakker-ste Dalen (Drenthe)', *Paleo-Aktueel*, 1: 64–7.

KOOISTRA, L. 1996, *Borderland Farming: Possibilities and Limitations of Farming in the Roman Period and Early Middle Ages Between the Rhine and Meuse*, Amersfoort/Assen: van Gorcum.

KOSSACK, G. 1984, 'Hausfleiß und Verkehrswirtschaft', in Kossack *et al.* (eds.): 305–9.

——K.-E. BEHRE, and P. SCHMID (eds.) 1984, *Archäologische und naturwissenschaftliche Untersuchungen an ländlichen und frühstädtischen Siedlungen im deutschen Küstengebiet vom 5. Jh. vor Chr. bis zum 11. Jh. n. Chr., Bd 1: ländliche Siedlungen*, Weinheim: Deutsche Forschungsgemeinschaft.

KROLL, H. 1986, 'Zur Bearbeitung der Pflanzenfunde der Ausgrabungen von Kosel, Schwansen', *Berichte der Römisch-Germanischen Kommission*, 67: 445–53.

——1990, 'Zum vorgeschichtlichen Ackerbau von Kosel', in D. Meier (ed.), *Niende Tvaerfaglige Vikingesymposium*, Kiel: University of Kiel: 43–7.

KROMANN, A., P. O. NIELSEN, K. RANDSBORG, P. VANG PETERSEN, and P. O. THOMSEN 1991, 'Gudme and Lundeborg—et fynsk rigdomscenter i jernalderen', *Nationalmuseets Arbejdsmark 1991*: 144–61.

KÜHN, H. J. 1993, 'Ausgrabung einer Siedlung des frühen und des hohen Mittelalters bei Schuby, Kr. Schleswig-Flensburg', in D. Meier (ed.), *Archäologie in Schleswig 1/1991*, Kiel: Christian-Albrechts Universität: 45–8.

KURZE, F. and G. PERTZ 1895 (eds.), *Annales regni Francorum, inde ab a. 741 usque ad a. 829*, repr. 1950, Hannover: Hahn.

LANTING, J. 1983, 'Kroniek van opgravingen en vondsten in Drenthe in 1980 en 1981', *Nieuwe Drentse Volksalmanak*, 100: 211–12.

LAVER, H. 1909, 'Ancient type of huts at Athelney', *Proc. Somerset Archaeological Soc.* 55: 175–80.

LAYTON, R. 1995, 'Functional and historical explanations for village social organization in northern Europe', *Journal of the Royal Anthropological Institute*, NS 1 (4): 703–23.

LEACH, E. 1976, *Culture and Communication: The Logic By Which Symbols Are Connected*, Cambridge: Cambridge University Press.

LEBECQ, S. 1983, *Marchands et navigateurs frisons du haut moyen âge*, Lille: Presses Universitatires de Lille.

LEBLAY, J.-C., S. LEPETS, and J.-H. YVINEC, 1997, 'L'Élevage dans l'Antiquité tardive en Île-de-France', in P. Ouzoulias and P. van Ossel (eds.), *Les Campagnes de l'Île-de-France de Constantin à Clovis*, Paris: 50–67.

LEEDS, E. T. 1947, 'A Saxon village at Sutton Courtenay, Berks.: a third report', *Archaeologia*, 112: 73–94.

LERCHE, G. 1996, 'Radiocarbon dating of agricultural implements in *Tools & Tillage*, 1968–95: revised calibrations and recent additions', *Tools & Tillage*, 7 (4): 172–206.

LETHBRIDGE, T. and C. TEBBUTT 1933, 'Huts of the Anglo-Saxon period', *Cambridge Antiquarian Society's Communications*, 33: 133–51.

LØKEN, T. 1987, 'The settlement at Forsandmoen: An Iron Age village in Rogaland, southwest Norway', *Studien zur Sachsenforschung* 6, Hildesheim: Verlag August Lax: 155–68.

——1992*a*, 'Ullandhaug sett i lys av Forsandundersøkelsene', in A. Skår (ed.), *Ams-Småtrykk 26 Gammel gård gjenoppstår*, Stavanger: Arkologisk museum I Stavanger: 31–45.

——1992*b*, 'Settlement pattern through 2000 years of the Bronze Age and Early Iron Age at Forsandmoen in Rogaland, Norway', paper presented at the forty-third meeting of the Arbeitsgemeinschaft für Sachsenforschung, Aalborg.

LORREN, C. 1989, 'Le Village de St. Martin de Trainecourt à Mondeville (Calvados) de l'Antiquité au Haut Moyen Âge', in H. Atsma (ed.), *La Neustrie: les pays au nord de la Loire de 650 à 850: colloque historique international*, Thorbecke: Sigmaringen: 439–66.

——1996, 'Einige Beobachtungen über das frühmittelalterliche Dorf in Nordgallien', in A. Wieczorek, P. Périn, K. v. Welck, and W. Menghin (eds.), *Die Franken: Wegbereiter Europas*, Mainz: Philipp von Zabern: 745–53.

——and P. PÉRIN, (eds.) 1995, *L'Habitat rurale du haut-moyen âge (France, Pays-Bas et Danemark)*, Actes des XIVe journées internationales d'archéologie mérovingienne, Paris 1993 (Rouen 1995) Mémoires AFAM 6.

——1997, 'Images de la Gaule rurale au VIᵉ siecle', in N. Gauthier and H. Galinié (eds.), *Grégoire de Tours et l'Espace Gaulois*, Tours: Revue archéologique du Centre de la France: 93–109.

LOSCO-BRADLEY, S. 1977, 'Catholme', *Current Archaeology*, 59: 358–63.

——and H. WHEELER 1984, 'Anglo-Saxon settlement in the Trent Valley: some aspects', in M. Faull (ed.), *Studies in Late Anglo-Saxon Settlement*, Oxford: Oxford University Dept of External Studies: 101–14.

LOVELUCK, C. 1998, 'A high-status Anglo-Saxon settlement at Flixborough, Lincs.', *Antiquity*, 72 (275): 146–61.

——2001, 'Wealth, waste and conspicuous consumption. Flixborough and its importance for mid and late Saxon settlement studies', in H. Hamerow and A. MacGregor (eds.), *Image and Power in the Archaeology of Early Medieval Britain: Essays in Honour of Rosemary Cramp*, Oxford: Oxbow: 78–130.

LÜDTKE, H. 1989, 'Fünf Karten zur Verbreitung mittelalterlichen Keramik in Skandinavien', *Hammaburg NF*, 9: 215–26.

McDONNELL, G. 1989, 'Iron and its alloys in the fifth to eleventh centuries AD in England', *World Archaeology*, 20 (3): 373–82.

MACKRETH, D. 1996, *Orton Hall Farm: A Roman and Early Anglo-Saxon Farmstead*, Manchester: University of Manchester.

MALIM, T. and J. HINES 1998, *The Anglo-Saxon Cemetery at Edix Hill (Barrington A), Cambridgeshire*, CBA Research Report 112, York: Council for British Archaeology.

MARSHALL, A. and G. MARSHALL 1993, 'Differentiation, change and continuity in Anglo-Saxon buildings', *Archaeological Journal*, 150: 366–402.

MARX, K. 1964, *Pre-Capitalist Economic Formations* (trans. J. Cohen; ed. E. J. Hobsbawm), London: Lawrence and Wishart.

MATTHEWS, C. and S. HAWKES 1985, 'Early Saxon settlements and burials on Puddlehill, near Dunstable, Bedfordshire', in S. Hawkes, J. Campbell, and D. Brown (eds.), *Anglo-Saxon Studies in Archaeology and History*, 4, Oxford: Oxford University Committee for Archaeology: 59–116.

MEIER, D. 1990*a* (ed.), *Beretning fra niende tvaerfaglige vikingesymposium*, Kiel: University of Aarhus and Christian-Albrechts University, Kiel.

——1990*b*, 'Ländliche wikingerzeitliche und hochmittelalterliche Siedlungen im Umland von Haithabu', in Meier (ed.): 16–32.

——1991, 'Ausgrabungen in Kosel', in Müller-Wille and Hoffmann (eds.): 114–34.

——1994, *Die wikingerzeitliche Siedlung von Kosel (-West), Kreis Rendsburg-Eckernförde*, Neumünster: K. Wachholtz.

METCALF, M. 1996, 'Viking-Age numismatics 2: coinage in the northern lands in Merovingian and Carolingian times, *Numismatic Chronicle*, 156: 399–428.

MILES, D. 1984, *Archaeology at Barton Court Farm, Abingdon, Oxon.*, Oxford: Oxford Archaeological Unit.

MILLETT, M. 1990, *The Romanisation of Britain*, Cambridge: Cambridge University Press.

——with S. JAMES 1984, 'Excavations at Cowdery's Down, Basingstoke, 1978–1981, *Archaeological Journal*, 140: 151–279.

MILOJČÍC, V. 1983, 'Handwerk auf dem Runden Berg bei Urach: Zusammenfassung', in Jankuhn *et al.* (eds.): 90–2.

MØLLER HANSEN, K. and H. HØIER 2000, 'Næs: a Viking Age settlement with flax production', *KUML 2000*: 59–89.

MORELAND, J. 2000, 'The significance of production in eighth-century England', in L. Hansen and C. Wickham (eds.), *The Long Eighth Century: Production, Distribution and Demand*, Leiden: Brill: 69–104.

MORTIMER, R. 2000, 'Bloodmoor Hill, Carlton Colville, Suffolk: excavation of the early Anglo-Saxon settlement. An interim statement, 1998–2000'. Unpublished report of the Cambridge Archaeological Unit.

MÜLLER-WILLE, M. 1973, 'Acker- und Flurformen', in J. Hoops, *Reallexicon der Germanischen Altertumskunde*, Bd. 1, Berlin: W. de Gruyter: 45–53.

——1979, 'Siedlungs und Flurformen als Zeugnisse frühgeschichtlicher Betriebsformen der Landwirtschaft', in Jankuhn and Wenskus (eds.): 355–72.

——1983, 'Der Schmied im Spiegel archäologischer Quellen: zur Aussage von Schmiedegräbern der Wikingerzeit', in Jankuhn *et al.* (eds.): 216–60.

——1988, 'Hedeby und sein Umland', in B. Hårdh (ed.), *Trade and Exchange in Prehistory, Archaeologia Lundensia*, 16, Lund: Lunds Universitets Historiska Museum: 271–8.

——1994/5, 'Archäologische Untersuchungen ländlicher Siedlungen der Wikingerzeit im Umland des Frühstädischen Handelsplatz Hedeby', *Acta Praehistorica et Archaeologica*, Bd. 26/7: 39–56.

——1999, 'Settlement and non-agrarian production from the high mountain region to the shoreline: an introduction', in C. Fabech and J. Ringtved (eds.), *Settlement and Landscape: Proceedings of a Conference in Århus, May 4–7 1998*, Moesgård: Jutland Archaeological Society: 205–11.

——and D. HOFFMANN (eds.) 1992, *Der Vergangenheit auf der Spur: Archäologische Siedlungsforschung in Schleswig-Holstein*, Neumünster: K. Wachholtz Verlag.

——W. DÖRFLER, D. MEIER, and H. KROLL 1988, 'The transformation of rural society, economy and landscape during the first millennium A.D.: Archaeological and palaeobotanical contributions from northern Germany and southern Scandinavia', *Geografiska Annaler*, 70B: 53–68.

MURPHY, P. 1994, 'The Anglo-Saxon landscape and rural economy: some results from sites in East Anglia and Essex', in Rackham (ed.): 23–39.

MYHRE, B. 1978, 'Agrarian development, settlement history and social organization in southwest Norway in the Iron Age', in K. Kristiansen and C. Paludin-Muller (eds.), *New Directions in Scandinavian Archaeology*, Copenhagen: National Museum of Denmark: 224–65.

——1982, 'Settlements of Southwest Norway during the Roman and Migration Periods', *Offa*, 39: 197–215.

——1987, 'Chieftain's graves and chiefdom territories in southern Norway in the Migration Period', *Studien zur Sachsenforschung*, 6, Hildesheim: Verlag August Lax: 169–88.

MYRES, J. N. L. 1977, *A Corpus of Anglo-Saxon Pottery*, 2 vols., Oxford: Oxford University Press.

NÄSMAN, U. 1983, review of B. Myhre, *The Farm at Ullandhaug I: Farm Houses in the Iron Age and Early Middle Ages in Southwest Norway* (Stavanger, 1980), *Norwegian Archaeological Review*, 16 (1): 62–7.

——1987, 'House, village and settlement', in *Danmarks længste udgravning: arkæologi på naturgassens vej 1979–86*, Herning: Poul Kristensen: 457–65.

——1989, 'The Germanic Iron Age and Viking Age in Danish archaeology', *Journal of Danish Archaeology*, 8: 159–87.

NÄSMAN, U. 2000, 'Exchange and politics: the eighth–early ninth centuries in Denmark', in L. Hansen and C. Wickham (eds.), *The Long Eighth Century: Production, Distribution and Demand*, Leiden: Brill: 35–68.

——and E. ROESDAHL 1993, 'The late Germanic and Viking Period', in Hvass and Storgaard (eds.): 181–6.

——and B. RASMUSSEN (eds.) 1998, *Settlement and Cultural Landscape: A Report*, Århus: University of Århus.

NEHLSEN, H. 1981, 'Die rechtliche und soziale Stellung der Handwerker in den germanischen Leges', in Jankuhn *et al.*

NEWMAN, J. 1989, 'East Anglian Kingdom Survey—final interim report on the Southeast Suffolk Pilot Field Survey', *Bull. Sutton Hoo Research Committee*, 6, Woodbridge: Sutton Hoo Research Trust: 17–20.

——1992, 'The late Roman and Anglo-Saxon settlement pattern in the Sandlings of Suffolk', in M. Carver (ed.), *The Age of Sutton Hoo: The Seventh Century in North-Western Europe*, Woodbridge: The Boydell Press: 25–38.

——1999, '*Wics*, trade and hinterlands: the Ipswich region', in M. Anderton (ed.), *Anglo-Saxon Trading Centres: Beyond the Emporia*, Glasgow: Cruithne Press: 32–48.

——forthcoming, 'Barham, Suffolk: Middle Saxon market or meeting place?'

NICE, A. 1992, 'L'Habitat et la nécropole de Goudelancourt-les-Pierrepont (Aisne), VIᵉ–VIIᵉ siècle: état de la recherche', in *Archéologie Mérovingien, Bulletin de Liaison*, 16: 40–5.

NIELSEN, L. C. 1980, 'Omgård', *Acta Archaeologica*, 50: 173–208.

NIELSEN, P., K. RANDSBORG, and H. THRANE (eds.) 1993/4, *The Archaeology of Gudme and Lundeborg: Papers Presented at a Conference at Svendborg, October 1991*, Copenhagen: Universitetsforlaget.

NILSSON, T. 1990, 'Stentinget: an inland site with trade and handicrafts from the later Iron Age', *KUML 1990*: 3–9.

NISSEN JAUBERT, A. 1998, 'Habitats ruraux et communautés rurales', *Ruralia II: Conference Ruralia II—SPA, 1–7 September 1997*, Prague: Archeologický ústav AV ČR: 213–25.

——1999, 'Ruptures et continuités de l'habitat rural du haut Moyen Âge dans le nord-ouest de l'Europe', in F. Braemer, S. Cleuziou, and A. Coudart (eds.), *Habitat et société: Actes des Rencontres 22–23–24 Octobre 1998*, Antibes: Association pour la promotion et la diffusion des connaissances archéologiques: 519–33.

NØRBACH, L. 1999, 'Organizing iron production and settlement in northwestern Europe during the Iron Age', in Fabech and Ringtved (eds.): 237–47.

NORR, S. and A. SUNDKVIST 1995, 'Valsgärde revisited. Fieldwork resumed after 40 years', *TOR* 27 (2): 395–418.

O'BRIEN, C. and R. MIKET, 1991, 'The early medieval settlement of Thirlings, Northumberland', *Durham Archaeological Journal* 7: 57–92.

O'CONNOR, T. 1994, '8th–11th century economy and environment in York', in Rackham (ed.): 136–47.

OP DEN VELDE, W., W. J. DE BOONE, and A. POL 1984, 'A survey of sceatta finds from the Low Countries', in D. Hill and D. M. Metcalf (eds.), *Sceattas in England and on the Continent: The Seventh Oxford Symposium on Coinage and Monetary History*, BAR British Series, 128, Oxford: British Archaeological Report: 117–45.

ORWIN, C. and C. ORWIN 1938, *The Open Fields*, Oxford: Clarendon Press.

OUZOULIAS, P. 1997, 'La Déprise agricole du Bas-Empire: un mythe historiographique?', in P. Ouzoulias and P. van Ossel (eds.), *Les Campagnes de l'Île-de-France de Constantin à Clovis*, Paris: 10–20.

PAGE, R. 1970, *Life in Anglo-Saxon England*, London and New York: Batsford.

PALMER, J. B. O. 2002, *The Emporia of Mid-Saxon England: Hinterlands and Trade*, unpublished D. Phil. thesis, University of Oxford.

PALS, J. 1987*a*, 'Reconstruction of landscape and plant husbandry', in Groenman van Waateringe and van Wijngaarden-Bakker (eds.): 52–96.

——1987*b*, 'Observations on the economy of the settlement', in Groenman van Waateringe and van Wijngaarden-Bakker (eds.): 118–29.

PARKHOUSE, J. 1997, 'The distribution and exchange of Mayen lava quernstones in early medieval northwest Europe', *Papers of the 'Medieval Europe Brugge 1997' Conference*, vol. 3, *Exchange and Trade in Medieval* Europe, Zellik: Instituut voor het Archeologisch Patrimonium: 97–106.

PAULSEN, P. 1967, *Alamannische Adelsgräber von Niederstotzingen*, Stuttgart: Müller & Graf.

——1992, *Die Holzfunde aus dem Gräberfeld bei Oberflacht und ihre Kulturhistorische Bedeutung*, Stuttgart: K. Theiss.

——and H. SCHACH-DÖRGES 1972, *Holzhandwerk der Alamannen*, Stuttgart: W. Kohlhammer.

PÉRIN, P. 1992, 'La Part du Haut Moyen Âge dans le genèse des terroirs de la France médiévale', in M. Parisse and X. Barral i Altet (eds.), *Le Roi de France et son royaume autour de l'an Mil*, Paris: Picard: 225–35.

PEYTREMANN, E. 1992, 'L'Habitat rural du Haut Moyen Age (V^e–Xe siècle): un état de la recherche', 2 vols., unpublished thesis, University of Paris I.

PILET, C., A. ALDUC-LE-BAGOUSSE, J. BLONDIAUX, L. BUCHET, and J. PILET-LEMIÈRE 1992, 'Le Village de Sannerville, "Lirose" fin de la période gauloise au VIIe siècle ap. J.-C.', *Archéologie Médiévale*, 22: 1–97.

PIRLING, R. 1986, *Römer und Franken am Niederrhein: Katalog-Handbuch des Landschaftsmuseums Burg Linn in Krefeld*, Mainz: Philip von Zabern.

——H.-J. HUNDT, and B. WINTER 1989, *Das römisch-fränkische Gräberfeld von Krefeld-Gellep, 1966–1974*, Stuttgart: Franz Steiner.

PLINY, *Natural History*, H. Rackham (ed.), Loeb Classical Library, 1971.

POWLESLAND, D. 1990, 'West Heslerton: The Anglian settlement. Interim report on excavations in 1989', *Medieval Settlement Research Group Annual Report*, 4: 46.

——1997, 'Anglo-Saxon settlements, structures, form and layout', in J. Hines (ed.), *The Anglo-Saxons from the Migration Period to the Eighth Century: An Ethnographic Perspective*, Woodbridge: Boydell Press: 101–16.

PRUMMEL, W. 1983, *Excavations at Dorestad 2: an archaeozoological study*, Amersfoort: ROB.

RACKHAM, J. 1994*a* (ed.), *Environment and Economy in Anglo-Saxon England* (CBA Res Rept. 89), York: Council for British Archaeology.

——1994*b*, 'Economy and environment in Saxon London', in Rackham (ed): 126–35.

RADFORD, C. R. 1958, 'The Saxon house: a review and some parallels', *Medieval Archaeology*, 1: 27–38.

RAHTZ, P. 1976, 'Buildings and rural settlement', in D. Wilson (ed.), *The Archaeology of Anglo-Saxon England*, Cambridge: Cambridge University Press: 49–98.

RAMQVIST, P. 1983, *Gene: On the Origin, Function and Development of Sedentary Iron Age Settlement in Northern Sweden*, Umeå: University of Umeå.

——1992, 'Building traditions in northern and northeastern Europe during the Iron Age', in B. Hårdh and B. Wyszomirska-Werbart (eds.), *Contacts Across the Baltic Sea During the Late Iron Age (5th–12th centuries)*, University of Lund, Inst. of Archaeology Report, 43: 73–83.

RANDSBORG, K. 1980, *The Viking Age in Denmark: The Formation of a State*, London: Duckworth.

——1985, 'Subsistence and settlement in northern temperate Europe in the first millennium AD', in G. Barker and C. Gamble (eds.), *Beyond Domestication in Prehistoric Europe: Investigations in Subsistence Archaeology and Social Complexity*, London: Academic Press: 233–65.

——1989 (ed.), *The Birth of Europe: Archaeology and Social Development in the First Millennium A.D.*, Rome: 'L'Erma' di Bretschneider.

——1994, 'Gudme-Lundeborg: Interpretative scenarios and thoughts', in P. Nielson *et al.* (eds.): 209–13.

——1998, 'The Migration Period: model history and treasure', in R. Hodges and W. Bowden (eds.), *The Sixth Century: Production, Distribution and Demand*, Leiden: Brill: 61–88.

RAPOPORT, A. 1979, 'Cultural origins of architecture', in J. Snyder and A. Catanese (eds.), *Introduction to Architecture*, New York: McGraw-Hill: 2–20.

——1980, 'Cross-cultural aspects of environmental design', *Human Behaviour and Environment*, 4: 7–46.

REGTEREN ALTENA, C. VAN 1990, 'On the growth of young medieval archaeology: a recollection', in Besteman *et al.* (eds.): 1–8.

REICHMANN, C. 1981, 'Siedlungsreste der vorrömischen Eisenzeit, jüngeren römischen Kaiserzeit und Merowingerzeit in Soest-Arday', *Germania*, 59 (1): 51–77.

——1982, 'Ländliche Siedlungen der Eisenzeit und des Mittelalters in Westfalen', *Offa*, 39: 163–82.

——1984, 'Zur Entstehungsgeschichte des Niederdeutschen Hallenhauses', *Rheinisch-westfälische Zeitschrift für Volkskunde*, 29. Jahrgang: 31–64.

——1991, 'Der ländliche Hausbau in Niederdeutschland zur Zeit der Salischen Kaiser', in Böhme (ed.): 277–98.

REICHSTEIN, J. 1987, 'Ausgrabungen in Alt-Archsum auf Sylt', *Berichte der Römisch-germanischen Kommission*, 67: 373–84.

REICHSTEIN, H. 1991, *Die Fauna des germanischen Dorfes Feddersen Wierde*, Stuttgart: F. Steiner.

——1994, *Die Saugtiere und Vögel aus der frühgeschichtlichen Wurt Elisenhof*, Frankfurt: Peter D. Lang.

——and M. TIESSEN 1974, *Berichte uber die Ausgrabungen in Haithabu 7: Untersuchungen an Tierknochenfunden*, Neumünster: K. Wachholtz.

RENFREW, C. 1975, 'Trade as action at a distance: Questions of integration and communication', in J. Sabloff and C. Lamberg-Karlovskey (eds.), *Ancient Civilisation and Trade*, Albuquerque: University of New Mexico Press: 3–59.

—— 1986, 'Introduction: peer-polity interaction and socio-political change', in C. Renfrew and J. Cherry (eds.), *Peer polity interaction and socio-political change*, Cambridge: Cambridge University Press.

RIVERS, T. 1977 (ed. and trans.), *Laws of the Alamans and Bavarians*, Philadelphia: University of Pennsylvania Press.

—— 1986 (ed. and trans.), *Laws of the Salian and Ripuarian Franks*, New York: AMS Press.

RÖBER, R. 1990, *Die Keramik der frühmittelalterlichen Siedlung von Warendorf: ein Beitrag zur Sächsischen Siedlungsware Nordwestdeutschlands*, Bonn: Habelt.

ROBINSON, D. 1991, 'Plant remains from the late Iron Age/early Viking Age settlement at Gammel Lejre', *Journal of Danish Archaeology*, 10: 191–8.

—— 1994, 'Botanical investigations at Lundeborg I: some preliminary findings', in Nielsen *et al.* (eds.): 98–102.

ROE, F. 1997, 'The worked stone from Yarnton, Worton Rectory Farm', unpublished report of the Oxford Archaeological Unit.

ROWLEY, T. 1981, *The Origins of Open-Field Agriculture*, London: Croom Helm.

ROYMANS, N. 1996, 'The sword or the plough: regional dynamics in the romanisation of Belgic Gaul and the Rhineland area', in N. Roymans (ed.), *From the Sword to the Plough*, Amsterdam: Amsterdam University Press: 9–126.

RUAS, M.-P. 1988, 'Alimentation végétale, pratiques agricole et environment, du VIIᵉ au Xᵉ siècle (Villiers-le-Sec et Baillet-en-France)' in *Un village au temps de Charlemagne: Moines et paysans de l'abbaye de Saint-Denis du VIIᵉ siècle à l'An Mil*, Paris: éditions de la Réunion des musées nationaux: 203–17.

RUSSEL, A. 1984, 'Early Anglo-Saxon Ceramics from East Anglia: A Microprovenience Study', unpublished Ph.D. thesis, University of Southampton.

SAMSON, R. 1987, 'Social structure from *Reihengräber*: Mirror or mirage?', *Scottish Archaeological Review*, 4: 116–26.

SAWYER, P. 1968, *Anglo-Saxon Charters: An Annotated List and Bibliography*, London: Royal Historical Society.

SCHIEK, S. 1992, *Das Gräberfeld der Merowingerzeit bei Oberflacht*, Stuttgart: Theiss.

SCHLÜTER, W. 1975, 'Vorbericht über die Ausgrabungen auf der Pipinsburg bei Osterode am Harz im Jahre 1974, *Nachrichten aus Niedersachsens Urgeschichte*, 44: 113–40.

SCHMID, P. 1977, 'Zur chronologische Auswertung von Siedlungskunden des 4.–5. Jhs. n. Chr. im Küstengebiet zwischen Elbe und Weser', in G. Kossack and J. Reichstein (eds.), *Archäologische Beiträge zur Chronologie der Völkerwanderungszeit*, Bonn: Rudolf Habelt Verlag: 29–41.

—— 1982, 'Ländliche Siedlungen der vorrömischen Eisenzeit bis Völkerwanderungszeit im niedersächsischen Küstengebiet', *Offa*, 39: 73–96.

—— 1995, 'Archäologische Ergebnisse zur Siedlungs- und Wirtschaftsweise in der Marsch', in Dannenberg und Schulze (eds.): 221–50.

—— and W. H. ZIMMERMANN 1976, 'Flögeln: Zur Struktur einer Siedlung des 1. bis 5. Jhs. n. Chr. im Küstengebiet der südlichen Nordsee', *Probleme der Küstenforschung*, 11: 1–77.

SCHMIDT, H. 1990, 'Viking Age buildings', *Journal of Danish Archaeology*, 9: 194–202.

—— 1991, 'Reconstruction of the Lejre hall', *Journal of Danish Archaeology*, 10: 186–90.

SCHMIDT, H. 1994, *Building Customs in Viking Age Denmark* (trans. J. Olsen), Herning, Denmark: Poul Kristensen Forlag.

SCHMIDT-WIEGAND R. 1977, 'Das Dorf nach dem Stammesrechten des Kontinents', in H. Jankuhn, R. Schützeichel, and F. Schwind (eds.), *Das Dorf der Eisenzeit und des frühen Mittelalters: Siedlungsform, wirtschaftliche Funktion, soziale Struktur*, Göttingen: Vandenhoeck and Ruprecht: 408–43.

SCHÖN, M. 1988. Gräberfelder der Römischen Kaiserzeit und frühen Völkerwanderungszeit aus dem Zentralteil der Siedlungskammer von Flögeln, Landkreis Cuxhaven', *Neue Ausgrabungen und Forschungen in Niedersachsen*, 18: 181–297.

——1999, *Feddersen Wierde, Fallward, Flögeln: Archäologie im Museum Burg Bederkesa*, Museum Burg Bederkesa: Bederkesa.

SCHULZE, M. 1982, 'Die Wüstung Wülfingen in Nordwürttemberg', *Offa*, 39: 235–43.

SCHUSTER, J. and P. DE RIJK 2001, 'Zur Organisation der Metallverarbeitung auf der Feddersen Wierde', *Probleme der Küstenforschung im südlichen Nordseegebiet*, 27.

SCHÜTTE, S. 1995, 'Continuity problems and authority structures in Cologne', in Ausenda (ed.): 163–9.

SCHWIND, F. 1977, 'Beobachtungen zur inneren Struktur des Dorfes in karolingischer Zeit', in H. Jankuhn, R. Schützeichel, and F. Schwind (eds.), *Das Dorf der Eisenzeit und des frühen Mittelalters: Siedlungsform, wirtschaftliche Funktion, soziale Struktur*, Göttingen: Vandenhoeck und Ruprecht: 444–93.

SCOTT, I. 1993, 'The evidence from excavations for Late Iron Age, Roman and Saxon occupation in Romsey', unpublished report of the Test Valley Archaeological Trust.

SCULL, C. 1991, 'Post-Roman Phase I at Yeavering: a re-consideration', *Medieval Archaeology*, 35: 51–63.

——1997, 'Urban centres in pre-Viking England?', in J. Hines (ed.), *The Anglo-Saxons From the Migration Period to the Eighth Century*, Woodbridge: Boydell Press: 269–97.

——2001, 'Burials at emporia in England', in D. Hill and R. Cowie (eds.), *Wics: The Early Mediaeval Trading Centres of Northern Europe*, Sheffield: Sheffield Academic Press: 67–74.

SELKIRK, A. 1989, 'Rook Hall', *Current Archaeology*, 115: 262–4.

SIEMEN, P. 1990, 'House-type chronology in southwest Jutland', *Norwegian Archaeological Review*, 23 (1–2): 161–71.

SMITH, C. 1976, 'Regional economic systems: linking geographical models and socio-economic problems', in C. Smith (ed.), *Regional Analysis*, vol. 1, *Economic systems*, New York and London: Academic Press: 3–63.

SØRENSEN, P. Ø. 1993, 'Jernalderhof udgravet i Gudme', *Nyt fra Nationalmuseet*, 59: 4.

——1994, 'Gudmehallerne: Kongeligt byggeri fra jernalderen', *National Museets Arbejdsmark* 1994: 25–39.

SPEAKE, G. 1989, *A Saxon Bed Burial on Swallowcliffe Down*, London: English Heritage.

STAFFORD, P. 1985, *The East Midlands in the Early Middle Ages*, Leicester: Leicester University Press.

STAMM, O. 1955, 'Zur Karolingischen Königspfalz in Frankfurt am Main', *Germania*, 33: 391–401.

STEEDMAN, K. 1995, 'Excavation of a Saxon site at Riby Cross Roads, Lincolnshire', *Archaeological Journal*, 151: 212–306.

STEUER, H. 1979, *Elisenhof Bd. 3: Die Keramik aus der frühgeschichtlichen Wurt Elisenhof*, Frankfurt: Lang.

——1982, *Frühgeschichtliche Sozialstrukturen in Mitteleuropa: Eine Analyse der Auswertungsmethoden des archäologischen Quellenmaterials*, Göttingen: Abhandlungen der Akademie der Wissenschaften.

——1987, 'Der Handel der Wikingerzeit zwischen Nord- und Westeuropa aufgrund archäologischer Zeugnisse', in Düwel *et al.* (eds.): 112–97.

——1989, 'Archaeology and history: Proposals on the social struture of the Merovingian kingdom', in Randsborg (ed.): 100–22.

——1994, 'Handwerk auf spätantiken Höhensiedlungen des 4./5. Jh. in Südwestdeutschland', in Nielsen *et al.* (eds): 128–44.

STORK, I. 1989, 'Die frühmittelalterliche Siedlung zum Gräberfeld bei Lauchheim, Ostalbkreis', *Archäologische Augrabungen in Baden-Württemberg 1989*: 212–17.

——1990, 'Weitere Untersuchungen in der frühmittelalterlichen Siedlung «Mittelhofen» bei Lauchheim, Ostalbkreis', *Archäologische Augrabungen in Baden-Württemberg 1990*: 209–15.

——1991, 'Neues aus Lauchheim, Ostalbkreis', *Archäologische Augrabungen in Baden-Württemberg 1991*: 187–92.

——1992, 'Zum Fortgang der Untersuchungen im frühmittelalterlichen Gräberfeld, Adelshof und Hofgrablege bei Lauchheim, Ostalbkreis', *Archäologische Augrabungen in Baden-Württemberg 1992*: 231–9.

STOUMANN, I. 1980, 'Sædding: a Viking-age village near Esbjerg', *Acta Archaeologica*, 50: 95–118.

SYKES, N. 2001, 'Animal Bones and the Norman Conquest: a zooarchaeological perspective', unpublished Ph.D. thesis, University of Southampton.

SZABÓ, M., G. GRENANDER-NYBER, and J. MYRDAL 1985, *Die Holzfunde aus der frühen Wurt Elisenhof (Elisenhof V)*, Frankfurt: P. Lang.

TACITUS, *The Agricola and the Germania*, 1970, H. Mattingly (trans.), London: Penguin Books.

TAYLOR, C. 1983, *Village and Farmstead: A History of Rural Settlement in England*, London: George Philip.

THEUWS, F. 1986, 'The integration of the Kempen region into the Frankish Empire (550–750): some hypotheses', *Helinium*, 26: 121–36.

——1990, 'Centre and periphery in northern Austrasia, sixth to eighth centuries: an archaeological perspective', in Besteman *et al.* (eds): 41–69.

——1991, 'Landed property and manorial organisation in northern Austrasia', in N. Roymans and F. Theuws (eds.), *Images of the Past: Studies on Ancient Societies in Northwest Europe*, Amsterdam: Instituut voor Pre- en Protohistorische Archeologie: 299–407.

——1994, 'Elites and the transition from Merovingian to Carolingian', in P. Nielsen *et al.* (eds.): 195–201.

——1996, 'Haus, Hof und Siedlung im nördlichen Frankenreich (6.–8. Jh)', in A. Wieczorek, P. Périn, K. v. Welck and W. Menghin (eds.), *Die Franken: Wegbereiter Europas*, Mainz: Philipp von Zabern: 754–68.

THEUWS, F. 1998, 'Changing settlement patterns, burial grounds and the symbolic construction of ancestors and communities in the late Merovingian southern Netherlands', in C. Fabech and J. Ringtved (eds.), *Settlement and Landscape: Proceedings of a Conference in Århus*, Moesgård: Jutland Archaeological Society: 337–49.

THOMSEN, P. 1994, 'Lundeborg: an early port of trade in south-east Funen', in P. Nielson *et al.* (eds.): 23–9.

THRANE, H. 1987, 'Das Gudme-Problem und die Gudme-Untersuchung', *Frühmittelalterliche Studien*, 21: 1–48.

—— 1994. 'Gudme: a focus of archaeological research 1833–1987', in P. Nielsen *et al.* (eds.): 8–16.

TRIER, B. 1969, *Das Haus im Nordwesten der Germania Libera*, Münster: Aschendorff.

TUMMUSCHEIT, A. 1995, 'Ländliche Siedlungen des 5.–7. Jh. in England unde ihre kontinentalen Vorgänger', unpublished MA thesis, Christian-Albrechts University, Kiel.

UCKO, P., G. DIMBLEBY, and R. TRINGHAM 1972 (ed.), *Man, Settlement and Urbanism*, London: Duckworth.

UNVERHAU, H. 1990, 'Das südöstliche Schleswig in der Wikingerzeit und dem hohen Mittelalter', in Meier (ed.): 48–58.

VANG PETERSEN, P. 1994, 'Excavations at sites of treasure trove finds at Gudme', in P. Nielsen *et al.* (eds.): 30–40.

VINCE, A. 1984, 'New light on the Saxon pottery of the London area', *London Archaeologist*, 4 (16): 431–9.

—— 1985, 'The Saxon and medieval pottery of London: a review, *Medieval Archaeology*, 29: 25–93.

VITA-FINZI, E. and E. HIGGS 1970, 'Prehistoric economy in the Mount Carmel area of Palestine: site catchment analysis', *Proc. Preh. Soc.*, 36: 1–37.

VOSS, O. 1993, 'Iron Smelting', in Hvass and Storgaard (eds.): 206–9.

WADE, K. 1980, 'A settlement site at Bonhunt Farm, Wicken Bonhunt, Essex', in D. Buckley (ed.), *Archaeology in Essex to A.D. 1500*, CBA Research, Report, 34, London: Council for British Archaeology: 96–102.

—— 1988, 'Ipswich', in R. Hodges and B. Hobley (eds.): 93–100.

WALLIS, S. 1998, 'Excavations at Slough House Farm', in S. Wallis and M. Waughman, *Archaeology and the Landscape in the Lower Blackwater Valley*, East Anglian Archaeology, 82: 5–58.

WAMERS, E. 1994, 'Fibel und Fibeltracht: Karolingerzeit', in *Reallexicon der Germanischen Altertumskunde*, Bd. 8 Berlin: Walter de Gruyter: 586–602.

WATERBOLK, H. T. 1973, 'Odoorn im frühen Mittelalter: Bericht der Grabung 1966', *Neue Ausgrabungen und Forschungen in Niedersachsen*, 8: 25–89.

—— 1975, 'Evidence of cattle stalling in excavated pre- and protohistoric houses', in A. Clason (ed.), *Archaeozoological Studies: Papers of the Archaeological Conference 1974*, Amsterdam and New York: American Elsevier: 383–94.

—— 1982, 'Mobilität von Dorf, Ackerflur und Gräberfeld in Drenthe seit der La Tènezeit', *Offa*, 39: 97–137.

—— 1989, 'Siebzig Jahre archäologische Sieldungsforschung durch das Biologisch-Archäologische Institut der Universität Groningen', in K. Fehn, H. Bender, K. Brandt, D. Denecke (eds.), *Siedlungsforschung. Archäologie-Geschichte-Geographie*, Bd. 7, Bonn: Verlag Siedlungsforschung: 285–320.

——1991*a*, 'Das mittelalterliche Siedlungswesen in Drenthe: Versuch einer Synthese aus archäologischer Sicht', in Böhme (ed.): 47–108.

——1991*b*, 'Ezinge', in H. Jankuhn, H. Steuer, and R. Wenskus (eds.), *Reallexicon der Germanischen Altertumskunde*, Bd. 8, Berlin: Walter de Gruyter: 60–76.

——1995, 'Patterns of the peasant landscape,' *Proc. Preh. Soc.*, 61: 1–36.

——1999, 'From Wijster to Dorestad and beyond', in H. Sarfatij, W. Verwers, and P. Woltering (ed.), *In Discussion With the Past: Archaeological Studies Presented to W. A. van Es*, Zwolle: SPA: 107–18.

——forthcoming, 'Odoorn', in J. Hoops, *Reallexicon der Germanischen Altertums-kunde*, Berlin: W. de Gruyter.

——and O. HARSEMA 1979, 'Medieval farmsteads in Gasselte (Province of Drenthe)', *Palaeohistoria*, 21: 228–65.

WATT, M. 1999, 'Kings or gods? The iconographic evidence of Scandinavian gold foil figures', in T. Dickinson and D. Griffiths (eds.), *The Making of Kingdoms: Papers From the 47th Sachsensymposium, Anglo-Saxon Studies in Archaeology and History*, 10, Oxford: Oxford University Committee for Archaeology: 173–84.

WEBSTER, L. 1993, 'The brooch-mould', in Hamerow (1993): 62–3.

WELCH, M. 1992, *Anglo-Saxon England*, London: English Heritage.

WERNER, J. 1980, 'Der goldene Armring des Frankenkönigs Childerich und die german-ischen Handgelenkringe der jüngeren Kaiserzeit', in *Frühmittelalterliche Studien*, 14: 1–49.

WEST, S. 1986, *West Stow: The Anglo-Saxon Village*, 2 vols., *East Anglian Archaeology*, 24, Ipswich: Suffolk County Planning Department.

WHITELOCK, D. 1955 (ed.), *English Historical Documents*, vol. 1, London: Eyre & Spottiswoode.

WICKER, N. 1994, 'The organization of crafts production and the social status of the Migration Period goldsmith', in P. Nielsen *et al.* (eds.): 145–50.

WICKHAM, C. 1985, 'Pastoralism and underdevelopment in the early Middle Ages', in *L'Uomo di fronte al mondo animale nell'Alto Medioevo 1*, (Settimane di Studio del Centro Italiano di Studi sull'Alto Medioeve 31): 401–55.

——2000*a*, 'Introduction', in I. L. Hansen and C. Wickham (eds.), *The Long Eighth Century: Production, Distribution and Demand*, Leiden/Boston/Cologne: Brill: pp. ix–x.

——2000*b*, 'Overview: production, distribution, demand II', in I. L. Hansen and C. Wickham (eds.): 345–78.

WIJNGAARDEN-BAKKER, L. VAN 1987, 'Experimental zoology', in Groenman van Waateringe and van Wijngaarden-Bakker (eds.): 101–17.

WILLEMS, W. 1989, 'An officer or a gentleman? A late Roman weapon grave from a villa at Voerendaal', in C. van Driel-Murray (ed.), *Roman Military Equipment: The Sources of Evidence*, BAR International Series, 476, Oxford: British Archaeological Reports: 143–56.

WILLIAMS, D. and A. VINCE 1998, 'The characterization and interpretation of Early to Middle Saxon granitic-tempered pottery in England', *Medieval Archaeology* 4:1: 214–19.

WILLIAMS, R. 1993, *Pennylands and Hartigans: Two Iron Age and Saxon Sites in Milton Keynes*, Aylesbury: Buckinghamshire Archaeological Society.

WILLIAMSON, T. 1988, 'Settlement chronology and regional landscapes: the evidence from the claylands of East Anglia and Essex', in D. Hooke (ed.), *Anglo-Saxon Settlements*, Oxford: Blackwell: 153–75.

WILLROTH, K.-H. 1990, 'Zur Besiedlungsgeschichte des östliche Schleswig im ersten nachchristliche Jahrtausend', in Meier (ed.): 7–15.

WINGHART, S. 1984, 'Frühmittelalterliche Siedlungen von Eching und München-Englschalking', *Das Archäologische Jahr in Bayern 1983*: 139–44.

WINKELMANN, W. 1958, 'Die Ausgrabungen in der frühmittelalterlichen Siedlung bei Warendorf', *Neue Ausgrabungen in Deutschland*, Berlin: Römisch-Germanisch Kommission: 492–517.

——1971, 'Die frühgeschichte im Paderborner Land', *Führer zu vor- und frühgeschichtlichen Denkmälern*, Bd. 20, Mainz: Philip von Zabern: 87–121.

——1977, 'Archäologische Zeugnisse zum frühmittelalterlichen Handwerk in Westfalen', *Frühmittelalterliche Studien*, 11: 92–126.

WITTE, H. 1992/3, 'Ausgrabung 1991/92 in der Siedlung Bremen-Grambke', *Bremer Archäologische Blätter N.F.*, 2: 23–30.

——1994/5, 'Ausgrabung 1993 in der Siedlung Bremen-Grambke', *Bremer Archäologische Blätter N.F.* 3: 25.

WORMALD, P. 1994, Review of R. Bartlett, *The Making of Europe: Conquest, Colonisation and Cultural Change, 950–1350, London Review of Books*, 24 February 1994.

WULF, F.-W. 1991, 'Karolingische und Ottonische Zeit', in H.-J. Häßler (ed.), *Ur- und Frühgeschichte in Niedersachsen*, Stuttgart: Theiss: 321–68.

YPEY, J. 1973, 'Das Fränkische Gräberfeld zu Rhenen, Prov. Utrecht', *Berichten der Rijksdienst voor Oudheidkundig Bodemonderzoek*, 23: 289–312.

ZADORA-RIO, E. 1989, 'La Formation des campagnes médiévales', in C. Goudineau and J. Guilaine (eds.), *De Lascaux au Grand Louvre: Archéologie et Histoire en France*, Paris: Errance: 112–15.

——2000, 'Burials in the landscape: cemeteries and rural territories', lecture given to the Society for Medieval Archaeology.

ZEIST, W. VAN 1988, 'Botanical evidence of relations between the sand and clay districts of the north of the Netherlands in medieval times, in H.-J. Küster (ed.), *Der Prähistorische Mensch und seine Umwelt*, Stuttgart: Theiss: 335–48.

——and R. PALFENIER-VEGTER 1979, 'Agriculture in medieval Gasselte', *Palaeohistoria*, 21: 267–99.

——G. J. DE ROLLER, R. PALFENIER-VEGTER, O. HARSEMA, and H. DURING 1986, 'Plant remains from medieval sites in Drenthe, the Netherlands', *Helinium*, 26: 226–74.

ZIMMERMANN, C. 1998, 'Zur Entwicklung der Eisenmetallurgie in Skandinavien und Schleswig-Holstein', *Praehistorische Zeitschrift*, 73, Heft 1: 70–99.

ZIMMERMANN, W. H. 1974, 'A Roman Iron Age and early Migration settlement at Flögeln, Kr. Wesermünde, Lower Saxony', in T. Rowley (ed.), *Anglo-Saxon Settlement and Landscape*, BAR 6, Oxford: British Archaeological Reports: 56–73.

——1982, 'Archäologische Befunde frühmittelalterliche Webhäuser', *Jahrbuch der Männer von Morgenstern*, 61: 111–44.

——1984, 'Nährungsproduktion', in Kossack *et al.* (eds.): 246–63.

——1986, 'Zur funktionalen Gliederung völkerwanderungszeitlicher Langhäuser in Flögeln-Eekhöltjen, Kr. Cuxhaven', *Probleme der Küstenforschung*, 16: 55–86.

——1988, 'Regelhafte Innengliederung prähistorischer Langhäuser in den Nordseean-rainerstatten: Ein Zeugnis enger, langandauender kultureller Kontakte', *Germania*, 66 (2): 465–89.

——1991a, 'Die früh- bis hochmittelalterliche Wüstung Dalem, Gem. Langen-Neuenwalde, Kr. Cuxhaven', in Böhme (ed.): 37–46.

——1991b, 'Erntebergung in Rutenberg und Diemen aus Archäologischer und Volkkundlicher Sicht', in A. Kovács (ed.), *Néprajzi Értesítö a Néprajzi Muzeum Évkönyve*, Budapest: Magyar Nemzeti Muzeum: 71–104.

——1992a, *Die Siedlungen des 1. bis 6. Jh. n. Christus von Flögeln-Eekhöltjen, Niedersachsen: Die Bauformen und ihre Funktionen. Probleme der Küstenforschung im Südlichen Nordseegebiet*, Bd. 19, Hildesheim: Verlag August Lax.

——1992b, 'The "Helm" in England, Wales, Scandinavia and North America', *Vernacular Architecture*, 23: 34–43.

——1995a, 'Haus, Hof und Siedlungsstruktur auf der Geest vom Neolithikum bis in das Mittelalter', in Dannenberg and Schulze (eds.): 251–88.

——1995b, 'Ackerbau in ur- und frühgeschichtlicher Zeit auf der Geest und in der Marsch', in Dannenberg and Schulze (eds.): 289–315.

——1999a, 'Favourable conditions for cattle farming, one reason for the Anglo-Saxon migration over the North Sea?', in H. Sarfatij, W. Verwers, and P. Woltering (eds.), *In Discussion with the Past: Archaeological studies presented to W. A. van Es*, Zwolle: SPA: 129–44.

——1999b, 'Why was cattle-stalling introduced in prehistory? The significance of byre and stable and of outwintering', in Fabech and Ringtved (eds.): 295–312.

——2001, 'Loxstedt, Ldkr. Cuxhaven', in *Reallexicon der Germanischen Altertumskunde* Bd. 18, pp. 629–33, Berlin: W. de Gruyter.

ZIMMERMANN-HOLT J. 1996, 'Beyond optimization: alternative ways of examining animal exploitation', *World Archaeology*, 28: 89–109.

Index

Bold numbers denote references to illustrations